Powers
of Congress

Congressional Quarterly Inc.

Congressional Quarterly Inc. is an editorial research service and publishing company serving clients in the fields of news, education, business and government. Congressional Quarterly, in its basic publication, the CQ *Weekly Report*, covers Congress, government and politics. Congressional Quarterly also publishes hardbound reference books and paperback books on public affairs. The service was founded in 1945 by Henrietta and Nelson Poynter.

An affiliated service, Editorial Research Reports, publishes reports each week on a wide range of subjects. Editorial Research Reports also publishes hardbound and paperback books.

Editor: Robert A. Diamond
Contributors: Margaret Thompson, Elder Witt, Michael A. Carson, Prentice Bowsher, Mary Cohn, David Tarr. **Editorial Coordinator:** Mary Neumann. **Art Director:** Howard Chapman. **Production Manager:** I.D. Fuller. **Assistant Production Manager:** Kathleen E. Walsh.

Library of Congress Cataloging in Publication Data

Congressional Quarterly Inc

Powers of Congress.

Bibliography: p. 327.

Includes index.

1. United States. Congress—Powers and duties.

I. Title.

JK1061.C59 1976 328.73'07'4 76-32556

ISBN 0-87187-095-9

Table of Contents

PART I - Fiscal Powers

PART II - Foreign Affairs

PART III - Commerce Power

PART IV - Impeachment

PART V - Investigations

PART VI - Confirmations

PART VII - Amending Power

PART VIII- Electing the President

Preface

The broadest grant of authority to the federal government is set forth in Article I, Section 8 of the Constitution, which enumerates the powers of Congress. A more modest list of powers for the President is contained in Article II, Sections 2 and 3. Nevertheless, the general trend throughout the 20th century has been just the reverse. There has been an enormous growth of presidential and executive branch power, while Congress has long been considered to be the comparatively passive branch of government.

This pattern has been modified in the past six years as Congress has taken significant actions to challenge executive supremacy. In an effort to restore its power of the .purse, Congress in 1974 devised a new method of dealing with the federal budget. The 1973 War Powers Act, enacted over President Nixon's veto, set limits on the authority of the President to commit American forces to combat abroad without congressional approval. The 1973 Watergate hearings and the 1974 impeachment proceedings proved to be successful challenges to an abuse of presidential power.

These developments of the past few years make it appropriate to take a fresh look at congressional power. *Powers of Congress* provides a detailed examination of the constitutional origins, the evolution and current status of major congressional powers. The Introduction presents an overall survey. Parts I through VIII examine fiscal powers, foreign affairs, commerce powers, impeachment, investigations, confirmations, amending the Constitution and electing the President and Vice President. Reference notes and a selected bibliography appear at the end of the book.

Robert A. Diamond
August 1976

Introduction

The powers of Congress are numerous and they are carefully detailed in the Constitution. Whereas presidential power has been enhanced by precedent and by law since 1789, Congress has not always chosen to exercise its powers. The result of this has been that congressional strength, particularly in the area of foreign policy, has been less than was envisioned by the drafters of the Constitution. Nevertheless, it has always been true that executive power cannot easily circumvent Capitol Hill unless the Congress is willing to be bypassed.

Article I, Section 1 of the Constitution grants to Congress "all legislative powers." These are set forth in detail, in the remaining nine sections of Article I. The fiscal powers—to tax and to spend—are the most important because they permit Congress to determine policy in many different areas.

Congress also has major powers in the areas of foreign policy (declarations of war and treaty-making); confirmation of nominations of public officials; investigations; impeachment of federal officers; regulation of foreign and interstate commerce; amending the Constitution; election of the President in the case of an electoral college deadlock; and in seating and disciplining of its own members.

Fiscal Powers

The congressional "power of the purse" includes raising revenues through various taxes and direction, through the appropriations process, of the spending of those revenues. The taxing and appropriating powers are granted to Congress by various provisions of the Constitution. These powers were long exercised separately, but a 1974 budget control law established a mechanism to help Congress coordinate all federal spending and taxing.

The budget law, fully implemented for the first time in 1976, set up House and Senate Budget Committees to formulate overall spending and tax goals and a Congressional Budget Office to provide Congress with technical information about the economy and the budget.

The law also created a complicated series of deadlines for congressional action on the budget. The key dates each year are May 15, when Congress is supposed to have completed action on a resolution setting targets for spending and revenues to guide committees as they process fiscal legislation during the summer months, and Sept. 15, when Congress is to replace the targets with a ceiling on spending and a floor on revenues for the fiscal year beginning Oct. 1.

If the amounts adopted in the fall differ from those adopted during the summer in actual spending and tax bills, Congress must reconcile the amounts. Once this reconciliation process is completed, the limits become binding unless Congress itself revises them.

In addition to forcing Congress to compare total spending with total receipts, the budget process required members for the first time to vote on a budget deficit. Although the budget resolutions also included an "appropriate" level for the national debt, Congress ignored suggestions that it abolish the statutory limit on the amount of debt the government might incur and rely instead on its new budget procedures to exert fiscal control.

Taxes on the income and profits of individuals and corporations have become the federal government's basic source of revenue since the Sixteenth Amendment (income tax) was ratified in 1913. In addition, Congress has imposed an excess profits tax on corporations during wartime, has levied a variety of excise taxes under powers authorized by the Constitution, has authorized estate and gift taxes and has imposed payroll taxes to underpin the old-age insurance and unemployment compensation systems.

Tax legislation must, under a constitutional provision, originate in the House of Representatives. Tax bills and bills having to do with tariffs are handled there by the Ways and Means Committee. After the House acts, such bills go to the Senate and are referred to that chamber's Finance Committee where further amendments may be proposed. Amendments adopted by the Senate may be far-reaching. Thus the Senate also has important control over tax legislation.

Generally, the initiative on raising, lowering or enacting new taxes in the post-war period has been taken by the administration; it has prepared the basic proposals and Congress has acted on them. There is no requirement that this be the case. Congress itself initiated a major tax reform bill in 1969.

Revenue raised through the taxing system is not available in the Treasury to be disbursed by the executive branch to meet governmental needs simply as agency officials deem proper. The Constitution gives to Congress the basic authority to determine how monies collected shall be expended and requires a regular statement of expenditures.

The appropriations procedure works in two steps after the President presents his annual budget requests to Congress. First, the various congressional committees consider the parts of the request which fall under their jurisdictions and report out bills authorizing programs and setting a ceiling on the amount of funds that can be spent for the programs. Second, in separate legislation after the authorization is law, Congress actually provides (appropriates) the money. The amount of money appropriated often is less than the maximum amount specified in the authorization for the program.

Appropriation of the money is initially considered by the relevant subcommittee of the House Appropriations Committee and then a bill is sent to the House floor by the full committee. The bulk of the basic appropriations decisions are usually made in the subcommittees. The general structure of any appropriations bill is derived from House consideration of the measure. What the Senate does in effect is to review the House action and hear appeals from agencies seeking changes in the allotments accorded them by the House.

Presidential refusal to spend funds appropriated by Congress became an issue during the Nixon administration. The 1974 budget control law curtailed the President's power to impound appropriated funds, a practice previously sanctioned by tradition rather than law. Impoundment was also limited by the Supreme Court in the 1974-75 term. *(Fiscal Powers, Part I, pp. 1-48)*

Foreign Affairs

While initiative in foreign relations is generally taken by the President, Congress has enormous powers which are indispensable to the support of foreign policy. These include the constitutional powers to raise taxes (which finance war), create and maintain an army and navy, regulate foreign commerce and make treaties. With the exception of a few votes during the Vietnam War in the early 1970s, Congress in the 20th century has chosen to use its powers to support the President rather than to challenge him.

While the Constitution gives Congress the power to declare war and "provide for the common defense," both the initiation and conduct of war have come to be directed largely by the President.

In October 1973, Congress cleared a resolution restricting the President's authority to commit U.S. troops only to respond to an "attack upon the United States, its territories or possessions or its armed forces." The resolution became law after Congress overrode President Nixon's veto of the measure.

Congressional power over some other aspects of foreign policy has greatly increased in recent years. Legislative authority over the massive, post-World-War-II foreign aid and military assistance programs is a case in point. The programs have required specific congressional authorizations and repeated congressional appropriations, and in recent years Congress has refused to give the President all he wanted for foreign aid.

The Constitution gives the President the power to make treaties if two-thirds of the Senate concurs. For years this clause served as a cornerstone of American foreign policy. Treaties forged peace agreements with other nations, supported American territorial expansion, established national boundaries, protected U.S. commerce and regulated government affairs with Indian tribes. Membership in the United Nations was accomplished by Senate consent to ratification of the U.N. Charter.

In recent years treaties have in part been replaced by executive agreements with foreign countries; such agreements do not require Senate approval. Except for rejection of the Versailles Treaty, Senate action on treaties has not been a major factor in foreign policy; only 11 treaties have been rejected since 1789. *(Foreign Affairs, Part II, pp. 51-98)*

Commerce Power

The Constitution gives Congress a broad and positive grant of power to regulate commerce, but gives few details. Therefore the extent of power over commerce has been established largely by precedent and judicial determination. As a result of Supreme Court decisions, it has been established that Congress has the power to regulate both interstate and foreign commerce, including manufacture of goods.

In its first century, Congress made little use of its power to regulate interstate commerce. But with the passage of the Interstate Commerce Act of 1887, Congress moved decisively into the area of domestic regulation. The act was prompted by the inability of the states to curb increasing abuses by the railroads. It was ultimately broadened to include all interstate commerce carried by railroads, trucking companies, bus lines, freight forwarders, water carriers, oil pipelines, transportation brokers and express agencies.

In 1890, Congress moved into federal regulation of commercial enterprise with enactment of the Sherman Antitrust Act, "to protect commerce against unlawful restraints and monopolies." After 1900 it expanded its regulatory authority over commerce into almost every area of the commercial and industrial life of the nation. Between 1903 and 1917 it enacted laws prohibiting the interstate transportation of explosives, diseased livestock, insect pests, falsely stamped gold and silver articles, narcotics, prostitutes and adulterated or misbranded foods and drugs.

Introduction

Many of the New Deal economic recovery programs (1933-39) were launched under the commerce clause. More recently, the scope of the commerce clause was enlarged to include civil rights. In the Civil Rights Act of 1964, Congress found sanction in the commerce clause and the "equal protection" clause of the Fourteenth Amendment for a ban on racial discrimination in most public accommodations. In 1968, Congress used the commerce clause as the basis for legislation making it a federal crime to travel in interstate commerce to incite or participate in a riot.

Congressional power to regulate foreign commerce is tied to its powers over foreign relations and fiscal affairs. The earliest actions in this field were efforts to replace markets lost when the nation won its independence from England. Modern laws have ranged from antitrust exemptions for exporters to use of tariff reductions to stimulate trade. While the Constitution gives Congress the power to set all tariffs, since 1934 general tariff agreements have been negotiated with foreign countries by the executive. *(Commerce Power, Part III, pp. 101-123)*

Impeachment

Impeachment is perhaps the most awesome, though the least used, power of Congress. It is specifically granted by the Constitution, which provides that the House should consider an impeachment resolution (usually reported by the House Judiciary Committee). If the resolution is adopted by the House, a trial is held by the Senate with the House acting as prosecutor. Conviction requires approval of two-thirds of the senators present. It provides for removal from office and disqualification from further federal office. There is no appeal.

The two most famous impeachment cases were acquitted by the Senate after sensational trials. They were President Andrew Johnson—accused of violating the Tenure of Office Act—and Supreme Court Justice Samuel Chase—accused of partisan conduct on the bench. Prior to 1974, 13 officers had been impeached by the House. Of the 12 cases that reached the Senate, two were dismissed, six resulted in acquittal and four ended in conviction. President Nixon's resignation in 1974 terminated House action on impeachment articles approved by the Judiciary Committee. *(Impeachment, Part IV, pp. 127-151)*

Investigations

The much publicized power of Congress to mount investigations is not specified in the Constitution. The first congressional investigation was held in 1792, justified by the tradition of investigative actions in the House of Commons. In 1927 a landmark Supreme Court decision upheld the constitutionality of investigations, contending that they were often indispensable to the effective exercise of "all legislative powers" granted to Congress by the Constitution.

No period of American history has been without congressional investigations. They have gathered information on the need for possible future legislation, tested the effectiveness of past legislative action, questioned executive branch proceedings and laid the groundwork for impeachment proceedings. Investigations have elevated comparatively minor political figures to national fame, broken the careers of important public men and captured the attention of millions of newspaper readers and television viewers.

The congressional investigative power has been given wide berth by the judiciary. In May 1975 the Supreme Court ruled that subpoenas issued by investigating committees may not be limited by courts, even where constitutional rights may be endangered. The justices said that the Constitution bars courts from interfering with a subpoena that is issued within the "sphere of legislative activity" of a committee or member. Furthermore, the court said, courts may not question the motives behind a congressional subpoena.

Congressional investigative power goes hand in hand with congressional power to punish for contempt. Such power is also not specifically granted by the Constitution, but an 1821 Supreme Court decision confirmed Congress' power to punish a person for contempt of its authority. Congress has since then voted contempt citations in cases where a witness refused to appear before a committee, refused to answer questions before a committee or refused to produce documents for a committee. *(Investigations, Part V, pp. 155-199)*

Confirmations

The Constitution provides for Senate approval of presidential nominations of federal officers. Most nominations involve military promotions of officers in various specialized services and Senate action is only a formality. But each year there are several hundred nominations to major federal posts which are subjected to varying degrees of individual scrutiny by the Senate. These include nominations to Cabinet and sub-Cabinet positions, independent boards and agencies, major diplomatic and military posts and the federal judiciary.

The Senate role in Supreme Court appointments is particularly important. It may not be able to dictate Supreme Court appointments, but historically it has not been afraid to reject them. Roughly one in five nominations to the Supreme Court has failed to win Senate confirmation.

Appointments to lower federal courts are another matter. Historically the President has used these judgeships, especially for the district courts, to please members of Congress. In general a district court judge is nominated by the President at the request of a congressman from that district. Thus lower court appointments provide presidential patronage—an opportunity for the President to win the goodwill of a congressman or a vote on a crucial issue.

Nominations of Cabinet officers are carefully considered by the Senate but such officers are usually confirmed with little difficulty, on the theory that the President should have great leeway in selecting the members of his official "family." Since 1789, only eight men nominated to the Cabinet have been rejected by the Senate. Major diplomatic nominations normally encounter little difficulty.

Appointments to independent boards and commissions offer a somewhat different situation. Usually created by act of Congress and not subordinate to any executive department, they frequently are viewed as an arm of Congress rather than the executive, and members of Congress expect to play a large role in the selection process. Contests over these nominations have been frequent, although few nominees actually have been rejected. *(Confirmations, Part VI, pp. 203-241)*

Amending Power

Congress shares with the state legislatures the power of proposing amendments to the Constitution. The Constitution provides that amendments may be proposed by two-thirds vote of both houses of Congress, or by a convention called by the legislatures of two-thirds of the states. Amendments must be ratified by the legislatures or conventions of three-fourths of the states as directed by Congress.

Although this envisioned a substantial role for the states in the amendment process, Congress has dominated the rewriting of the Constitution. Not once have the states been successful in calling for a convention to propose an amendment to the Constitution. The states have approved 26 of the amendments proposed by Congress, failing to ratify only five. The last amendment to be turned down was submitted in 1924. The states have until 1979 to ratify the proposed Equal Rights Amendment.

Restrained use of the amendment procedure of the Constitution has enabled it to remain the fundamental law of the land even though the United States has been transformed beyond recognition since it was drafted. Major amendments include: Extending the vote to blacks (Fifteenth) and women (Nineteenth) and levying the income tax (Sixteenth). The Fourteenth Amendment altered the relationship between national and state governments, the most fundamental formal revision of the Constitution; its consequences are still unfolding in Supreme Court decisions based on the amendment. *(Amending Power, Part VII, pp. 245-259)*

Electing the President

Congress under the Constitution has two key responsibilities relating to the election of the President and Vice President. First, it is directed to receive and in joint session count the electoral votes certified by the states. Second, if no candidate has a majority of the electoral vote, the House must elect the President and the Senate the Vice President.

In modern times the formal counting of electoral votes has been largely a ceremonial function. The House actually has chosen a President only twice, in 1801 and 1825. However, in the course of the nation's history a number of campaigns have been deliberately designed to throw elections into the House. Apprehension over this has nurtured many electoral reform efforts; the most recent was killed by a filibuster by southern and small-state senators in 1970.

In addition to its role in electing the President, the Twentieth and Twenty-fifth Amendments give Congress authority to settle problems arising from the death of candidates and disputes over presidential disability.

The Twenty-fifth Amendment, ratified in 1967 to cover what its authors considered would be rare contingencies, was applied twice in 12 months and gave rise to executive branch leadership unique in the nation's history. The amendment provides that whenever the office of Vice President becomes vacant, the President shall appoint a replacement, subject to confirmation by both houses.

Gerald R. Ford was the first Vice President to take office under the amendment, when he was sworn in Dec. 6, 1973. Nelson A. Rockefeller, was sworn in as Vice President on Dec. 19, 1974, to succeed Ford following the resignation of President Richard M. Nixon on Aug. 8, 1974. Thus, neither of the nation's two top leaders in 1975-76 was elected by the people. The situation prompted calls in 1975 for repeal or revision of the amendment, but little support for change developed. *(Electing the President, Part VIII, pp. 263-283)*

PART I
Fiscal Powers

Chapter 1

Taxation and Spending

Of the numerous powers of Congress, the "power of the purse" is the most important. All of the other powers—such as regulating commerce, conducting investigations, even declaring war—are as nothing without the power to finance the business of government. As George Galloway has remarked, "Perhaps nine-tenths of the work of Congress is concerned, directly or indirectly, with the spending of public money. The spending power is the constitutional birthright of Congress, for that document provides that 'no money shall be drawn from the Treasury, but in consequence of appropriations made by law' and that 'all bills for raising revenue shall originate in the House of Representatives; but the Senate may propose or concur with amendments as on other bills.' "[1] *(Footnotes, p. 309)*

The "power of the purse" includes both the raising of revenue through taxes, tariffs and other levies, and direction through the appropriations process of the spending of the funds raised. They are opposite sides of the same coin, although until 1975, Congress rarely considered them as an entity.

The taxing and appropriating powers are granted to Congress by various provisions of the Constitution. Over the years, Congress has jealously guarded these powers with the relatively recent exception of the tariff power, the exercise of which was delegated to the executive branch nearly 40 years ago. Occasional proposals that Congress also delegate to the President limited authority to alter tax rates have been ignored by the legislators. While Congress has always been dedicated to preserving its authority over spending, it has had difficulty in maintaining close control over government outlays since President Franklin D. Roosevelt launched the New Deal. In spite of an apparent desire on the part of many members of Congress—particularly those handling appropriations bills—to hold down government spending, it has continued to rise. From an outlay of $567-million in fiscal year 1900, federal expenditures have grown to an estimated outlay of $349.4-billion in fiscal 1976—21.9 per cent of the gross national product.

A related subject over which Congress has power is the national debt. The debt total has grown enormously as a result of government spending in excess of government revenue in most years since the early 1930s. Congress has imposed a statutory ceiling on the amount of debt which the government may incur, but the ceiling has been revised upward time and again as budget deficits have required more borrowing. The debt ceiling has been an unusually controversial and visible issue in Congress because it has given opponents of deficit spending an opportunity to vent their displeasure over constantly rising government outlays. But efforts to use the debt ceiling as a lid on spending have been fruitless.

Separation of Taxing and Spending

Until 1975, Congress rarely considered the two parts of government financing as an integrated whole. An effort in the late 1940s to tie spending and taxing together was unsuccessful, in large part because the resulting bill—and the committee formed to handle it—proved unwieldy.

The task of relating spending to revenue thus fell to the executive branch, which attempted to accomplish it through preparation of the federal budget.

A major reason for the difficulty in obtaining an overview of the budget in Congress is the fact that tax bills and appropriations bills are referred to different committees and are taken up and acted upon separately, even though the level of spending (without deficit financing) is dependent on the amount of revenue raised.

With passage of the 1974 Congressional Budget and Impoundment Control Act (PL 93-344), however, Congress took a potentially momentous step toward more coordinated action on federal economic policy by revising the procedures it uses to handle the government's budget.

The measure, which was to be fully implemented in 1976, established a framework for more timely and better-considered congressional action on legislation approving or amending the appropriations, spending, revenue and debt figures set out in the President's annual budget message to Congress.

In doing so, the measure spelled out a timetable for congressional actions affecting the federal budget and required that those decisions be reviewed in light of their impact on overall fiscal policy. It created House and Senate Budget Committees to supervise the new process. *(Details, p. 32)*

Congress and the Taxing Power

Financing of the federal government is carried out under authority granted to Congress in the first article of the Constitution. That authority is specific with regard to raising money, somewhat vague but nevertheless sweeping with regard to spending it. Article I, Section 8, Clause 1 reads:

The Congress shall have power to lay and collect taxes, duties, imposts and excises, to pay the debts and provide for the common defense and general welfare of the United States....

Under this basic authorization, with a monumental assist from the Sixteenth Amendment (income tax), Congress over the years has devised a taxing system that produced in fiscal 1976 an estimated total revenue of no less than $297.5-billion. Generally, the taxing power has been liberally construed by both Congress and the courts (the most important exception being a Supreme Court decision in 1895 that overturned an attempt by Congress to impose an income tax and which led finally to adoption of the Sixteenth Amendment). The constitutional historian C. H. Pritchett, in his book *The American Constitution,* noted that adequate sources of funds and broad authority to use them were "essential conditions for carrying on an effective government." "Consequently," he observed, "the first rule for judicial review of tax statutes is that a heavy burden of proof lies on anyone who would challenge any congressional

3

exercise of fiscal power. In almost every decision touching the constitutionality of federal taxation, the Supreme Court has stressed the breadth of congressional power and the limits of its own reviewing powers."[2]

The terms used in Article I, Section 8 granting the taxing power were broad enough to include all known forms of taxation. Customs levies, or tariffs, on goods imported from abroad were covered by "duties" and "imposts." "Excises" covered taxes on the manufacture, sale, use or transfer of property within the United States.

Limitations. Although the power of Congress to tax is broad, it is not unlimited. There are constitutional provisions, for example, on direct and indirect taxation.

Article I, Section 9, Clause 4 states: "No capitation, or other direct, tax shall be laid, unless in proportion to the census or enumeration hereinbefore directed to be taken." And Article I, Section 8, Clause 1 states: "...all duties, imposts and excises shall be uniform throughout the United States." The Supreme Court in 1895 laid out a rule to distinguish between these taxes. It said a tax "which cannot be avoided, is a direct tax, while a tax paid primarily by persons who can shift the burden upon others...is an indirect tax."

This rule came in the case which overturned the attempt by Congress to impose a personal income tax, *Pollock v. Farmers' Loan and Trust Co.*, 157 U.S. 429, 158 U.S. 601 (1895). The decision led to the Sixteenth Amendment to the Constitution which says: "The Congress shall have power to lay and collect taxes on incomes, from whatever source derived, without apportionment among the several States, and without regard to any census or enumeration." The amendment, ratified in 1913, opened up a revenue source that has since become the principal one for the government by eliminating the requirement that an income tax be apportioned among the states by population. Wealth is not distributed the same as population. As a result, an apportioned income tax—with high population states paying a larger share than less populated but perhaps richer ones—would be virtually impossible to obtain because of the political opposition that could be expected.

The other provision, dealing with uniformity, concerned the type of tax that is now considered indirect. The language means that the tax must apply equally—with the same force—in any location that the item to be taxed is located. Thus, the provision has come to mean geographical uniformity and has guided Congress in its passage of customs and excise levies that were the primary source of revenue for the national government until World War I.[3]

These constitutional provisions, including the Sixteenth Amendment, give Congress the right to enact virtually any taxes except for export duties, which are specifically prohibited (Article I, Section 9, Clause 5), and direct taxes not covered by the Sixteenth Amendment such as poll or property taxes which are still subject to the apportionment requirement.

Implied Limitations. In addition to specific restrictions, there are implied limitations on the taxing power of Congress. A major limitation extends immunity from federal taxation to state and local governments, their property and activities. A second limitation has exempted from federal taxation the income from state and municipal bonds. These limitations are based on the doctrine of intergovernmental tax immunity laid down in 1819 by Chief Justice Marshall in the Supreme Court's opinion in the case of *McCulloch v. Maryland*,[4] 4 Wheat. 316. That doctrine rested on the theory of state sovereignty and on the belief that, because "the power to tax involves the power to destroy," neither the federal nor a state government could tax the property or instrumentalities of the other without infringing on its sovereignty. The doctrine was applied even to the salaries of public employees.

Regulation Through Taxation

Congress has the power, confirmed by use over the years, to impose taxes for regulatory rather than revenue purposes. The leading example is the imposition of tariffs not for revenue only but also for the protection of domestic industries against competition from imports. Although the first tariff law was enacted in 1789, the Supreme Court did not have occasion to consider (and uphold) the constitutionality of this form of taxation until 1928.[5]

Regulation through taxation has been employed in other situations even to the extent of destroying a business enterprise. In 1863, Congress enacted a National Banking Act providing for the incorporation of national banks with authority to issue currency notes. In 1866, it imposed a 10-per cent tax on new state bank notes with the avowed purpose of driving such notes out of existence—which it did.[6] There were numerous laws of this kind in ensuing years. Among the best known were: a stiff excise tax on oleomargarine colored to resemble butter; a tax on the manufacture of poisonous white phosphorous matches (which virtually killed the industry); taxes on registered dealers in narcotic drugs; and a special tax (later overturned by the Supreme Court) on the profits of companies employing children under 16 years of age.[7]

Uses of the Tariff

Tariffs for Revenue. The first congressional measure to raise revenue was a tariff act approved July 4, 1789.[8] The revenue from customs duties proved adequate to meet most of the fiscal needs of the federal government until the Civil War. A wartime income tax and numerous excises were then imposed to help defray war costs. However, the pattern of substantial dependence on customs receipts, supplemented increasingly by excise taxes, continued up to World War I, when income and profits taxes became the mainstay of federal revenue. Customs receipts accounted for more than 90 per cent of total federal revenue until the Civil War. Their importance declined gradually after that, but in 1910 they still made up 49 per cent of the federal government's revenue. In contrast, by the late 1960s, the revenue from import duties had shrunk to little more than 1 per cent of the total.

Tariffs for Protection. As long as customs receipts were sufficient to meet government needs, the tariff in effect killed two birds with one stone. It supplied a large part of federal revenue while in the process of carrying out its principal purpose, which was to protect domestic producers, especially of manufactured goods, from a flood of foreign imports. Many of the so-called infant industries grew strong as they matured, but few reached the point of considering themselves able to get along without tariff protection. Thus, revenue considerations aside, the duties in numerous cases did more than put domestic producers on a basis of equality with foreign producers; they gave the American producers a competitive advantage. *(Additional details on tariffs, p. 122)*

Components of Federal Tax System

Taxes on the income and profits of individuals and corporations have become the federal government's basic source of revenue.[9] Such taxes yielded only modest amounts of revenue before American entry into World War I. Sharply increased rates then pushed up the yield from $360-million in fiscal 1917 to $2.3-billion in fiscal 1918. Since that time, income and profits taxes have produced annually more revenue than all excise and other internal revenue taxes combined except in the nine fiscal years from 1933 through 1941. During those years the Depression was holding down incomes and numerous new excise taxes were levied to bolster federal revenues.

In World War II, high rates and a broadened tax base doubled and redoubled the receipts from income and profits taxes. Following a downward movement after World War II and again after the Korean War, these receipts climbed year by year almost uninterruptedly to the huge net (minus refunds) total of $154-billion projected for fiscal 1976. That sum accounted for about 51.8 per cent of the government's net budget receipts of an estimated $297.5-billion in fiscal 1976. Social Security taxes and contributions of an estimated $91.6-billion made up the next largest share of net budget receipts. Net excise taxes were projected to yield $32.1-billion; estate and gift taxes, $3.6-billion; customs receipts, $4.3-billion; and miscellaneous receipts, $10.9-billion.

Individual Income Tax. A federal tax on personal income was first imposed during the Civil War. Pressed by the wartime need for additional funds, Congress in 1862 levied a tax on individual incomes in excess of $600. The personal exemption was raised to $1,000 in 1867, two years after the war ended, and then to $2,000 in 1870. At one point the tax was graduated up to a rate of 10 per cent. Total revenues under this tax amounted to $376-million. At its peak in 1866, it accounted for almost 25 per cent of internal revenue collections. The law imposing the tax expired by limitation in 1872.[10] The levy had been challenged as violative of the constitutional requirement that direct taxes be apportioned

7

among the states according to population, but the Supreme Court of that day ruled that it was not a direct tax.

During the 1870s and 1880s, little interest was shown in enactment of a new income-tax law. But growth of the country and accumulation of large fortunes began in the 1890s to generate pressure for a return to income taxation. After the depression of 1893 had reduced federal revenues, Congress yielded and in 1894 levied a tax of 2 per cent on personal incomes in excess of $3,000. Before the new tax law became operative, it was challenged, and this time the Supreme Court held that an income tax was a direct tax and therefore unconstitutional without apportionment *(Pollock v. Farmers' Loan & Trust Co.,* 1895).

Although the court had blocked the road to this attempted expansion of the tax system, a solution was afforded by the power of Congress and the states to revise the Constitution. A campaign to do so was begun immediately, and on Feb. 25, 1913, the Sixteenth Amendment was officially declared ratified. The one-sentence amendment stated tersely: "The Congress shall have power to lay and collect taxes on incomes from whatever source derived, without apportionment among the several states, and without regard to any census or enumeration."

Thus the problem of apportioning income taxes was swept away and Congress was left free to do what it had tried to do two decades earlier. The new grant of power came at a providential time, for the great expansion of federal revenue soon required by World War I would have been difficult, if not impossible, to achieve by any other means.

Congress instituted the income tax in the year the Sixteenth Amendment was ratified. The new levy applied to wages, salaries, interest, dividends, rents, entrepreneurial income and capital gains. The law contained certain exemptions (such as interest on federal, state and municipal bonds and salaries of state and local government employees) and allowed deductions for personal interest and tax payments and business expenses. Taxes were collected at the source on incomes in excess of $3,000. A personal exemption of $3,-000 for a single person and $4,000 for a married couple was allowed. Rates were set initially at only 1 per cent for the normal tax plus 1- to 6-per cent surtax on larger incomes.

In the following half-century, Congress made numerous changes in the income-tax law. Joseph A. Pechman, one of the nation's leading tax authorities, cites in his book *Federal Tax Policy* the following "most significant changes" since the original 1913 act: allowance of a credit for dependents and a deduction for charitable contributions in 1917; elimination of collection at the source in 1916 and its reinstatement in 1943 for wages and salaries of state and local government employees and discontinuance of the sale of tax-exempt federal securities in 1941; adoption of the standard deduction in 1944; enactment of the principle of "income-splitting" for married couples in 1948; introduction of an average plan for certain taxpayers and a minimum standard deduction in 1964; and in the 1969 act, the minimum standard deduction was replaced by a low-income allowance, and a minimum tax on selected preference incomes and a top marginal rate on earned income of 50 per cent were adopted.[11]

Rates and exemptions have changed frequently. According to Pechman, maximum marginal rates reached 77 per cent during World War I, 94 per cent during World War II, and 92 per cent during the Korean War. They declined to 24 per cent in the 1920s and rose to 79 per cent in the 1930s. In the late 1950s and early 1960s, the maximum rate was 91 per cent.[12] At present (1976), the maximum rate is 70 per cent.

Corporation Income and Profits Taxes. Congress did not encounter with a corporation income tax the constitutional difficulty that it had experienced with the tax on individual income. A corporation income tax was levied in 1909 in the guise of "a special excise tax" at a rate of 1 per cent of net income in excess of $5,000. That tax, like the 1894 individual income tax, was challenged in the courts, but the Supreme Court let it stand as an excise on the privilege of doing business as a corporation.[13]

Following ratification of the Sixteenth Amendment, an outright corporation income tax at the same rate was made a part of the Revenue Act of 1913 alongside the individual income tax. The two taxes together, broadened and modified through the years as circumstances required, became basic elements of the nation's revenue system.

During World War I, World War II, and the Korean War, the corporation income tax was supplemented by an excess profits tax. In most other years, revenue from taxation of corporation income has been less than that from taxation of individual income. Particularly in the past decade, the individual income tax has been far and away the greater revenue producer. In fiscal 1974, the individual tax yielded $119-billion, the corporation tax only $38.6-billion.

Excise and Other Taxes. Excise taxes have always been a part of the federal tax system; they were mentioned specifically in Article I, Section 8 of the Constitution among the various levies that Congress was authorized to impose. The excises levied upon ratification of the Constitution included taxes on carriages, liquor, snuff, sugar and auction sales. These and similar taxes have been controversial throughout the Republic's history, in important part because they were considered unfair and burdensome to the poor. Over the years, excises have been imposed and repealed or lowered; during every major war, the perennial liquor and tobacco taxes were supplemented by taxes on manufactured goods, licenses, financial transactions, services, luxury articles and dozens of other items that lent themselves to this form of taxation.[14]

Congress considerably expanded the excise-tax structure during World Wars I and II and the Korean War. The present system was enacted in 1965, when Congress scaled down the Korean War excises to all but a few major taxes. The law (PL 89-44) called for a staged reduction in excise levies that would terminate Jan. 1, 1969. As the Vietnam War grew in scale, however, President Johnson asked for and received extensions on excise items already scheduled for repeal.

President Nixon in 1969 asked, and Congress provided, for extension through calendar 1970 of the 7 per cent excise tax on automobiles. At his request, the tax was repealed in 1971.[15]

The power of Congress to tax in other areas has become well established over the years. One of the most important areas has been payroll taxes, which financially underpin the old-age insurance and unemployment compensation systems.[16] Estate taxes were imposed originally in the Civil War period, and they have been a permanent part of the national tax structure since 1916. The gift tax, levied to check avoidance of the estate tax, has been imposed on a permanent basis since 1932.[17]

Chapter 2

Tax Bills in Congress

Because tax proposals are among the most complicated pieces of legislation considered by Congress, close cooperation between the executive branch and Congress is always required when a tax bill is being drafted. Generally, the initiative on taxes in the post-World-War-II period has been taken by the administration; it has prepared the basic proposals and Congress has acted on them.[18] There is no legal or other requirement that this be the case. Congress itself initiated a major tax-reform bill in 1969. In December 1975, the House passed comprehensive tax revision legislation, the product of several years' study by the House Ways and Means Committee, but the Senate Finance Committee deferred action on the 674-page bill until 1976.

Constitutional Requirement. Tax legislation must, under a constitutional provision (Article I, Section 7, Clause 1), originate in the House of Representatives. Tax bills and bills having to do with tariffs are handled there by the Ways and Means Committee. After House passage, such bills go to the Senate and are referred to that chamber's Finance Committee, where amendments may be proposed. Amendments adopted by the Senate may be far-reaching. As in the case of all legislation, Senate-House differences over tax bills or measures involving tariff matters have to be resolved in conference. The final version, when agreed to by both houses, must then be approved by the President.

House Action

Ways and Means Committee. This committee, one of the most powerful and prestigious in the House, handles tax matters. It was created in 1802 with responsibility for both taxing and spending. Its authority over spending was gradually diminished over the years until an Appropriations Committee was created in 1865. Today the Ways and Means Committee has jurisdiction over revenue, debt, customs, trade and Social Security legislation. In addition, between 1911 and 1975, the Democratic members served as a committee on committees; they decided committee assignments for House Democrats.

The committee has had six chairmen since 1947, four Democrats and two Republicans. Of these, one—Wilbur D. Mills (D Ark.)—gained extraordinary authority over tax legislation. This was because of his length of service (he became chairman in 1958 and served until late 1974), his vast knowledge of the tax laws, his position as head of the committee which considered all tax bills as a whole (until 1975, the committee did not operate through subcommittees, although there were rare exceptions in the postwar years when special subcommittees were created to study a specific problem and then disbanded), and his renowned ability to sense the sentiment of the House and the committee and to draft tax and other measures to suit the sentiment.

Ways and Means has prided itself on its careful and professional work on tax legislation. This helped to earn it a favorable reputation in the House and resulted in House passage of almost all of the bills it has brought to the floor in the decade prior to 1975.

By 1974, however, there was growing dissatisfaction with the power of the committee and its chairman. This, coupled with disclosures concerning Mills' personal and health problems, prompted House Democrats in October and December of that year to institute far-reaching changes in the complexion and operations of the committee. Subsequently, Mills resigned the chairmanship and was succeeded by Rep. Al Ullman (D Ore.).

The changes included:

● Enlarging the committee to 37 from 25 members.

● Requiring the establishment of subcommittees, and giving members of the committee the power to determine the number and jurisdiction of its subcommittees.

● Providing that senior members of the committee would be allowed first choice for only one subcommittee slot and could not make a second choice until the junior members had each made one.

● Stripping Ways and Means of its Democratic committee assignment power and transferring it to the Democratic Steering and Policy Committee.

● Transferring revenue sharing from Ways and Means to the Government Operations Committee and export control legislation to the Foreign Affairs Committee (renamed the International Relations Committee).

As a consequence, the committee was in a great state of flux in 1975, with the "new subcommittee structure having a dramatic impact," according to Barber B. Conable Jr. (R N.Y.), a committee member.[19]

The full committee continued to handle tax legislation, but welfare, trade, Social Security, unemployment compensation and health legislation in 1975 was being written by the panel's six subcommittees. The new setup has increased the workload of committee members. Subcommittees in 1975 met on Monday and Friday and the full committee met Tuesday through Thursday. "The subcommittees are generating more legislation, which would not have been achieved without subcommittees," Conable said. The new subcommittee structure also has let Ways and Means engage in its first oversight of the Social Security program and the Internal Revenue Service.

Hearings. A bill starts on its way through Ways and Means in the normal congressional manner: testimony is collected from interested witnesses, usually leading off with the Secretary of the Treasury as the prime administration witness. Hearings often are lengthy: they consumed almost eight weeks on the controversial Revenue Act of 1964. Sometimes, however, the group will act without hearings on relatively noncontroversial bills or on questions that were the subject of previous hearings.

After hearings, the committee normally will begin mark-up sessions to draft the bill. The Treasury Department may have submitted its own bill, but preparation of

13

legal language often is left to congressional and Treasury experts working together after the hearings have delineated the general scope of the proposals to be put into a bill. Until 1973, mark-ups generally were held in executive (closed) session, but following House passage of new rules on committee secrecy in March of that year, most of the mark-up sessions have been open. (In 1974, the committee opened all but four of its 98 mark-up sessions.)

Floor Action. Once a tax bill has been drafted, approved and reported by the Ways and Means Committee, it is brought to the floor for consideration by the House. However, prior to 1973, it was taken up under special procedures which had become traditional for Ways and Means bills and all but guaranteed acceptance of the committee's work without change. Technically, under House rules, revenue legislation was "privileged" business, which meant that it could be brought up for consideration on the floor ahead of other measures and without a rule. In practice, the committee did not take advantage of this privilege because its bill would then be open to amendment. Instead, the committee obtained from the Rules Committee a "closed rule" for floor action. Under this procedure, the bill was not open to amendment in the course of House debate; essentially, the House had to accept or reject the bill as a whole. The minority party had one opportunity, at the end of debate, to try to make changes in the bill, but significant revisions seldom resulted.

There was one exception to the prohibition against floor amendments. Amendments which were approved by the Ways and Means Committee (separately from the bill) could be offered on the floor by a committee member and voted on. This gave the committee an opportunity to backtrack on any provision which appeared to be in danger of drawing unusual House opposition.

Use of a closed rule was justified on the ground that tax, trade and other Ways and Means bills were too complicated to be opened to revision on the floor, particularly because many of the proposed changes probably would be special-interest provisions designed to favor a small number of persons or groups; such floor proposals, it was argued, might upset carefully drafted legislation approved by the committee.

Nonetheless, the closed rule tradition came under attack as members of the House began to criticize the powers of the Ways and Means Committee. Finally in 1973, Democrats modified the closed rule by adopting a proposal that allowed 50 or more Democrats to bring amendments to Ways and Means bills to the party caucus for debate. If the caucus voted to approve them, the Rules Committee was instructed to write a rule permitting the amendments to be offered on the floor. In 1975, the House went a step further by changing its rules to require that all Ways and Means revenue bills must receive a rule prior to floor action and no longer had "privileged" status.

The impact of these reforms was vividly demonstrated in 1975 during consideration of two tax bills. The House Feb. 27 passed a Ways and Means Committee tax cut bill, but tacked on a provision repealing the oil depletion allowance, despite Chairman Ullman's objections. The issue was forced by the House Democratic Caucus which voted to allow a floor vote on amendments repealing the depletion allowance offered by dissident Ways and Means members. In a long-sought victory for tax revision advocates, the full House accepted the amendment by a 248-163 vote.[20]

Later that year, to assure committee approval of a tax revision package, Ways and Means Democrats agreed on floor procedures allowing their liberal members to offer floor amendments to tighten some provisions as written by the full panel. The House accepted three proposals, which further tightened the minimum tax provisions, deleted repeal of a withholding tax on foreigners' portfolio investments and removed a controversial provision allowing capital loss carrybacks worth $167-million to wealthy investors.[21]

Senate Action

Finance Committee. A House-passed tax bill is referred to the Senate Finance Committee. This committee, created in 1816, in 1975 had a membership of 18 senators. It has the same jurisdiction as the House Ways and Means Committee. The Finance Committee—like its House counterpart—until 1970 did not operate through subcommittes. In 1975, there were nine subcommittees.

Compared to Ways and Means, the Finance Committee's power and influence on revenue and related matters are limited. Moreover, the committee, through the years, has acquired something of a reputation as a haven for special-interest tax schemes. The primary reason for this trait is found in the second part of the Constitution's Article I, Section 7 on revenue matters: "...but the Senate may propose...amendments...." Because the major work on a tax bill normally is done by the House, the Finance Committee of the Senate is left with relatively little to do (compared to Ways and Means) except to tinker with the House's work and add provisions of special interest to individual senators. As a result of the Senate's power to amend House bills, the committee takes on something of a review or appellate role.

The Finance Committee holds hearings on bills sent to it by the House. As a rule, the first witnesses are administration officials led by the Secretary of the Treasury. The principal testimony of these officials and witnesses who follow after is directed to specific parts of the House bill. In addition, they may repeat much of the testimony they gave to House taxwriters. Administration witnesses of both parties who have gone through the complete tax process say that it is a grueling experience, the more so when it has to be done twice.

The committee eventually will go into mark-up session and make changes it deems necessary in the House bill. It may, and sometimes does, write basic changes into the measure sent to it by the House, but its revisions often will be primarily addition of new material. The committee, like Ways and Means, is assisted in its work by congressional tax experts (many of the same ones who assist Ways and Means) and by Treasury Department experts. Thus, the bill reported by the Finance Committee can be expected to have the characteristics of a professionally prepared tax measure which has been written after due deliberation (even though it may differ in important respects from the House bill).

Finance Committee mark-up sessions generally have been closed (in 1974, 37 per cent of 90 committee sessions were closed); but Senate approval of new open-committee rules in 1975 could change this in the future.

Floor Action. When the tax bill reaches the floor of the Senate for debate, there may be a radical departure from the careful consideration given the measure during the three previous steps. The Senate has no applicable procedures or rules to ward off amendment of a tax bill on the floor. Considering the number of tax and other financial bills that go through Congress, the Senate does not often use its amendment prerogative to basically rewrite House bills or load them with unrelated provisions. But when it does so, the event may be spectacular.

A striking example of what can happen occurred in 1966 on a bill called the Foreign Investors Tax Act.[22] It was one of the gems of legislative logrolling and mutual accommodation among members of Congress. The bill started out as a measure ostensibly intended to help the United States solve its balance-of-payments problems. But after the Finance Committee and the Senate itself had finished adding amendments, the bill contained provisions to help presidential candidates, self-employed individuals, persons in the mineral ore business, big-time investors, an aluminum company and even hearse owners. These amendments, called riders because they were germane to the purpose of the bill only to the extent that they would amend the Internal Revenue Code, earned the measure the appellation of the "Christmas-tree bill" in recognition of the numerous special tax benefits it would bestow on various groups. Many of the amendments were the product of intensive lobbying by individual groups and were attached to this particular bill because it was the last measure of the session—"the last train out of the station," as one senator put it.

One of the key provisions would have established a Presidential Election Campaign Fund in the Treasury to subsidize the costs of presidential election campaigns; the fund was to be financed by taxpayers who voluntarily designated $1 or $2 of their income-tax payments for that purpose. President Johnson called the proposal "precedent-setting." The plan was rendered inoperative in 1967 but was re-enacted in slightly different form in 1972.

The fund was a pet project of Finance Committee Chairman Russell B. Long (D La.), who worked diligently to get it added to the House bill. Efforts such as this, particularly by powerful senior senators, suggest one reason why special provisions may be added by the Senate to a tax bill. Senate riders sometimes are the result of simple logrolling, sometimes are accepted simply out of courtesy to the sponsoring senator who has a strong interest in the proposal, and sometimes are approved only because they have popular appeal and it is certain that they will be quietly dropped later in conference.

All of these reasons, especially the last-mentioned, were evident in Senate action on the tax-reform bill in 1969. The House-passed measure had emerged from the Finance Committee relatively intact, but when it reached the floor, amendments began to be proposed and accepted in considerable number. Among the more popular were: an amendment to liberalize medical deductions for elderly persons; an amendment to increase minimum Social Security payments; an amendment to allow parents a tax credit for college expenses of their children; an amendment to continue for small business the benefits of the investment tax credit (which the bill repealed); and an amendment by a senator from Alaska to retain the investment tax credit for economically depressed areas (which included all of Alaska).

This performance represented an exercise of the time-honored practice of going on record for an amendment which has considerable constituent appeal but which, many senators know, will be killed in conference. Few will publicly admit to such conduct. However, Sen. John J. Williams (R Del.), who was the senior GOP tax expert at the time and who had always taken a dim view of such activity, sharply criticized senators "who can vote for (amendments) and then go home and tell their constituents how much they wanted to help them" but who knew all the time that the proposa s would be scrapped in the end. Williams said he had already been approached by a number of senators who wanted him, as a conferee on the bill, to help kill amendments they voted for on the floor. "This is nothing but sheer political hypocrisy," he said. Williams refused to serve as a conferee on the tax-reform bill because he said he could not defend the Senate bill (as expected of a conferee); as it turned out, virtually all of the foregoing and other special-interest amendments were dropped from the final bill.[23]

The length of time the Senate may spend debating a tax bill is governed by the amount of interest in the measure and the number of amendments to be disposed of. The Senate spent more than five weeks debating a 1967 tax bill which dealt with a temporary suspension of the investment tax credit (which was repealed outright in 1969). Senate action generally runs only a few days except on tax bills of the first importance.

Conference Action

The final step in the process is a conference between senior members of the House Ways and Means Committee and of the Senate Finance Committee to resolve differences between the House- and Senate-approved versions of the bill. The conference sessions have usually been held in a small room maintained in the Capitol off the House floor by the Ways and Means Committee. The committee is presided over by the Ways and Means chairman. As a rule, there are three members from the majority and two members from the minority of the Ways and Means and the Finance Committees. The number may be enlarged for major bills, but a larger number for one side or the other makes no difference because each side votes as a unit with the majority vote controlling each group.

The conference may last from a day or two to several weeks on major or controversial bills. Congressional and Treasury tax experts are present to assist the conferees. Once all differences are resolved, the bill is sent back to each chamber for approval of the conference agreement. The House files a conference report (for both chambers) listing the differences and their resolution; it is a rather technical document and of most use to an expert; simpler explanations of conference decisions are given by senior committee members during floor discussion of the bill in both houses. If the conference agreement is approved by both, the bill is sent to the President to be signed into law.

Joint Internal Revenue Committee

One of the most important actions taken to improve the handling of tax matters by the legislative branch was the creation in 1926 of the Joint Committee on Internal Revenue Taxation. The committee itself has only 10 members—the senior members of the Ways and Means and Finance Committees. However, this is of no importance because the Joint Committee's purpose is to maintain a staff to study tax policies and problems and make recommendations to the two tax-writing committees. The Joint Committee does not have power to report bills. Over the years, it has developed a professional and highly competent staff, which in 1975, according to the *Congressional Staff Directory,* consisted of some 47 attorneys, economists and clerical assistants, who provide much of the expert knowledge needed by the House and Senate committees in formulating tax legislation. The joint committee's staff engages in all aspects of tax work from making revenue estimates to drafting tax-bill language. Members of the staff normally are present throughout the consideration of tax bills by both committees.

Congressional Initiative: the Exception

Although in most years since World War II, the administration has taken the initiative in setting tax policy, there were two major exceptions when Congress used its constitutional power to originate tax legislation. The first instance was in 1948 when a Republican Congress passed over President Truman's veto a bill reducing individual income-tax rates, increasing the personal exemption and allowing income-splitting for married couples. The second instance was in 1969 when a Democratic Congress seized the initiative on tax reform and reduction from the newly elected Republican Nixon administration, which did not have tax revision at the top of its list of priorities.

As time passed, the Nixon administration gave its support to the tax-reform bill and made recommendations of its own (many of which were adopted), but it labored under the image of being a few steps behind Congress. This was particularly true of actions in the House. The Ways and Means Committee opened tax-reform hearings at the beginning of the session, several months before the new administration was able to prepare its own proposals. In early summer the committee reported a bill with both revenue-raising reforms and revenue-losing tax cuts that went far beyond the Treasury Department's expectations. Later in the year, the administration brought itself more or less in line with the action of the Congress, but when the tax bill became law, most of the credit for its enactment (and the credit due was substantial because it was the most far-reaching tax-reform bill in decades) rested with Congress and especially the Ways and Means Committee.[24]

Chapter 3

Power Over Spending

Revenue raised through the taxing system is not available in the Treasury to be disbursed by the administration to meet governmental needs simply as agency officials deem proper. The Constitution gives to Congress the basic authority to determine how monies collected by the government shall be expended. Control of government spending is one of the most important powers of Congress. It is protected in the Constitution by Article I, Section 9, Clause 7, which states: "No money shall be drawn from the Treasury, but in consequence of appropriations made by law; and a regular statement and account of the receipts and expenditures of all public money shall be published from time to time."

Elsewhere in the Constitution (Article I, Section 8, Clause 12) a prohibition is laid down against appropriating money "to raise and support armies" for a period longer than two years. But this limitation and the Section 9 requirement of a "regular" accounting of public funds constitutes the specific authority for and limitations on spending. However, much more is implied. The Constitution directs the government to do various things, such as establish post offices, roads, armed forces and courts and take a decennial census, none of which could be done without expenditures of money. But until fairly recently there was always deep disagreement about the extent of the spending power of Congress. Only in the past few decades has

Congress used that power to finance a vast array of activities touching most aspects of the nation's life.

Welfare Clause Meaning

The constitutional provision, Article I, Section 8, Clause 1, which grants the taxing authority, ties the "power to lay and collect taxes" to the need to "pay the debts and provide for the common defense and general welfare of the United States." From the beginning, there were differences over what spending for the general welfare meant. One view was that it was limited to spending for purposes connected with the powers specifically mentioned in the Constitution; this was the strict interpretation and was associated with Madison. "Nothing is more natural nor common," he wrote in No. 41 of *The Federalist*, "than first to use a general phrase, and then to explain and qualify it by recital of particulars." The other view, associated with loose constructionists like Hamilton, was that the general welfare clause conferred upon the government powers separate and different from those specifically enumerated in the Constitution. Under the latter interpretation the federal government was potentially far more powerful than the strict constructionists intended; in fact, it was something more than a government of delegated powers.[25]

The broad interpretation came to be the generally accepted view, but it was not until 1936 that the Supreme Court had an opportunity to give its opinion on the meaning of the controversial wording. In a decision that year *(United States v. Butler*, 297 U.S. 1) the court invalidated the Agricultural Adjustment Act of 1933, which had provided federal payments to farmers who participated in a program of production control for the purposes of price stabilization. Although this law was held unconstitutional, the court construed the general welfare clause to mean that the congressional power to spend was not limited by the direct grants of legislative power found in the Constitution. Rather, an expenditure was constitutional "so long as the welfare at which it is aimed can be plausibly represented as national rather than local." The 1933 law was overturned on other grounds but was later re-enacted on a different constitutional basis and was sustained by the court. Decisions in the immediately following years upheld the tax provisions of the Social Security Act, thus confirming the broad scope of the general welfare clause.[26]

Appropriations and Budget Process Before 1921

The Constitution gives the House power to originate tax bills, but it contains no specific provision to that effect concerning appropriations (this is true also of tariff policy). However, the House has traditionally assumed the responsibility for initiating all appropriations, as well as tariff, bills and has jealously guarded this self-assumed prerogative whenever the Senate (as it has from time to time) has attempted to encroach upon it. The practical result, as far as appropriations are concerned, is that the House Appropriations Committee is more powerful than its counterpart on the Senate side. The bulk of basic appropriations decisions are made in the House committee. The general shape of any appropriations bill is derived from House consideration of the measure; what the Senate does in effect is to review the House action and hear appeals from agencies seeking changes in the allotments accorded them by the House. The Senate is free to make alterations as it deems necessary, but important changes usually are limited to revisions in the financing for a relatively small number of significant or controversial government programs.[27]

Prior to World War I, neither the expenditures nor the revenues of the federal government exceeded $800-million a year. No comprehensive system of budgeting had been developed, although the methods of handling funds had undergone various shifts within Congress. During the pre-Civil-War period, both taxing and spending bills were handled in the House by the Ways and Means Committee. That eventually proved too difficult a task for a single committee, and in 1865 the House Appropriations Committee was created. A similar situation existed in the Senate, where an Appropriations Committee was created in 1867.

In neither chamber did the appropriations power remain exclusively in the hands of these two committees. Between 1877 and 1885, the House removed from the Appropriations Committee jurisdiction over eight of 14 annual appropriations bills. These bills were placed with the substantive legislative committees. The action was taken, at least in part, to deal with what was considered an excessively independent Appropriations Committee. The Senate eventually followed the House's lead and dispersed the appropriation bills among the legislative committees. Though this division of labor allowed committees most familiar with a subject to consider the pertinent appropriations, it resulted in a division of responsibility that prevented any unified consideration or control of financial policy as a whole.[28]

The federal government has operated under a budget only since 1921—a period embracing only about one-fifth of the nation's history. However, as Louis Kimmel has noted, "The budget idea...was clearly in the minds of leading political and financial leaders as early as the Revolutionary and formative periods. The absence of logical or systematic budget methods during the early years and throughout the nineteenth century should not be construed as a lack of appreciation of the role of public finance."[29]

Ratification of the Constitution cleared the path toward establishment of a government financial system. In September 1789, Congress enacted a law establishing the Treasury Department and requiring the Secretary of the Treasury "to prepare and report estimates of the public revenues, and the public expenditures." However, according to Kimmel, "Alexander Hamilton's efforts in the direction of an executive budget were unsuccessful, mainly because of congressional jealousy and existing party divisions."[30]

Because the federal government relied on customs duties for the bulk of its revenues throughout the 19th century, and because there was an abundance of these revenues, there was no need to weigh expenditures against revenues. Consequently, the budget-making process underwent a progressive deterioration.[31]

According to Kimmel, the first important step toward establishing a federal executive budget was taken in 1910, when President Taft appointed a Commission on Economy and Efficiency to study the need for a federal budget. The commission concluded that a restructuring of the system for determining and providing for the financial needs of the government was of paramount importance. But Congress resented the commission's proposed system, and its report was not even considered by the House Appropriations Committee to which it was referred.[32]

Modern Budgeting Procedure

The diffuse appropriations system that had grown up in the first 130 years of the nation's life could no longer meet the financial needs of an increasingly complex government after World War I. Federal receipts exceeded $4-billion in all except two years in the 1920s, and expenditures dropped only to about $3-billion at the lowest point (fiscal 1927). Having seen the government spend $18.5-billion in fiscal 1919, which included the last 4¹₂ months of the war, and having appropriated $6.5-billion for fiscal 1920, the first full postwar year, Congress decided it must reorganize its financial machinery, both to retrench on expenditures and to tighten control over the execution of fiscal policy.[33]

The reorganization was accomplished through enactment of the Budget and Accounting Act of 1921. First, however, the House on June 1, 1920, restored exclusive spending powers to its Appropriations Committee and enlarged the committee from 21 to 35 members (55 in 1975). The Senate on March 6, 1922, similarly concentrated spending powers in its Appropriations Committee but left the membership at the existing total of 16 (in 1975 it was 26).

In the Budget and Accounting Act, Congress sought also to reform the financial machinery of the executive branch. The 1921 act established two important offices—the Bureau of the Budget and the General Accounting Office (GAO). The former was created to centralize fiscal management of the administration directly under the President; the latter was designed to strengthen the oversight of spending.

Bureau of the Budget. With passage of the 1921 act, Congress ended the right of federal agencies to decide for themselves what appropriations levels to ask of Congress; the Budget Bureau, serving under the President's direction, was to act as a central clearinghouse for administration budget requests.

Budget Circular 49, approved by President Harding on Dec. 19, 1921, required that all agency proposals for appropriations be submitted to the President prior to presentation to Congress. Agency proposals were to be studied for their relationship to "the President's financial program" and were to be sent on to Capitol Hill only if approved by the President. The bureau, though placed in the Treasury, was kept under the supervision of the President."[34]

In 1935, President Roosevelt broadened the clearance function to include other legislation as well as the appropriations requests.

Roosevelt in 1939 issued, and Congress approved, Reorganization Plan No. 1, creating the executive office of the President and transferring the Budget Bureau from the Treasury to the new office. By presidential directive, Roosevelt also broadened the bureau's clearance function by making it responsible for coordination of department views on all measures sent to the White House for the President's signature or veto. That responsibility had been limited previously to views on appropriations bills. Any recommendation that the President withhold his approval of a bill was required to have to be accompanied by a draft veto message or, in the case of a pocket veto, a memorandum of disapproval. These procedures were further strengthened by later Presidents.[35]

In 1970, President Nixon streamlined the budget process by restructuring the Bureau of the Budget.[36] The new office, called the Office of Management and Budget (OMB), was given sweeping authority to coordinate the execution of government programs as well as the Budget Bureau's old role of advising the President on agency funding requests. In 1974, Congress enacted legislation making future OMB directors and deputy directors subject to Senate confirmation.

The Government Accounting Office. Congress, in setting up the GAO, was attempting to strengthen its surveillance of spending. The GAO is headed by the comptroller general and assistant comptroller general, appointed by the President with the advice and consent of the Senate, for a period of 15 years. They can be removed only by joint resolution of Congress, thus making the agency responsible to Congress rather than the administration. The comptroller general was granted wide powers to investigate all matters relating to the use of public funds and was required to report annually to Congress, including in his report recommendations for greater economy and efficiency in public expenditures.

Many of the auditing powers and duties of the comptroller general had already been established by the

Dockery Act of 1894, which assigned them to the new office of the comptroller of the Treasury. But under that act the comptroller and his staff remained executive branch officers, and Congress lacked its own agency for independent review of executive expenditures.

In their book, *Federal Budget Policy,* David J. Ott and Attiat F. Ott describe the three major types of audits made by the GAO. "Recently, the *comprehensive audit* has become the most important. This audit concentrates on the accounting and reporting system used by a particular agency and checks transactions selectively. The *general audit* examines the accounts of agency disbursing and certifying officers to determine the legality of each transaction. If illegal or improper handling of receipts or expenditures is discovered, recovery procedures are instituted against the responsible officer. The *commercial audit* is applied to government corporations and enterprises. No recovery is possible in this case, but Congress is informed of questionable or improper practices."[37]

The results of GAO audits are transmitted to Congress by the comptroller general. The results of special investigations of particular agencies and the annual report are referred to the House and Senate Committees on Government Operations.

Appropriations Procedures

The complex budgetary process begins in the various agencies of the executive branch as estimates are made of the funds needed to carry out government programs. All of the estimates are brought together in the White House (previously by the Budget Bureau but under the 1970 reorganization by the Office of Management and Budget). At this point, the requests of the agencies are coordinated with presidential policies and expected revenues.

The President presents his budget to Congress in January. The estimates and requests that it contains are for the fiscal year which will begin the following July 1. (In 1976, the government changed from a fiscal year of July through June to one beginning Oct. 1 and ending the following Sept. 30.)

The expenditure of money by a government agency is the last of three main steps: Congress first authorizes a program of activity for which funds will be needed and sets a ceiling on the amount of these funds. Second, Congress provides the authority to spend money, usually through appropriations but sometimes through other means; the amount of money provided often is less than the maximum amount specified in the authorization for the program. Third, the agency in the government spends the money on the program.

Once funds have been appropriated or otherwise made available, their expenditure is under the control of the departments and agencies in the executive branch, although the congressional committees—particularly the Appropriations Committees—generally keep close track of how the officials are using the funds.

Authorization Requirement

The congressional procedure which leads to the expenditure of funds is a multi-step process. The substantive legislative committees of each chamber of Congress consider the proposed programs; this is the start of the authorizing step. Once the respective programs have been authorized by vote of the two houses and the President's approval, it is up to the Appropriations Committees of each chamber to recommend appropriations for the programs. Passage of the appropriations bills follows. Each step, first as to authorization and then as to appropriation of funds, is an essential part of the congressional process.[38]

The Appropriations Committees cannot act until the authorization has been signed into law. The House has had a rule since 1837 which provides that "No appropriation shall be reported in any general appropriation bill, or be in order as an amendment thereto, for any expenditure not previously authorized by law...." The Senate had a similar rule, but because appropriations bills originate in the House, the House rule is governing. There are some exceptions, such as a portion of the annual military spending that is authorized by the Constitution, but generally appropriations must await authorizations.

This requirement has led to conflict in Congress on numerous occasions. In the 1950-1970 period, Congress required to be authorized annually more and more programs that previously had permanent or multi-year authorization.

The trend to annual authorizations represented a victory for the legislative committees—such as the Committee on Education and Labor in the House for matters under its jurisdiction—which felt that they had lost effective control over their programs to the Appropriations Committees. The Appropriations Committees, particularly in the House, took a dim view of the annual authorizations, in part because they tended in some degree to diminish their power.

The annual authorization trend contributed important-ly to delaying the enactment of appropriations bills beyond the July 1 beginning of the new fiscal year. Rarely since the late 1950s has Congress completed action on more than one or two appropriations bills by July 1. This was due in part to the prohibition against appropriations action before an authorization bill is enacted. Another factor was the in-creasing number and complexity of government programs that required more time for congressional review.

The result has been to force the government to go into its new financial year without most of its regular funding bills enacted into law. Congress has got around the problem by adopting continuing resolutions that allow agencies to spend at certain levels (usually that of the previous fiscal year) for a specified time, which often has to be extended. This practice pleased hardly anyone. In an attempt to rec-tify the situation, Congress in the 1974 Congressional Budget and Impoundment Control Act established deadlines for clearing authorization and appropriations bills. It also changed the date on which the new fiscal year begins to Oct. 1.

House Appropriations Action

Although the President's budget is sent to Congress at the beginning of each regular session in massively detailed form (the President also submits an economic report at the beginning of each session), until 1975 it was seldom debated or considered as a whole. The detailed business of studying the budget proposals and preparing the appropriations bills was done piecemeal in subcommittees.

The House Appropriations Committee, like the Ways and Means Committee, is one of the most powerful and prestigious. It has been composed in large part of senior members of the House elected from safe congressional districts. It is a conservative body which believes it has a duty to reduce the budget requests submitted to it. This, it usually does—at least overall.

The true power of the committee resides in its 13 (in 1975) subcommittees. When the President's budget reaches Congress, it is divided among the subcommittees which function largely as independent kingdoms. The subcommittees are set up along functional lines: Agriculture, Defense, Interior, Labor-HEW and so on, roughly paralleling the 14 (in 1975) regular appropriations bills cleared by Congress. Generally, the members of the subcommittees become very knowledgeable and often expert in their assigned areas. The subcommittees, and particularly their chairmen, consequently wield substantial power over spending.

House Appropriations subcommittee hearings were traditionally closed, with testimony almost always restricted to that given by agency officials. A voluminous record of the hearings, along with the parent committee's report, usually was not made public until shortly before House floor action on an appropriation bill. As a result, few if any members not on the subcommittee were prepared to challenge the bill. The Legislative Reorganization Act of 1970 provided that all House committee and subcommittee hearings must be open, but not if a majority determines otherwise. In 1974, the Appropriations Committee opened 90 per cent of its hearings, but closed almost half of its mark-ups. Nine of the panel's 13 subcommittees opened all of their mark-ups in 1974, compared with only two in 1973.[39]

The 1970 act provided also that the House Appropriations Committee hold hearings on the President's budget as a whole within 30 days of its receipt; directed the setting up of a standardized data processing system for federal budgetary and fiscal data; and directed the President to send Congress five-year forecasts of the fiscal impact of all federal programs.

As a result of congressional reform efforts, the House Appropriations Committee underwent substantial changes in 1974-75. As of the beginning of the 94th Congress, chairmen of all the appropriations subcommittees had to be approved by the House Democratic Caucus. The caucus also voted in late 1974 to restrict senior Democrats to membership on only two of a committee's subcommittees.

This was aimed mainly at the Appropriations Committee, where senior conservative Democrats dominated important subcommittees handling defense, agriculture, and labor, health, education and welfare appropriations.

Instead of fragmenting the committee, the strengthening of subcommittees in 1975 made the committee much more active by giving its liberals a greater voice in the panel's work. Rep. David R. Obey (D Wis.), an Appropriations member who was a prime mover in reforming the panel, called the subcommittee changes "absolutely crucial" to loosening the control of conservative Chairman George Mahon (D Texas) "and the college of cardinals [the conservative subcommittee chairmen]" over the committee.[40]

House procedure on appropriation bills permits amendments from the floor. However, the prestige of the Appropriations Committee is such that few major changes are ever made. By and large, the amounts endorsed by the Appropriations Committee during the post-World War II period have been accepted by the House; administration efforts to win "restoration" of cuts in the budget estimates have been concentrated on the Senate.

Senate Appropriations Action

Once an appropriations bill has passed the House, it is sent to the Senate and referred to the Appropriations Committee where a parallel system of subcommittees exists. The Senate subcommittees review the work of the House at hearings which are open to the public. The Senate subcommittees do not attempt to do the same amount of work on a bill that the House has already done; the time required (often it is getting late in the year by the time the Senate receives appropriations bills) and the heavy workload of most senators preclude the same detailed consideration that is given in the House. The Senate subcommittees are viewed more as appellate groups which listen to administration witnesses requesting the restoration of House-cut funds. The subcommittee normally will restore some of the funds denied by the House, although it may make cuts in other places. The Senate itself may add or restore more when the bill reaches the floor. Most appropriations bills carry larger total amounts when they pass the Senate than when they passed the House. The differences are resolved in conference, generally by splitting the difference between the two.

Chapter 4

1974 Budget Act

The "power of the purse"—defined broadly to include both receipts through taxes and outlays through appropriations—clearly is a basic power which the framers of the Constitution intended to impart to Congress. Over the years, Congress has jealously and successfully guarded its powers of taxation from encroachment by the executive branch; this is the basic reason why Presidents Kennedy and Johnson were unsuccessful in obtaining standby authority to alter tax rates for economic purposes.

However, Congress has been much less successful, at least since New Deal days, in retaining control over government expenditures. And, until 1975, it was totally unsuccessful in relating expenditures to revenues even though the two are intrinsically linked. The responsibility for doing so thus fell to the administration.[41]

Efforts to Control Spending

Prior to 1974, efforts had been made in Congress to exert overall control over appropriations (and in turn, therefore, government spending)—basically with the intention of holding appropriations to a minimal level. Attempts were made also to use the tax system to hold down government outlays and to tie the two together in Congress. But none of these undertakings met with great success, and most were dismal failures during the Johnson and Nixon administrations and the first year of Ford's administration.

Well aware of the unfortunate record and the need to do something about it, Congress in 1974 enacted legislation to reform its budget procedures. At the end of its first year of (partial) operation in 1975, Congress' attempt to launch a revolutionary new federal budget system appeared to be working.

Background

Setting the framework for reasserting congressional control over government spending, Congress June 21, 1974, completed action on legislation (HR 7130—PL 93-344) that revised and elaborated the procedures by which Congress considers the federal budget.

As written, the Congressional Budget and Impoundment Control Act would force Congress into more measured and timely action on budgetary legislation, tying its separate spending decisions together with fiscal policy objectives in a congressionally determined budget package.

Following a budget reform format prepared in 1973 by a joint study committee, the law required Congress before acting on appropriations and spending measures to adopt a budget resolution setting target figures for total appropriations, total spending and appropriate tax and debt levels. The measure created new House and Senate Budget Committees to analyze budget options and prepare the budget resolutions. The committees are assisted by a new Congressional Budget Office (CBO).

While building on the existing committee structure in considering authorization and appropriations bills, the act established a detailed timetable setting deadlines for floor action on various spending measures. To fit the expanded budget-making procedures into the yearly congressional session schedule, the act shifted the federal government onto an Oct. 1-Sept. 30 fiscal year, giving Congress an additional three months to wrap up its budget review. Before the fiscal year begins, Congress must reconsider its budget targets and reconcile its spending actions.

Correcting existing practices that foiled congressional control over federal spending levels, the law provided procedures for putting limits on backdoor spending programs and for forcing the President to spend impounded funds. *(Box on backdoor spending, p. 34)*

However, the act allowed a waiver of its procedural and deadline requirements at several stages. Thus, the success of the new budget process depended on Congress' determination to discipline its spending decisions.

The process was a sweeping reform designed to focus Congress' attention in a systematic way on two broad budgetary concerns: national fiscal policy and national priorities.

The process requires members of Congress for the first time to vote on a deficit. Instead of treating spending and

Backdoor Spending

One form of spending authority was particularly controversial in the 1950s and 1960s. It went under the general name of "backdoor spending," a label applied by its opponents, but it included different types of authority.

In general, backdoor spending reduced the control of Congress over government spending, and it virtually wiped out the authority of the Appropriations Committees over the programs which it covered.

By 1974 only about 60 per cent of federal spending was subject to annual appropriations. The rest either did not require yearly appropriations or created obligations that Congress had no choice but to meet through appropriations. This "backdoor spending" authority was provided through such devices as the following:

● *Borrowing authority,* which permits an agency to borrow either from the Treasury or the public.

● *Contract authority,* which allows agencies to enter into contracts that require future appropriations.

● *Permanent appropriations,* in which funds are made available under basic legislation and no further appropriations action is required. Authority to pay interest on the public debt is one example.

● *Mandatory spending (entitlement programs),* in which basic legislation requires payments—such as Social Security, welfare or veterans' benefits—and forces the enactment of appropriations.

tax measures individually and separately, Congress is forced to compare total spending with total receipts. In doing so, Congress must confront such fiscal policy issues as the effect of the budget on inflation, unemployment and economic growth.

The Budget Act also required members for the first time to make choices and thereby set priorities. For example, if Congress calls for more spending for health programs, it now must increase revenues through higher taxes, accept a larger deficit, or balance the addition by cutting other programs.

So Congress in 1975 began viewing the federal budget as a balloon, which when squeezed in one place would pop up in another. "People are seeing for the first time where all the money is going, and I'm not sure they like it," said House Budget Committee Chairman Brock Adams (D Wash.).

In reforming its budget procedures, Congress in 1974 undertook a task that it tried and abandoned nearly 25 years before.

In three years of trying, the House and Senate never got together to fully implement a legislative budget created by the Legislative Reorganization Act of 1946 (PL 79-601). After unsuccessful attempts in 1947, 1948 and 1949, Congress abandoned the experiment as an unqualified failure.

Similar in some respects to the reform procedures adopted by Congress in 1974, the 1946 act required that Congress set by concurrent resolution a maximum amount to be appropriated for each fiscal year.

That appropriations ceiling was part of a legislative budget based on revenue and spending estimates prepared by a massive Joint Budget Committtee composed of all members of the House and Senate Appropriations Committees and of the tax-writing House Ways and Means and Senate Finance Committees.

In 1947, conferees failed to agree on Senate amendments to the budget resolution providing for use of an expected federal surplus for tax reductions and debt retirement.

In 1948, Congress appropriated $6-billion more than its own legislative budget ceiling, and in 1949 the legislative budget never was produced as the process broke down completely.

One of the principal reasons the legislative budget failed was the inability of the Joint Budget Committee to make accurate estimates of spending so early in the session and before individual agency requests had been considered in detail. In addition, the committee was said to be inadequately staffed and, with more than 100 members, to be much too unwieldy for effective operation.[42]

Failure of the legislative budget prompted a serious effort in Congress in 1950 to combine the numerous separate appropriations bills into one omnibus measure.

The traditional practice of acting on the separate bills one by one made it difficult to hold total outlays in check. In 1950, the House Appropriations Committee agreed to give the omnibus-bill plan a trial. The overall bill was passed by Congress about two months earlier than the last of the separate bills had been passed in 1949. The appropriations totaled about $2.3-billion less than the President's budget requests. The omnibus approach was praised by many observers. It was particularly well received by persons or groups seeking reductions in federal spending.

Nevertheless, the House Appropriations Committee in January 1951 voted 31 to 18 to return to the traditional method of handling appropriations bills separately. Two years later, in 1953, the Senate proposed a return to the omnibus plan, but the House did not respond. The plan was dead. Opponents said the omnibus bill required more time and effort than separate bills. Equally important was the opposition of the House Appropriations subcommittee chairmen, who feared that some of their power would be eroded under the omnibus-bill plan.[43]

In addition to the legislative budget and omnibus plan, other proposals to control federal spending were made during the post-war period. None of these was enacted; and Congress had to fall back on its traditional practice of adding to appropriations bills specific restrictions on how the money provided in the bills could be spent.

Congress began another effort to strengthen its control over the budget process in 1972 when it established a Joint Study Committee on Budget Control. The 32-man committee held hearings and in 1973 made recommendations which were incorporated in the 1974 act. Impetus for action was provided by struggles between Congress and the Nixon administration over presidential impoundment of funds.

Major Provisions of the 1974 Act.

The final version of the 1974 Budget Act was the product of intense staff negotiations both during Senate consideration and in conference. As it emerged from conference, the bill tended to follow more detailed Senate provisions where the two versions differed. Following is a summary of the major provisions of the act.[44]

Budget Committees. To give Congress a more expert perspective on budget totals and on fiscal policy requirements, the budget reform act established House and Senate Budget Committees to study and recommend changes in the President's budget.

Assuring that existing House committees concerned with budgetary matters would be represented on the 23-member House Budget Committee, the act assigned five seats to Ways and Means Committee members and five to Appropriations Committee members. The remaining seats are occupied by one member from each of the eleven legislative committees, and by one member from the majority leadership and one from the minority leadership of the House.

The act rotated House Budget Committee membership by prohibiting any member from serving for more than four years out of a 10-year period. Members on the committee must serve for a full Congress.

The 15-member Senate Budget Committee is picked by normal Senate committee selection procedures. No rotation is required, but after 1976, any member holding seats on two other major committees must drop one.

Budget Submission. In moving to an Oct. 1-Sept. 30 fiscal year, the act established a timetable to assure orderly action on spending measures before the fiscal year began.

To give Congress a quicker start in shaping the budget, the act required the executive branch to submit a "current services" budget by Nov. 10 for the fiscal year that would start the following Oct. 1.

Building on the programs and funding levels in effect for the ongoing fiscal year that had started the month before, the November current services budget projects the spending required to maintain those programs at existing commitment levels without policy changes through the following fiscal year. The Joint Economic Committee reviews the current services budget outlook and reports its evaluation to Congress by Dec. 31.

As under existing law, the President submits his revised federal budget to Congress about Jan. 20. In addition to the customary budget totals and breakdowns, however, the act required the budget document to include a list of existing tax expenditures—revenues lost to the Treasury through preferential tax treatment of certain activities and income—as well as any proposed changes.

The measure also required that the budget include estimates of costs for programs whose funds were required to be appropriated one year in advance before they were obligated. Thus the budget would include projections for spending during fiscal 1980, for example, of funds provided under an advance appropriation requested from Congress for fiscal 1979.

Other provisions directed that the budget figures be presented in terms of national needs, agency missions and basic federal programs. The budget also has to include five-year projections of expected spending under federal programs.

Budget Office. The act established an office within Congress to provide the experts and the computers needed to absorb and analyze information that accompanied the President's budget. The act required the Congressional Budget Office to make its staff and resources available to all congressional committees and members, but with priority given to work for the House and Senate Budget Committees. (The CBO also assumed the functions and staff of the Joint Committee on Reduction of Federal Expenditures, which was abolished.)

The office is run by a director appointed for a four-year term by the Speaker of the House and the president pro tempore of the Senate and paid $42,000 annually.

Budget Resolution. After reviewing the President's budget proposals—and considering the advice of the budget office and other committees—the House and Senate Budget Committees draw up a concurrent resolution outlining a tentative alternative congressional budget.

Under the law's timetable, congressional committees have until March 15 to report their budget recommendations to the budget committees. The budget office report is due on April 1.

By April 15, the budget committees must report concurrent resolutions to the House and Senate floors. By May 15, Congress must clear the initial budget resolution.

The initial resolution, a tentative budget, sets target totals for appropriations, spending, taxes, the budget surplus or deficit and the federal debt.

Within those overall targets, the resolution breaks down appropriations and spending among the functional categories—defense, health, income security and so forth—used in the President's budget document.

The resolution also includes any recommended changes in tax revenues and in the level of the federal debt ceiling. If Congress so chooses, the first resolution also could direct that appropriations bills and bills creating federal entitlement programs when cleared by Congress be withheld from the President until Congress had completed its budget reconciliation process in September.

The budget targets are broken down in another way reflecting the congressional committee structure once House and Senate conferees reach agreement on the final version of the first budget resolution. In their statement on the conference agreement, the conferees allocate the targets among committees in Congress that would consider legislation providing the funds to be spent within the total and functional category targets.

The Appropriations Committees, which would be considering the bulk of spending proposals requiring appropriations, would further subdivide their allocations among the 13 subcommittees that handle appropriations for different departments and agencies.

Each committee also would allocate its share of the spending targets between controllable spending and spending that was beyond immediate congressional control.

Appropriations Process. Once enacted, the budget resolution guides but does not bind Congress as it acts on appropriations bills and other measures providing budget authority for spending on federal programs.

No measure appropriating funds, changing taxes or the public debt level or creating a new entitlement program committing the government to pay certain benefits may be considered on the floor before adoption of the first budget resolution. In the Senate, however, that prohibition may be waived by majority vote.

To clear the way for prompt action on appropriations before the fiscal year begins, the law requires that all bills authorizing appropriations be reported by May 15, the deadline for enactment of the budget resolution. That requirement may be waived, however, by majority vote in both the House and the Senate.

There are two exemptions from the May 15 deadline for reporting authorizing legislation: for Social Security legislation, dealing with a variety of trust funds and welfare programs, and for entitlement legislation that could not be considered on the floor until the budget resolution had been cleared.

Starting with programs for fiscal 1977, the law requires the administration to make requests for authorizing legislation a year in advance.

Under its terms, the administration would have to submit its requests by May 15 for the fiscal year following the fiscal year that would start on Oct. 1. That would give congressional committees a full year to study the requests before the following May 15 deadline for reporting authorization bills for the fiscal year in question.

For example, for fiscal 1977, which would start on Oct. 1, 1976, authorization requests would be submitted by May 15, 1975, and authorization bills reported by May 15, 1976.

After enactment of the budget resolution, Congress begins processing the 13 regular appropriations bills for the upcoming fiscal year through its customary appropriations process: House Appropriations subcommittee and full committee action, House floor action, Senate Appropriations subcommittee and full committee action, Senate floor action and conference action.

The law directs the House Appropriations Committee to try to complete action on all appropriations measures and submit a report summarizing its decisions before reporting the first bill for floor action.

All appropriations bills have to be cleared by the middle of September—no later than the seventh day after Labor Day. That deadline also applies to final action on entitlement bills.

The deadline may be waived, however, for any appropriation bill whose consideration was delayed because Congress had not acted promptly on necessary authorizing legislation.

If Congress so provides in its initial budget resolution, appropriations and entitlement bills may be held up after final action on conference reports. Under that procedure, no appropriations bills would be sent to the President until Congress had completed a September reconciliation of its initial budget targets with its separate spending measures.

Reconciliation. In mid-September, after finishing action on all appropriations and other spending bills, Congress takes another overall look at its work on the budget.

By Sept. 15, Congress must adopt a second budget resolution that could either affirm or revise the budget targets set by the initial resolution. If separate congressional decisions taken during the appropriations process do not fit the final budget resolution totals, the resolution may dictate changes in appropriations (both for the upcoming fiscal year or carried over from previous fiscal years), entitlements, revenues and the debt limit.

The resolution would direct the committees that had jurisdiction over those matters to report legislation making the required changes.

If all the required changes fell within the jurisdiction of one committee in each house—appropriations changes that the Appropriations Committees would consider, for example—those committees then would report a reconciliation bill to the floor.

If the changes involved two committees—appropriations changes by the Appropriations Committees and tax changes by the House Ways and Means and Senate Finance Committees, for example—those committees would submit recommendations to the Budget Committees. The Budget Committees then would combine the recommendations without substantial change and report them to the floor as a reconciliation bill.

If Congress withholds all appropriations and entitlement bills from the President, reconciliation may be accomplished by passage of a resolution directing the House clerk and secretary of the Senate to make necessary changes in the bills previously cleared. A reconciliation bill still could be needed, however, to change tax levels or other provisions already enacted into law.

Backdoor Spending. The law attempted to bring most forms of new backdoor spending programs under the appropriations process, but existing backdoor programs remained outside that process. The bill required annual appropriations of funds for spending from new contract authority or borrowing authority programs.

Contract authority permits federal officials to enter into contracts obligating the federal government to make certain payments before the money is appropriated; borrowing authority permits federal officials to incur indebtedness in advance of appropriations to pay back the money.

Entitlement programs commit the federal government to pay benefits to all eligible recipients. Because the government cannot control the number of eligible recipients—at least without tinkering with eligibility standards—it has little control under existing procedures over total spending on these programs. Congress has no choice but to appropriate the funds required to meet the obligations.

In devising special procedures for entitlement programs, the act relied on the initial budget resolution's allocations of spending limits for guidelines on how much spending would be permissible on new programs in the upcoming fiscal year.

Under the new procedures, a bill reported by an authorizing committee to establish a new entitlement program would be referred to the Appropriations Committee if the amount of the appropriations authorized by the bill exceeded the authorizing committee's allocation set out after adoption of the congressional budget resolution.

The Appropriations Committee then would have 15 days to consider the measure and report an amendment putting a limit on appropriations for the new program. If the Appropriations Committee did not act within 15 days, the measure would go on the calendar as reported.

To tie consideration of entitlement bills closely to the budget-making process, the act prohibited floor action on entitlement bills before adoption of the first budget resolution. And no entitlement legislation could go into effect before the start of the fiscal year, making the spending it provided subject to revision in the reconciliation stage.

Exempted from the act's backdoor spending procedures were all Social Security trust funds, all trust funds that received 90 per cent or more of their financing from designated taxes rather than from general revenues, general revenue sharing funds, insured and guaranteed loans, federal government and independent corporations and gifts to the government.

Impoundment. The act prescribed two different procedures for Congress to deal with impoundments (a tactic used by Presidents to withhold expenditures of previously appropriated funds): one for impoundments that simply delayed the spending of funds and a tougher procedure for impoundments made to cut total spending or to terminate programs.

For impoundments that merely deferred spending, Congress could force the President to release the funds if either the House or the Senate passed a resolution calling for their expenditure. No time limit for congressional action was set.

For impoundments that terminate programs or cut total spending for fiscal policy reasons, the act requires congressional action to rescind the previous appropriations action providing the funds. Unless both the House and Senate pass a rescission bill within 45 days, the President must spend the money.

To remove language in existing law that had been cited as justification for presidential impoundments, the act repeals a clause in the Anti-Deficiency Act of 1950 allowing the executive branch to withhold funds from obligation because of "other developments" as well as to save money or take account of changing requirements or improved efficiency.

To keep Congress informed on impoundment actions, the bill requires the President to report deferrals or to request rescissions. If the comptroller general finds that impoundments have been made without reports to Congress, he may report the impoundments himself and Congress then may act to force release of the funds.

If a President refuses to comply with a congressional action overruling an impoundment, the comptroller general may go to court for an order requiring spending of the funds.

Chapter 5

The National Debt

Through the years, and particularly since the New Deal days of the 1930s, the national debt and congressional control over it have been controversial subjects. The debt has become increasingly a political issue as compensatory fiscal policies and budget deficits have gained popular acceptance. Growth of the national debt gave legislators and other public officials a convenient opening to express their views on government spending; but expansion of the debt had little effect in curbing the spending.

Constitutional Authority. The Constitution, in Article I, Section 8, Clause 2, gives Congress the power "to borrow money on the credit of the United States." This is a very broad power.[45] Ogg and Ray's *Introduction to American Government* noted that the "power to borrow not only is expressly conferred in the Constitution, but is one of the very few federal powers entirely unencumbered by restrictions—with the result that Congress may borrow from any lenders, for any purposes, in any amounts, on any terms, and with or without provision for the repayment of loans, with or without interest."[46] Ogg and Ray noted also that the United States has no constitutional debt limit, whereas many state constitutions and state charters for counties and local governments impose debt ceilings. The United States has had a statutory debt ceiling for many decades, but the ceiling can be altered easily by Congress and, in fact, has been raised repeatedly—although seldom without an intense political fight in Congress.

Composition of the Debt

Debt has been incurred by the federal government when it has found it necessary to spend more than it has collected in tax and other forms of revenue. When expenditures outstrip revenues, the deficit must be made up by borrowing. Through much of the nation's history, a surplus resulting from an excess of revenues over expenditures has been used, at least in part, to reduce outstanding debt. Since the long string of federal budget deficits began in fiscal 1931, there have been budget surpluses in only seven years. It was during this period that the bulk of the national debt (estimated to reach $605.9-billion by the end of fiscal 1976) had been incurred.

The debt consists of various types of obligations. David J. Ott and Attiat F. Ott in *Federal Budget Policy* gave the following definitions: "The federal debt consists of direct obligations or debts of the U.S. Treasury and obligations of federal government enterprises or agencies. It is...broken down into 'public debt'—that part issued by the Treasury—and 'agency debt'—that part issued by federal agencies. The public debt consists of issues (that is, bonds, notes and bills), which are generally sold to the public (some are held by federal agencies and trust funds), and 'special issues,' which are held only by government agencies and trust funds. Of the issues sold to the public, some are 'marketable,' that is, they are traded on securities markets, and some are 'nonmarketable' and cannot be traded (for example, U.S. savings bonds). The latter may, however, be redeemed in cash or converted into another issue."[47]

Philosophy Prior to 1930s

Throughout most of the nation's history, the principal concern of government in regard to budget policy was to assure that revenues were sufficient to meet expenditure requirements. This philosophy, which in application meant an approximate balance between receipts and outlays, was generally accepted from the beginning until the early 1930s.

Lewis H. Kimmel wrote in *Federal Budget and Fiscal Policy, 1789-1958:* "From the beginning of our national history, ideas in public finance have been influenced by the unfolding of events. At the outset acceptance of the balanced budget philosophy was facilitated by the adverse financial experience during the Revolutionary War and under the Articles of Confederation. There was an awareness that the public credit is a valuable resource, especially in an emergency. The experience of the preceding fifteen years suggested to Hamilton and others that the preservation of the public credit depended on the consolidation of existing indebtedness and the provision of adequate revenues for debt service. The thought that the interests of the new nation would be best served if Hamilton's ideas were adopted was soon translated into policy."[48]

Kimmel pointed out that three key ideas were generally accepted by federal officials and economists alike during the period leading up to the Civil War: (1) a low level of public expenditures was desirable; (2) the federal budget should be balanced in time of peace; and (3) the federal debt should be reduced and eventually extinguished. "These ideas," he observed, "were a reflection of views that were deeply rooted in the social fabric."[49]

The Civil War, like other major wars of modern times, resulted in a much enlarged national debt. The reported debt in 1866 amounted to almost $2.8-billion in contrast to less than $90.6-million in 1861. The debt was gradually reduced after the war to a low of $961-million in 1893. However, after the Civil War, there was less concern about eliminating the outstanding debt; increasingly, the emphasis was on servicing the debt in an orderly manner. Proposals to liquidate it became fewer and fewer.

From the post-Civil War low point in 1893, the debt increased very slowly for half a dozen years and then hovered between $1.1-billion and $1.2-billion until 1917, when the United States entered World War I. The debt jumped from just under $3-billion in fiscal 1917 to a peak of $25.5-billion at the end of fiscal 1919. In the 1920s the debt receded steadily, year by year, down to $16.2-billion at the end of fiscal 1930.

Rise of Debt

In 1930 and following years, the nation was faced with the problems of the Great Depression. Kimmel noted of the early years of the Depression: "A concerted effort was made by the President and the leadership of both parties in Congress to adhere to the balanced-budget philosophy. Yet a balanced federal budget was almost impossible to attain—the annually balanced-budget dogma in effect gave way to necessity. Alternatives were soon suggested, and within a few years what came to be known as compensatory fiscal theory gained numerous adherents."[50]

The practice of using the federal budget to help solve national economic problems was increasingly accepted. Budget deficits and a rapidly increasing national debt were the result. The debt rose to nearly $50-billion—almost twice the World War I peak—at the end of fiscal 1941. Then came Pearl Harbor. The debt passed the $100-billion mark in fiscal 1943 and exceeded $269-billion in fiscal 1946. No steady reduction followed World War II. The debt total fluctuated for a few years but then began a new rise which took it past the World War II peak in fiscal 1954, past $300-billion in fiscal 1963 and all the way to $475-billion at the end of fiscal 1974.

Congress and the Debt

The first overall debt ceiling was established Sept. 25, 1917, by the Second Liberty Bond Act, which fixed a limit of $11.5-billion. By 1945, Congress had amended the act 16 times, and the ceiling had been lifted to $300-billion. In June 1946, the high World War II limit was reduced to a "permanent" $275-billion ceiling. However, as Congress continued to vote more appropriations than taxes, and the executive branch to spend more than it took in, budget deficits resulted and the debt continued to rise. There followed perforce repeated ceiling increases, almost all of which were accompanied by strong partisan activity in Congress and much sermonizing on the evils of federal expenditures and indebtedness.[51]

Although Congress actually had little choice but to increase the statutory debt limit, the heated debates —primarily in the House—suggested that the events were milestones in public financial affairs. The controversy over rising debt ceilings flowed essentially from the broader issue of government spending. The proponents of a statutory debt ceiling—including those who would refuse to raise it or who would lower it—saw the ceiling as a form of expenditure control. They believed that a firm commitment by Congress not to increase the limit would force a halt in spending, especially spending that exceeded tax revenues.

Officials in the executive branch responsible for paying the government's bills, as well as many members—indeed, a majority—of Congress, were convinced that a debt ceiling could not control expenditures. Throughout the postwar period, Secretaries of the Treasury expressed their opposition to use of the debt ceiling for that purpose.

A typical statement came from Treasury Secretary Douglas Dillon in a 1963 speech: "Let no one labor under the delusion that the debt ceiling is either a sane or an effective instrument for the control of federal expenditures. No one is more conscious than I of the need to keep government spending under firm control. But this cannot be done by trying to exert controls at the tag end of the expenditure process, when the bills are coming due. The debt limit is not and cannot be made a substitute for the control of expenditures at the decisive stage of the expenditure process—when the funds are being appropriated." Even a staunch critic of government spending, Rep. Thomas B. Curtis (R Mo., 1951-69), once said that trying to stop spending by use of the debt limit was like trying to stop an elevator from going up by grabbing the indicator arrow.[52]

One characteristic aspect of the debt-limit debate in postwar years was that the opposition to raising the limit was led by conservatives who sought to reduce government spending. But expenditures during these years—even during the Republican Eisenhower administration—showed a steady increase. The increase reflected not only the adoption of new government programs but also a buildup of political pressures on Congress that made it difficult to cut and relatively easy to add to existing levels of expenditures.

When it came down to the actual voting, Congress always raised the debt ceiling enough to enable the government to meet its financial obligations. But the attendant congressional debate gave members so inclined an excellent opportunity to throw the spotlight on the public indebtedness and government spending.

PART II
Foreign Affairs

Chapter 6

Legislative-Executive Antagonism

Historical practice and the rush of world developments have broadened immensely the late 18th century American attitudes which limited foreign policy to the making of treaties and, if necessary, the waging of war. Hence the division of foreign policy power between the President and Congress, as laid down in 1787 has been severely strained.

The Constitution assigned to Congress the powers "to...provide for the common defense and general welfare of the United States; ...to regulate commerce with foreign nations; ...to define and punish piracies and felonies committed on the high seas and offenses against the law of nations; to declare war...and make rules concerning captures on land and water; to raise and support armies; ...to provide and maintain a navy; ...to make all laws which shall be necessary and proper for carrying into execution the foregoing powers...."

The Constitution also states: "The President shall be Commander-in-Chief of the Army and Navy.... He shall have power, by and with the advice and consent of the Senate, to make treaties, provided two-thirds of the senators present concur; and he shall nominate and, by and with the advice and consent of the Senate, shall appoint ambassadors, other public ministers, and consuls.... He shall receive ambassadors and other public ministers; he shall take care that the laws be faithfully executed...."

The division of power over foreign affairs has stirred up antagonism between the legislative and executive branches of government on numerous occasions.[1] Two outstanding facts have emerged from the resulting picture of alternate tension and cooperation: first, the overwhelming importance of presidential initiative in this area of power; and second, the ever-increasing dependence of foreign policy on congressional cooperation and support. *(Footnotes, p. 311)*

Issuance of a Proclamation of Neutrality by President Washington in 1793, upon the outbreak of war between France and Great Britain, marked the start of the continuing struggle between the President and Congress for control of the nation's foreign policy. The proclamation was attacked by the pro-French Jeffersonian Republicans as a usurpation by the President of authority granted to Congress. In a series of articles published in a Philadelphia newspaper under the pseudonym "Pacificus," Alexander Hamilton defended Washington's action. He argued that the conduct of foreign relations was in its nature an executive function and therefore, except where the Constitution provided otherwise, belonged to the President, upon whom was bestowed "the executive power." Possession by Congress of the power to declare war, as well as other powers affecting foreign relations, did not diminish the discretion of the President in the exercise of the powers constitutionally belonging to him, Hamilton said.[2]

This view was disputed by James Madison, writing as "Helvidius." Emphasizing that the vital power to declare war was vested in Congress, Madison took the position that the powers of the executive in foreign relations were to be strictly construed. Doubt as to the exact location of any power in this field was to be resolved in favor of the legislature. Madison attempted to bolster his argument by pointing to the confusion likely to ensue if concurrent discretionary powers were exercised by different branches of the government. "A concurrent authority in two independent departments, to perform the same function with respect to the same thing," he declared, "would be as awkward in practice as it is unnatural in theory." Over time, however, Hamilton's view has prevailed.

Despite the widely recognized prerogatives of the President in foreign relations, the fact is that Congress has enormous powers which are indispensable to the support of any foreign policy. Moreover, congressional laws made in pursuance of these powers are the "supreme law of the land," according to the Constitution, and the President is bound constitutionally to "take care that" they "be faithfully executed."

As Louis Henkin has pointed out in his book, *Foreign Affairs and the Constitution*, "The vast legislative powers of Congress that relate particularly to foreign affairs do not begin to exhaust its authority to make law affecting foreign relations. Congress has general powers that, taken together, enable it to reach virtually where it will in foreign as in domestic affairs, subject only to constitutional prohibitions protecting human rights. The power to tax (Article I, Section 8, Clause 1) has long been a power to regulate through taxation, and could be used to control, say, foreign travel.... Major programs depend wholly on the 'spending power'...—to 'provide for the common Defence and general Welfare of the United States'—and it has been used in our day for billions of dollars in foreign aid.

"Other, specialized powers also have their international uses: Congress has authorized a network of international agreements under its postal power (Article I, Section 8, Clause 7), and there are international elements in the regulation of patents and copyrights. The express power to govern territory (Article IV, Section 3) may imply authority to acquire territory, and Congress determines whether territory acquired shall be incorporated into the United States. Congress can exercise 'exclusive legislation' in the nation's capital, its diplomatic headquarters (Article I, Section 8, Clause 17). The power to acquire and dispose of property has supported lend-lease and other arms programs, and sales or gifts of nuclear reactors or fissionable materials.... By implication in the Constitution's grant of maritime jurisdiction to the federal judiciary (Article III, Section 2), Congress can legislate maritime law."[3] In addition, the fact that the appointment of ambassadors, public ministers and other diplomatic officers requires the advice and consent of the Senate gives that body a considerable degree of control over foreign relations (Article II, Section 2, Clause 2).[4] Finally, the power to appropriate funds—for defense, war and general execution of foreign policy—rests solely with Congress (Article I, Section 9, Clause 7).[5]

Presidential Leadership

Early Presidents—Washington, Adams, Jefferson, Madison and Monroe—exercised dominant influence in determining the country's relations with other nations. Washington's Neutrality Proclamation and his Farewell Address, and Monroe's warning against foreign intervention in the Western Hemisphere, laid the basis for American foreign policy.[6]

Much of the 19th century was dominated by the twin domestic issues of slavery and development of the American West, which shifted national attention away from foreign affairs. Presidential authority in that field was somewhat less effective, and the executive branch suffered a number of serious setbacks. A major turn in foreign policy, strongly supported by Congress, was taken in 1898. The country dropped its traditional policy of nonintervention, went to war to rid Cuba of Spanish rule, and emerged from the conflict with overseas outposts as far distant as the Philippines in the western Pacific.

During most of the present century, particularly in the years since World War II, the President has been the leader in foreign affairs. An important exception was the 15-year period of commanding congressional influence following Senate rejection of the Treaty of Versailles after World War I. But on the eve of the next great conflict, the country's overseas interests as interpreted by the President began to dominate American foreign policy.

On balance, until the mid-1970s, the foreign affairs legislation enacted by Congress operated to increase presidential powers much more frequently than it operated to curtail them. A classic example of this tendency was the passage of the lend-lease act in the spring of 1941. It authorized the President to "sell, transfer title to, exchange, lease, lend, or otherwise dispose of" defense articles to any country "whose defense the President deems vital to the defense of the United States."

Changing Role of Congress

As American policies toward other nations have evolved, the role of Congress in foreign affairs has shifted. The Senate, which once claimed dominant influence because of its part in treaty making, plays no part in the making of the increasingly popular executive agreements with foreign countries; executive agreements do not require Senate approval. In addition, it has been argued that the power of Congress to declare war has lost significance as modern weapons have made surprise attack more and more advantageous, if not a matter of necessity, for an aggressor nation. The war power of Congress has been eroded also by actions taken under the constitutional authority claimed by the President as commander-in-chief.

At the same time, congressional influence over other aspects of foreign affairs has greatly expanded. Legislative authority over the massive, post-World War II foreign aid, defense and military assistance programs is an example. The programs have required specific congressional authorizations and repeated congressional appropriations. Furthermore, foreign policy implications surround much other legislation, such as Food for Peace, regulation of immigration, shipping subsidies, space exploration, the Peace Corps and import quotas. Meanwhile, the fundamental constitutional authority for a share of the treaty-making power and the war power continues to underlie this sweeping congressional involvement in foreign affairs.

Congressional Assertiveness

The period spanning the late 1940s and early 1950s was characterized by what Francis O. Wilcox, in his book *Congress, the Executive and Foreign Policy*, has called "extraordinary executive-legislative cooperation." "During this period," he said, "the bipartisan approach to foreign policy reached its zenith."[7] The Senate approved, by overwhelming votes, the United Nations Charter, the peace treaty with Italy, and the whole network of regional security treaties—the Rio Treaty, NATO, SEATO, and other collective and mutual security arrangements. Congress approved the Marshall Plan, aid to Greece and Turkey, and U.S. participation in a wide variety of U.N. specialized agencies.

By the late 1960s, however, Congress was increasingly restive with what many members considered the aggrandizement of presidential foreign policy power. Critics usually cited these examples of presidential actions: waging costly undeclared wars in Korea and Vietnam, sending troops to other parts of the world without first securing congressional consent and negotiating an array of international commitments through executive agreements not subject to congressional approval. As a result, Congress made several attempts to limit the President's power to send troops abroad, make defense commitments and wage war without legislative approval.

A first indication of congressional discontent occurred in 1951. During the "great debate" concerning Truman's authority to send troops to Europe, two resolutions were introduced to require congressional authorization for sending military forces abroad. Neither measure cleared Congress. Two years later, Sen. John W. Bricker (R Ohio) proposed a constitutional amendment intended to restrain the President's power to make executive agreements. The amendment was rejected in 1954.

Disillusionment with the Vietnam War in the 1960s prompted Congress to make new efforts to regain influence in foreign affairs. In June 1969, by an overwhelming 70-16 vote, the Senate adopted a "national commitments" resolution which declared the sense of the Senate that a national commitment by the United States results "only from affirmative action taken by the executive and legislative branches of the United States government by means of a treaty, statute, or concurrent resolution of both houses of Congress specifically providing for such commitment." In 1969 and 1970, Congress repeatedly attempted to terminate funds for U.S. military activities in Indochina. During that period, Congress used its investigative powers to probe the extent of American commitments abroad—particularly through a series of hearings conducted by the Senate Foreign Relations Subcommittee on United States Security Agreements and Commitments Abroad, chaired by Stuart Symington (D Mo.).[8]

Congressional action in the early 1970s was highlighted by passage of a tough war powers measure over the President's veto in July 1973. The measure set a 60-day limit on any presidential commitment of U.S. troops to hostilities abroad, or to situations where hostilities might be imminent, without specific congressional authorization.

In 1974, Congress passed a major trade reform bill only after approving an amendment linking trade concessions for Communist countries to their emigration policies. And throughout the 1970s, Congress played an important role in shaping U.S. policy in the Middle East by repeated calls for continued military support for Israel. In 1974, in reaction to the Turkish invasion of Cyprus, Congress imposed a ban on military aid and arms shipments to Turkey (the ban was partially lifted in October 1975). Congress in 1975 also began weighing new controls on the sale of U.S. weapons abroad.[9]

In 1975, committees in both chambers conducted a major probe of the American intelligence community—the first such investigation since establishment of the Central Intelligence Agency in 1947. The investigations brought to light numerous abuses of power by intelligence and law enforcement agencies and resulted in recommendations for structural changes in both Congress and the agencies so as to improve congressional oversight in the future.

These are but a few examples of congressional atttempts to fashion for itself a more influential role in foreign policy; they seem to indicate, as Wilcox has phrased it, that "a tide has clearly been running toward a larger congressional role in foreign policy and, perhaps more importantly, toward a new conception of that role."[10]

Chapter 7

The Treaty Power

The whole of the treaty-making power is contained in a single clause of the Constitution. Spelling out presidential authority, Article II, Section 2, Clause 2 declares: "He shall have power, by and with the advice and consent of the Senate, to make treaties, provided two-thirds of the Senators present concur...."

For years this clause served as a cornerstone of American foreign policy. It brought peace with other nations, supported American territorial expansion, established national boundaries, protected U.S. commerce and regulated government affairs with Indian tribes."

Despite its importance, the clause was ambiguous on some points, and the ambiguities led from the beginning to conflicts between the executive and legislative branches. Neither the Senate procedure for advising the President nor the stage of treaty making at which the Senate was to act in an advisory capacity was defined. And, the role of the House of Representatives in treaty making, to the extent that legislation or appropriations were needed to make a treaty effective, was ignored. The Constitution was silent on all of these points.

It is generally agreed that the main purpose of the advice-and-consent formula was to provide for democratic control of foreign policy. In the early years of the nation, the executive branch sought to incorporate Senate advice into the process of treaty negotiation by such means as presidential meetings with senators, Senate confirmation of negotiators, and special presidential messages. But as international relations became more complicated, the early administrations abandoned, one after the other, the various devices by which the Senate's advice had been obtained.

Deprived of opportunities to make its influence felt in treaty negotiations, the Senate resorted to advising the President through drastic amendment—or outright rejection—of completed treaties. The historically dramatic climax of senatorial dissatisfaction came in 1919 and 1920 with the prolonged debate on, and ultimate rejection of, the Treaty of Versailles, which embodied not only the World War I treaty of peace with Germany but also the Covenant of the League of Nations.

Senate's Ratification Record

Despite the shock caused by rejection of the Versailles pact, and consequent reinforcement of the Senate's popular reputation as a graveyard of treaties, its overall record on ratification has been overwhelmingly favorable. Between 1789 and 1976, only 11 treaties were rejected through failure to receive a two-thirds majority in the Senate.[12] The last treaty rejected was an optional protocol to the law-of-the-sea conventions, concerning compulsory settlement of disputes in 1960.

Presidential reaction to rejection of the Treaty of Versailles took two forms. On the one hand, the White House made renewed efforts to court Senate support of proposed treaties by reinstituting some of the old, and developing some new, methods of associating senators with the treaty-making process. On the other hand, there was a growing tendency to rely on the executive agreement as a vehicle of international accords, thus eliminating altogether the need for Senate approval. There was reaction also in Congress, where various constitutional amendments were proposed to curtail the power of the Senate in the making of treaties.

New Importance of Treaty Power

In the years following World War II, the treaty-making power took on added importance. Membership in the United Nations was accomplished by Senate consent to ratification of the U.N. Charter, while membership in an expanding number of international organizations was brought about either by treaty or by both House and Senate approval of appropriate legislation. Treaties were used to conclude the widening circle of U.S. mutual security agreements designed to provide collective defense against aggression. (By the mid-1970s, the United States was committed to the defense of 42 countries through eight mutual security treaties.)[13] Agreements aimed to guide the peaceful and restrict the military use of atomic energy were incorporated in treaties, as were agreements intended to curtail the spread and production of nuclear armaments. And as man opened new frontiers in space and under the oceans, additional treaties were concluded or proposed to govern his behavior there.

Old conflicts over treaty making were renewed in the postwar years. It was a time of strong executive branch leadership, producing congressional reaction which came to a head in 1953-54 with consideration of the Bricker amendment, a proposal to limit presidential treaty power.

Action of Constitutional Convention

At the root of the recurring conflict between the President and Congress over the treaty-making power has been the doctrine of separation of powers that is so basic to the governmental structure of the United States.

During the Constitutional Convention, the treaty power came up for discussion repeatedly. At first, it was assumed that the existing power of the Continental Congress to make treaties by a two-thirds majority would be transferred intact to the legislative branch of the new government. Continued legislative control of treaty making was taken for granted despite the fact that it was then the exclusive prerogative of the executive in all other governments at that time.

The first suggestion that the treaty power should be divided between the legislative and executive branches seems to have been made in the convention on June 18, 1787. Hamilton proposed an executive elected for life, who, along with many other powers, would have "with the advice and approbation of the Senate, the power of making all treaties."[14] There was no discussion of Hamilton's suggestion, and it appeared dead when the Aug. 6 report of the Committee of Detail proposed that "the Senate shall have power to make treaties." Debate on the committee's report failed to resolve the issue of who was to exercise the treaty power. The section was referred back to the committee. On Sept. 4, the report of the Committee of Eleven recommended that "the President, by and with the advice and consent of the Senate," would have the power to make treaties, and that no treaty could be made "without the consent of two-thirds of the members present." Several attempts were made to alter the proportion of the Senate whose consent would be required, and to add House participation in treaty making, but on Sept. 8 the provision as proposed in the report was finally agreed to.[15]

There was nearly unanimous support in the convention for some means of enabling the new government to require the states to honor treaty provisions. Although the Articles of Confederation entrusted the treaty-making power to Congress, fulfillment of Congress' promises to other nations was dependent on the state legislatures. Inaction, or adverse action, by certain states had led to violation of some articles of the Peace Treaty of 1783 with Great Britain. A solution was provided in the declaration of Article VI, Clause 2 of the Constitution that "all treaties made, or which shall be made, under the authority of the United States shall be the supreme law of the land...."

Exclusion of the House from the treaty-making process was defended by Hamilton and Jay in *The Federalist.* Using similar arguments, they contended that the legislative role in treaty making should be limited to the Senate because decisions on treaties would thus be placed in the hands of persons chosen by the "select assemblies" of the states instead of by the rank and file, because the longer and overlapping Senate terms would provide relatively greater continuity, because the smaller size of the Senate would aid "secrecy and dispatch," and because agreement among the President, the Senate and the House would be more difficult to obtain.[16]

Form of Senate Consent. In performing its constitutional treaty-making functions, the Senate merely consents to the ratification of a treaty; ratification itself is subject to executive action. Normally, the Senate considers a resolution of advice and consent to ratification of a pending treaty. In the case of the nuclear test-ban treaty, approved by the Senate on Sept. 24, 1963, the resolution of ratification read as follows:

"Be it resolved (two-thirds of the senators present concurring therein), that the Senate advise and consent to the ratification of the treaty banning nuclear weapons tests in the atmosphere, in outer space, and under water, which was signed at Moscow on Aug. 5, 1963, on behalf of the United States of America, the United Kingdom of Great Britain and Northern Ireland and the Union of Soviet Socialist Republics."

Consideration of First Treaties, 1789

The first treaties to be laid before the Senate under the Constitution were submitted on May 25, 1789.[17] They were a pair of treaties with Indian tribes negotiated and signed under the authority of the Continental Congress. It was not until June 12 that the two treaties were referred to a committee for study; in the meantime, the President had submitted another treaty, a consular convention with France, concluded under the Articles of Confederation. After a series of meetings with, and reports from John Jay, secretary of foreign affairs, an office held over from the Confederation, the Senate on July 29, 1789, unanimously consented to ratification of the consular treaty.[18] This was the first time the Senate had given its advice and consent to ratification of a treaty.

The committee studying the two Indian treaties finally reported on Aug. 12. Instead of recommending that the Senate advise and consent to ratification (as had been done with the consular treaty with France), the committee recommended that the President "be advised to execute and enjoin an observance" of the agreements. The Senate on Sept. 8 approved the committee recommendation for one of the treaties (that with the Wyandot, Delaware, Ottawa, Chippewa, Pattawattima and Sacs nations) but took no action on the other (that with the Six Nations, except the Mohawks).

The Senate action confused President Washington. He was not certain whether the Senate meant that he should merely see that the approved treaty went into operation or that he should proceed with a formal ratification. In a message to the Senate, Sept. 17, the President asked for a clarification. His own opinion, he said, was that treaties with Indian tribes should be ratified in the same way as treaties with European nations. The Senate disagreed. A committee that studied the President's message reported, Sept. 18, that since past Indian treaties never had been solemnly ratified, it was not "expedient or necessary" to ratify the present treaties. The committee proposed a resolution to advise the President "to enjoin a due observance" of the Wyandot treaty, passing over the treaty with the Six Nations. But on Sept. 22 the Senate substituted a resolution of advice and consent to the Wyandot treaty. No action was taken on the other agreement. Senate consent to ratification of the Wyandot treaty set a precedent that endured for more than 70 years. However, a rider to the Indian Appropriations Act of 1871 provided that in the future no American Indian nation or tribe was to be considered an independent nation with which the United States could conclude a treaty. Indian affairs were to be handled subsequently by statute.[19]

Advice of the Senate

The first treaties considered by the Senate had been negotiated under instructions from the Continental Congress because there was no executive in the confederation government. Although the new Constitution provided for an executive and authorized him to make treaties, with advice from the Senate, it failed to explain what kind of advice was appropriate or how it was to be offered. It was clear, however, that to be effective the advice would have to be given before the conclusion of negotiations.

In practice, procedures developed by Washington and the first Senate established precedents which have exerted varying degrees of influence. After an abortive attempt at personal consultation with the Senate as an executive council, Washington's usual practice, at least up to the Jay treaty negotiations with Great Britain in 1794, was to ask for advice about opening negotiations; to transmit the full instructions to be given to the negotiators; to submit their names for confirmation; and to keep the Senate fully informed of the progress of negotiations. If matters came up which were not covered in the original instructions,

Washington again would call for Senate advice.[20] When treaties would require subsequent appropriations to carry them into effect, he reported the proceedings to the House as well as to the Senate.

Additional procedures adopted by early administrations included requests for advance appropriations to cover the cost of negotiating, naming of senators and representatives to the negotiating team and consulting personally with key members of the Senate, and, after its establishment in 1816, with the Foreign Relations Committee. At times Congress took the initiative by considering resolutions to suggest or to oppose negotiations.

Consultation. While the Senate was considering the first treaties, it named a committee of three senators, Aug. 6, 1789, to meet with the President to establish ground rules for consultation on the making of treaties. Washington favored oral communications rather than written exchanges, and, following a committee recommendation, the Senate on Aug. 21 adopted a rule providing for meetings with the President either in the Senate chamber or elsewhere. Later the same day, the Senate received a message announcing that Washington was coming to the Senate chamber the next day "at half past 11 o'clock" to discuss proposed terms for a treaty with the southern Indians.

Unfamiliar with the background of the situation or with the proposed treaty terms, the Senate sought to refer the papers to a committee for study. Washington, who had hoped for prompt action, objected strenuously. He finally agreed to defer action to Aug. 24. The second meeting went more smoothly; the Senate agreed to vote its advice on each of the points raised by the President.[21] However, Washington never again went before the Senate to consult on treaty terms or discuss foreign policy, nor did any other President until Woodrow Wilson appeared on Jan. 22, 1917, to call for "peace without victory" and propose a League for Peace. President Truman also went to the Senate in person, July 2, 1945, to ask its early consent to ratification of the United Nations Charter. President Nixon appeared before Congress June 1, 1972, to urge approval of the U.S.-Soviet strategic arms limitation talks (SALT) accords.

President Washington, after his initial venture in direct consultation, relied on special messages in seeking the advice of the Senate. Tradition says that the chilling reception which he had met in the Senate chamber led him to swear that he would never go there again.[22]

Although Washington's general position was that he considered it advisable to postpone negotiations until he had received the advice of the Senate as to the propositions to be offered, he did not follow this course in the case of the Jay treaty. He submitted Jay's name as a negotiator for confirmation by the Senate but withheld the instructions to be given him.[23] The same procedure was adopted by Washington's immediate successors, Adams and Madison.

Polk returned to the earlier practice when in 1846 he asked the Senate's advice as to whether negotiations should be undertaken with Great Britain on the basis of proposals submitted from London for the settlement of the Oregon boundary question.[24] Similar requests for preliminary advice were sent to the Senate by Buchanan, Lincoln, Johnson, Grant and Cleveland. Harding, in 1922, asked advice as to revival of a patents treaty with Germany.

The right of the Senate to direct treaty making by proposing negotiations has been vigorously debated on the Senate floor. Proponents have defended such initiative as the right and duty of the Senate under the Constitution, and as helpful in showing the United States to be a unit in its demands. Opposition senators have contended that for the Senate to make the first move was "officious and disrespectful," and that it tended to "shelter" the President from responsibility in treaty making. In 1902 a report by the Committee on Foreign Relations declared: "The initiative lies with the President.... Whether he will negotiate a treaty, and when, and what its terms shall be are matters committed by the Constitution to the discretion of the President."[25]

Today the right of either house of Congress to offer advice about negotiations is not questioned, but the advice of the legislative branch is merely persuasive, and not compelling. In its landmark decision in the *Curtiss-Wright* case in 1936 *(U.S. v. Curtiss-Wright Export Corp.,* 299 U.S. 305) the Supreme Court ruled: "The President...alone negotiates. Into the field of negotiation the Senate cannot intrude, and Congress itself is powerless to invade it."[26]

The reaction of different administrations to Senate advice to negotiate has varied. President Jackson acted on a

Senate resolution in opening negotiations with Central American governments for an interoceanic canal. Cleveland replied with some asperity to a similar Senate suggestion for negotiations to limit Chinese labor. Harding refused to recognize that the Borah resolution for agreement with Great Britain and Japan on reduction of naval expenditures was responsible for the calling of the Washington Conference on the Limitation of Armament. Sponsored by Sen. William E. Borah (R Idaho), the resolution was adopted by the Senate May 26, 1921, and by the House on June 29. Formal invitations to the conference were issued Aug. 11, 1921.[27]

Confirmation of Negotiators. Up to the end of Madison's administration, the names of treaty negotiators were referred to the Senate for confirmation. Subsequent neglect of the practice was repeatedly protested in the Senate. In 1883, the Senate attempted in ratifying a treaty with Korea to revive the earlier practice by adopting a resolution which stipulated that the consent given to ratification did not "admit or acquiesce in any right or constitutional power in the President to employ any person to negotiate treaties...unless such person shall have been appointed...with the advice and consent of the Senate."[28] Cleveland's appointment of a special commissioner with "paramount authority" to negotiate with Hawaii was declared by the Republican members of the Foreign Relations Committee to be "an unconstitutional act in that such appointee was never nominated to the Senate.[29]

That confirmation of negotiators gave the Senate an important power was recognized by both the Senate and the executive branch. Commenting on the situation when one of Adams' nominations was under attack, Jefferson wrote that, were a large opposition vote registered, even if confirmation resulted, "it is supposed the President would perhaps not act under it, on the probability that more than a third would be against ratification."[30]

Abandonment of the practice of Senate confirmation of negotiators appears to have been due to the need for secrecy which led to employment of special agents whose appointment was recognized as the right of the executive in carrying out his constitutional duties, and to acceptance of the principle—in Jefferson's words to Citizen Genet, envoy to the United States from the first French Republic—that the

President is "the only channel of communication between this country and foreign nations."[31]

In later years, on various occasions, the executive sought Senate confirmation of treaty negotiators. Polk submitted the names of his appointees to negotiate a treaty with Mexico. Grant nominated to the Senate the commissioners who negotiated the Treaty of Washington with Great Britain. Harding submitted the names of his appointees to the World War Foreign Debt Commission in 1922, but such submission was required by a provision of the act creating the commission, which stipulated that its members be appointed by the President, "by and with the advice and consent of the Senate."[32]

The United Nations Participation Act of 1945 provided for Senate confirmation of the United States representatives to the United Nations, of members of the U.S. delegation to the General Assembly, and of delegates to various U.N. agencies.

Negotiators' Instructions. Submission of their instructions along with the names of negotiators, amounted, while Washington was President, to an opportunity for the Senate to advise on treaty proposals. No opportunity to consider the terms of a treaty not yet agreed upon was provided during ensuing administrations until Polk submitted the skeleton of a treaty ending the war with Mexico in 1846. Preliminary drafts of treaties were sent to the Senate in a few instances by four other executives—Buchanan, Lincoln, Johnson and Grant. In 1919, the Senate requested a copy of the Treaty of Versailles as presented to the representatives of Germany. The Secretary of State replied: "The President feels it would not be in the public interest to communicate to the Senate a text that is provisional and not definite, and finds no precedent for such a procedure."[33]

In at least two instances, the Senate (with the concurrence of the House) has "advised" the executive by specifying the limits within which negotiators of international agreements were to operate. In the act of February 9, 1922, creating the Foreign Debt Commission it was provided that "nothing contained in this act shall be construed to authorize...the commission to extend the time of maturity of...obligations due the United States...beyond June 15, 1947, or to fix the rate of interest at less than $4\frac{1}{4}$ per centum per annum."[34] In a joint resolution making funds available to send a delegation to the Opium Conference of 1924, Congress specified certain results to be obtained by the negotiators.

Members of Congress as Negotiators. The first two members of Congress to be selected to negotiate a treaty were Sen. James A. Bayard (Federalist Del.) and House Speaker Henry Clay (Ky.). Madison named them to help negotiate a treaty of peace with Great Britain in 1814.[35] Both resigned their places in Congress on the ground that the two offices were not compatible. On at least three occasions resolutions have been introduced in the Senate to prohibit members of that body from serving as treaty negotiators.[36] The first, in 1870, was defeated after a heated all-night debate, when it was turned into a question of confidence in President Grant. The second was occasioned by McKinley's appointment, following a series of such congressional appointments by himself and his predecessors, of three members of the Committee on Foreign Relations on the commission to negotiate the Treaty of Paris in 1898. The Committee on Foreign Relations, to which a resolution of protest was referred, hesitated to make a report that might appear to censure its own members, but it directed its chairman to visit the President and express the Senate's strong disapproval.[37] Theodore Roosevelt's selection of Sen. Henry Cabot Lodge (R Mass.) for the Alaskan boundary tribunal led to the third attempt of the Senate to prohibit such service by senators. The resolution introduced at that time was not acted upon.

Senate resentment of Wilson's failure to include any senators on the 1919 peace commission came as a sharp contrast to its previous position. To compensate for lack of representation on the commission, a resolution calling for the appointment of a bipartisan committee of eight senators to visit Paris during the sittings of the Peace Conference, to "make itself familiar with all facts" and report to the Senate "as often as it deemed desirable," was introduced but not acted upon.[38] Senate attempts to advise as to negotiations through debate on the floor and through a round-robin warning against inclusion of provisions for a League of Nations in the peace treaty proved to be without effect.

As a result of Wilson's experience, the appointment of senators to important international conferences has since been frequent. President Harding in 1921 chose the chairman of the Senate Committee on Foreign Relations, Sen. Henry Cabot Lodge (R Mass.), and the minority leader, Sen. Oscar W. Underwood (D Ala.), as delegates to the Conference on the Limitation of Armament, and members of both houses were appointed by Hoover to the American delegation to the London Naval Conference in 1930. President Roosevelt recognized Congress in his selection of commissioners to the World Monetary and Economic Conference, in 1933 and to the International Refugee Conference in 1943.

In 1945, the eight-member U.S. delegation to the United Nations founding conference at San Francisco included four members of Congress: Foreign Relations Committee Chairman Tom Connally (D Texas), Sen. Arthur H. Vandenberg (R Mich.), a committee member, and Reps. Sol Bloom (D N.Y.) and Charles A. Eaton (R N.J.), chairman and ranking minority member of the House Foreign Affairs Committee. Since organization of the United Nations, two senators and two representatives have alternated as members of the U.S. delegation.

During the postwar period, successive administrations have followed the practice of including members of Congress on delegations to international conferences. Wilcox offers this assessment of the practice: "On balance, congressional participation in international conferences seems to have done very little harm and some good. In a few cases...congressional cooperation has been of inestimable value, not only in the drafting process but in securing Senate approval of the finished product. Measured quantitatively over the years, it has most often simply been neutral, having no results commensurate with the time, trouble and money required."[39]

Consent of the Senate

Over the years, Senate action on treaties has led to recurring rounds of controversy. At issue traditionally have been rival claims by the President and the Senate with respect to the treaty power.

The Senate has adopted a simple resolution of consent to ratification on a vast majority of treaties submitted to it. It has modified or rejected relatively few.[40] But the significance of some of the rejected treaties has prompted criticism of the Senate's treaty-making role, as well as the two-thirds rule, and has spawned a variety of proposed constitutional amendments designed to modify its power.

Treaties are transmitted to the Senate by the President under an injunction of secrecy which normally is removed shortly after the Senate receives the treaty. Once a treaty is submitted, it remains before the Senate until it is disposed of favorably, or until the President requests its return and the Senate agrees.[41]

Senate Procedures. Senate consideration of a treaty is open to presidential discretion at a number of points. The President may refuse to submit a treaty; he may withdraw it after submission; or he may refuse to ratify it even after the Senate has given its consent.[42]

Within the Senate, treaties are subject to the jurisdiction of the Foreign Relations Committee whether or not they involve subjects that usually require consideration by another committee. The Foreign Relations Committee considers a treaty in much the same way that it considers proposed legislation. It may hold open or closed hearings and may recommend adoption or rejection, with or without modifications. Committee actions require a majority vote of the members present; to act, according to the Legislative Reorganization Act of 1946, a committee majority must be "actually present."[43]

After action by the Foreign Relations Committee, treaties are considered by the full Senate. The Senate used to debate treaties in closed executive session, preserving the cloak of secrecy. Pressures later developed to make public the Senate treaty debates. A fisheries treaty with Great Britain was considered—and defeated—in the first open executive session in 1888. Other public treaty debates followed, and the Senate on June 18, 1929, amended its rules to provide that all Senate business, including action on treaties, would be conducted in open session unless a Senate majority decided in a closed session to consider a particular matter in secret.[44]

After a brief experiment (1801 to 1803) with a rule requiring a two-thirds vote on all treaty action, the Senate limited the two-thirds rule to the final question of advice and consent and to a motion for indefinite postponement. All other questions are decided by majority vote.[45]

A separate vote normally is taken on each treaty. But that procedure is sometimes departed from when a large number of similar treaties, or a variety of noncontroversial treaties, is to be considered. It has become the practice in these cases to consider the group of treaties en bloc (taking one vote on several resolutions of consent) or to take a single vote, which by unanimous consent is shown separately in the *Congressional Record* for each resolution. Although Senate rules do not require roll-call votes on treaties, that practice has become customary. It grew out of a 1952 incident in which three noncontroversial consular conventions were approved, on June 13, when only two senators were present in the chamber. On July 20, 1953, acting Majority Leader William F. Knowland (R Calif.) announced that "as a matter of standard operating procedure in the future, we intend, in connection with all treaties...not only to ask for a quorum call, but to ask for a yea-and-nay vote...."[46]

Modification of Treaties. In the Constitution, there is no provision for or against amendment of treaties by the Senate. But since the time of the Jay treaty with Great Britain, the Senate has claimed authority to modify treaties after the completion of negotiations. The Senate on June 24, 1795, by a 20-10 vote consented to ratification of the Jay treaty on condition that an additional article be negotiated to suspend portions of the treaty's 12th article that related to trade between the United States and the British West Indies. Scores of later treaties have been subjected to amendments, reservations, conditions and qualifications, some of them added at the request of the President.[47]

The wisdom of the Senate practice of amending treaties was questioned as early as 1805 by John Quincy Adams. In a Senate debate, Adams said, "I think amendments to treaties imprudent. By making them you agree to all the treaty except the particular you amend, and at the same time you leave it optional with the other party to reject the whole."[48] A later opinion was voiced by Secretary of State Richard Olney, after Senate rejection of an Anglo-American arbitration treaty in 1897: "...Senators have exhausted their ingenuity in devising amendments to the treaty. Before the treaty came to a final vote, the Senate brand had been put upon every part of it, and the original instrument had been mutilated and distorted beyond all possibility of recognition."[49]

On two occasions the Supreme Court has sustained the power of the Senate to amend treaties. In 1869, in the case of *Haver v. Yaker* (9 Wall. 34), the court stated: "In this country a treaty is something more than a contract, for the federal Constitution declared it to be the law of the land. If so, before it can become a law, the Senate in whom rests the power to ratify it, must agree to it. But the Senate are not required to adopt or reject it as a whole, but may modify or amend it."[50] And in a 1901 opinion *(Fourteen Diamond Rings v. U.S.*, 183 U.S. 183) the court said: "The Senate may refuse its ratification or make it conditional upon adoption of amendments to the treaty."[51]

Probably the best known of recent Senate qualifications of U.S. international obligations is the Connally reservation to the compulsory jurisdiction clause of the statute of the International Court of Justice. In adhering to the U.N. Charter in 1945, the United States accepted membership in the court. President Truman contended that the country should also accept compulsory jurisdiction under terms of the court's statute, which excluded matters deemed to be within the domestic jurisdiction of any nation; and on July 31, 1946, the Senate took up a resolution to that effect.

Recalling fears which led to Senate refusal in 1935, after a decade of discussion, to approve adherence to the earlier World Court, some senators objected to letting the International Court of Justice determine what matters might or might not be within U.S. jurisdiction. To obviate this possibility, Sen. Tom Connally (D Texas) proposed adding after a clause excluding "matters which are essentially within the domestic jurisdiction of the United States" the words "as determined by the United States." The Senate agreed to the Connally reservation on Aug. 2, 1946, by a 51-12 vote, in effect negating the U.S. commitment in principle; it then adopted the amended resolution by a 60-2 vote. Attempts to repeal the reservation have failed.[52]

When the Senate adopts a treaty amendment, the amendment, if it is accepted by the President and the other parties to the treaty, changes it for all parties. A Senate reservation limits only the treaty obligation of the United States, although a reservation may be so significant that the other treaty parties may file similar reservations or refuse to ratify the treaty.

The Senate Foreign Relations Committee has identified four major forms which a treaty qualification may take.

● The Senate may consent to ratification and include its views or interpretations in a committee report accompanying the treaty.

● Senate "understandings" or "interpretations" may be included in the resolution of consent. Such language would have no legal effect on the treaty if it did not substantially affect the treaty's terms or U.S. obligations. Under normal practice, the executive branch would inform the other treaty parties of the interpretations or understandings.

● The Senate may add a "reservation" to the resolution of consent, involving some change in obligations under the treaty. Again, other parties would be informed of the reservation.

● The Senate may amend the terms of the treaty itself, requiring new negotiations with the other parties.[53]

From the point of view of the executive branch, Senate alteration of treaties has become an increasingly serious problem in view of a growing tendency to adjust international relations through multilateral treaties. Resubmission of an amended treaty to a number of foreign governments—any one of which may wish to alter other provisions of the treaty in view of U.S. changes—presents almost insuperable obstacles to final agreement. The substitution of reservations for amendments in recent years has not lessened the difficulty, for the Senate has demanded more and more formal recognition of such reservations.

Proposed Changes in Treaty Power

For more than 70 years attempts have been made to alter the treaty-making provisions of the Constitution.[54] Most of the proposals have been to eliminate the two-thirds rule governing Senate action on treaties or to require consent to ratification by the House as well as the Senate. The Bricker amendment of the 1950s, which sought to curtail the President's treaty power, was a marked exception to the pattern.

Following the war with Spain, two resolutions were introduced in the House of Representatives proposing a constitutional amendment giving the power of consent to a majority of the whole Senate. In 1920, amendments were offered in both houses stipulating that consent to ratification should be by majority vote of members present in the Senate.[55]

Between 1919 and 1928, five resolutions were introduced in the lower house to let that body share in giving "advice and consent" in the making of treaties. As Democratic candidate for President in 1924, John W. Davis endorsed the plan to substitute a majority for a two-thirds vote. William Jennings Bryan, in a Jackson day address in 1920, advocated associating the House with the Senate. An even more fundamental change was proposed in Congress in 1921 whereby certain treaties would have to be approved by popular vote.[56]

During World War II, recollection of Senate rejection of the Treaty of Versailles and the League of Nations prompted a number of proposals to change the provisions for treaty ratification so as to reduce the possibility that new postwar arrangements for enforcement of world peace would be rejected. Josephus Daniels, Navy Secretary in the Cabinet of Woodrow Wilson, suggested in a 1942 speech that the Constitution be amended to provide for consent to ratification by majority vote of both chambers. Proposed amendments to carry out his suggestion were introduced the following year in the House. In the Senate in 1943 a proposed amendment was introduced to allow Senate consent by a simple majority.[57]

In 1945, while the San Francisco conference was debating the charter of the United Nations, destined for consideration by the Senate alone, the House took up a resolution (H J Res 60) by Hatton Sumners (D Texas) to amend the Constitution to require that "Treaties shall be made by the President by and with the advice and consent of both houses of Congress." Despite general agreement that the Senate never would agree to share its treaty power, the House on May 9 adopted the resolution by a 288-88 vote.[58]

Bricker Amendment

During 1953 and 1954 (and briefly in 1956), Congress engaged in a heated debate on an amendment to the Constitution proposed by Sen. John W. Bricker (R Ohio) which would curb the executive's foreign-policy powers.[59] The

Bricker amendment reflected fears that American adherence to various United Nations covenants and conventions, such as the genocide convention (which had not been ratified, as of 1976) would enhance federal powers and possibly interfere with enforcement of state laws by reason of the constitutional provision making treaties the "supreme law of the land." The proposed amendment stemmed also from resentment at the tendency to substitute executive agreements, not subject to ratification, for treaties requiring Senate consent. The controversy surrounding the amendment pitted a majority in Congress against the President and turned a highly technical legal question into a wide-ranging debate between "isolationists" and "one-worlders."

On Jan. 7, 1953, Sen. Bricker and 63 cosponsors (45 Republicans and 19 Democrats) introduced S J Res 1, the revised version of a proposed constitutional amendment introduced by Bricker and 58 cosponsors on Feb. 7, 1952. As revised, the proposed amendment read:

"1. A provision of a treaty which denies or abridges any right enumerated in this Constitution shall not be of any force or effect.

"2. No treaty shall authorize or permit any foreign power or any international organization to supervise, control, or adjudicate rights of citizens of the United States within the United States enumerated in this Constitution or any other matter essentially within the domestic jurisdiction of the United States.

"3. A treaty shall become effective as internal law in the United States only through the enactment of appropriate legislation by the Congress.

"4. All executive or other agreements between the President and any international organization, foreign power, or official thereof shall be made only in the manner and to the extent to be prescribed by law. Such agreements shall be subject to the limitations imposed on treaties or the making of treaties in this article.

"5. The Congress shall have power to enforce this article by appropriate legislation."

On Feb. 16, Sen. Arthur V. Watkins (R Utah) introduced a variation of Bricker's amendment as S J Res 43, which had been drafted by the American Bar Association. It covered all except the second of Bricker's provisions.

The crux of the case for a constitutional amendment, as put by ABA spokesmen, was that some 200 treaties proposed or in preparation by UN agencies and covering a wide range of political, social and economic matters contained provisions at variance with federal or state law.

On June 15, the full Judiciary Committee, by a 9-5 vote, reported an amended version of S J Res 1 that, except for a slight change of wording, followed the text of S J Res 43. Its key provision still declared that "a treaty shall become effective as internal law only through legislation which would be valid in the absence of a treaty."

No further action was taken before Congress adjourned. Senate debate on S J Res 1 was resumed Jan. 27, 1954, and continued through Feb. 26. A final tally that day fell one vote short (60-31) of the two-thirds majority required for Senate approval. Before the next (84th) Congress adjourned July 27, 1956, it considered briefly the question of revising the Constitution's treaty provisions along the lines advocated by Bricker. But, faced with the absence of administration support and the prospect of a long debate, Democratic leaders refused to call up Bricker's latest proposal (again designated S J Res 1), and it died without coming to a vote.

Executive Agreements

Controversy over the extensive use in the post-war period of executive agreements as an alternative to treaties surfaced again in the 1970s, when Congress began to press for legislation that would afford it a voice in the making of such agreements.[60]

The courts repeatedly have upheld the authority of the President to enter into agreements or compacts with other governments without consulting the Senate.[61] The vast majority of executive agreements have concerned such routine matters as the regulation of fishing rights, private claims against another government and postal agreements. In other cases, however, major U.S. diplomatic policies have been carried out by executive agreements, sometimes with controversial results—as in the case of the World War II summit conference agreements at Cairo, Teheran, Yalta and Potsdam.[62] Still other executive agreements have been concluded under specific delegations of power by Congress, such as tariff agreements under the Reciprocal Trade Agreements Act of 1934 and wartime aid agreements under the Lend-Lease Act of 1941.

Executive agreements have been recognized as distinct from treaties since the presidency of George Washington. The Post Office Act of 1792 authorized the postmaster general to "make arrangements with postmasters in any foreign country for the reciprocal receipt and delivery of letters and packets, through the post offices."

But it was not until World War II that the executive agreement assumed a major role as a foreign policy tool. The number of international agreements increased dramatically in the late 1930s, according to statistics provided by the Senate Judiciary Subcommittee on Separation of Powers,[63] and has grown even more significantly since 1946, according to the State Department.

The growth of executive agreements alarmed many members of Congress, who felt that some of those agreements—for example, military base arrangements—involved major commitments of U.S. resources or represented significant policy decisions that were made without the consultation of Congress. As a result of this concern, members of both the House and Senate introduced various bills during the 1970-75 period to give Congress a veto over executive agreements. Foreign policy officials in the Ford administration in 1975 vigorously opposed such legislation on constitutional, foreign policy and pragmatic grounds. They suggested instead a more informal cooperative relationship between the two branches. But that approach failed to satisfy many members who pointed to what they considered were abuses of the use of executive agreements.

Legislative History

Under a law enacted in 1950 (PL 81-821), the Secretary of State was directed to compile and publish annually the contents of all treaties and executive agreements entered into the previous year. In practice, however, agreements considered sensitive to national security were withheld from Congress by the executive branch, even from the relevant committees on a classified basis.

Two years after rejecting the Bricker amendment, the Senate in 1956 passed by unanimous voice vote over the objections of the Eisenhower administration a bill requiring the submission of all executive agreements to the Senate within 60 days, but the House took no action on it.

In 1972 the issue of executive agreements arose again, this time in reaction to secret agreements uncovered by the Senate Foreign Relations Subcommittee on Security Agreements and Commitments Abroad. The subcommittee study, chaired by Stuart Symington (D Mo.) and conducted in 1969-70, found that commitments and secret conditions had been made throughout the 1960s to such countries as Ethiopia, Laos, Thailand, South Korea and Spain. Causing particular controversy was an agreement permitting U.S. use of Spanish bases in return for American grants, loans and improvements.[64]

Adding to congressional frustrations were agreements with Portugal made in 1971 by the Nixon administration on the use of an airbase in the Azores and with Bahrain for naval base facilities in the Persian Gulf. The two agreements raised important foreign policy questions and should have been submitted as treaties, argued members of the Senate Foreign Relations Committee. The Senate passed a sense of the Senate resolution to that effect.

A result of the controversy was congressional passage, over the initial opposition of the Nixon administration, of a measure (PL 92-403) introduced by Sen. Clifford P. Case (R N.J.) requiring the Secretary of State to submit to Congress within 60 days the final text of any international agreement made by the executive branch. Those having national security implications were to be submitted on a classified basis to the House and Senate foreign affairs committees.

Chapter 8

The War Power

The war power—like the treaty power—is divided between the Congress and the President. And, no less than the treaty power, it has been the subject of recurring controversy and debate involving rival claims by the executive and legislative branches.

Article II, Section 2 of the Constitution provides: "The President shall be Commander-in-Chief of the Army and Navy of the United States, and of the militia of the several states, when called into the actual service of the United States."

Article I, Section 8, provides: "The Congress shall have power...to declare war, grant letters of marque and reprisal, and make rules concerning captures on land and water; to raise and support armies...; to provide and maintain a navy; to make rules for the government and regulation of the land and naval forces; to provide for calling forth the militia to execute the laws of the Union, suppress insurrections and repeal invasions"; and "to provide for organizing, arming and disciplining the militia, and for governing such part of them as may be employed in the service of the United States, reserving to the states respectively, the appointment of the officers and the authority of training the militia according to the discipline prescribed by Congress."

At the time the American Constitution was framed, the war-making power in all other countries was vested in the executive. When the Convention at Philadelphia took up this question, at the session of Aug. 17, 1787, Pierce Butler, a delegate of South Carolina, proposed that the power to make war be granted to the President, "who will have all the requisite qualities and will not make war but when the nation will support it." Elbridge Gerry of Massachusetts thereupon objected that he "never expected to hear in a republic a motion to empower the executive alone to declare war." George Mason of Virginia also opposed "giving the power of war to the executive, because he is not safely to be trusted with it." He was "for clogging rather than facilitating war."[65]

Charles Pinckney of South Carolina contended that the proceedings of the House of Representatives were too slow and that it would be "too numerous for such deliberations." He accordingly suggested that the war power be placed in the Senate, which would be "more acquainted with foreign affairs and most capable of proper resolutions." The Convention nevertheless conferred the power on Congress as a whole. It changed the phrase "to make war," as reported by the Committee of Detail, to "to declare war," so as to leave the President the power to repel sudden attacks but not to commence war.[66]

The innovation of placing the war power in the legislative rather than the executive branch of the government was hailed by Jefferson as a valuable restraint upon exercise of the power. He wrote to Madison, Sept. 6, 1789: "We have already given, in example, one effectual check to the dog of war, by transferring the power of letting him loose from the executive to the legislative body, from those who are to spend to those who are to pay." Madison himself wrote: "The Constitution supposes what the history of all governments demonstrates, that the executive is the branch of power most interested in war and most prone to it. It has accordingly, with studied care, vested the question of war in the legislature."[67]

Writing in *The Federalist* (No. 69), Hamilton noted that the powers of the President as commander in chief would be "much inferior" to that of the British King; "it would amount to nothing more than the supreme command and direction of the military and naval forces, as first general and admiral...while that of the British King extends to the declaring of war and to the raising and regulating of fleets and armies—all which, by the Constitution...would appertain to the legislature."[68]

"Those who are to conduct a war cannot in the nature of things be proper or safe judges whether a war ought to be commenced, continued or concluded," wrote Madison. "They are barred from the latter functions by a great principle in free government, analogous to that which separates the sword from the purse, or the power of executing from the power of enacting laws."[69]

Thus was viewed the system of checks and balances on the war power at the founding of the republic. Writing nearly two centuries later, Prof. Raoul Berger noted: "The commander in chief, as conceived by the Framers, bears slight resemblance to the role played by the President today, when, in the words of (Supreme Court) Justice (Robert H.) Jackson, the clause is invoked for the 'power to do anything, anywhere, that can be done with an army or navy.' From history, the Framers had learned of the dangers of entrusting control of the military establishment to a single man who could commit the nation to war."[70]

"With few exceptions, the power to initiate and wage war has shifted to the executive branch," wrote Louis Fisher in his book, *President and Congress.* "The President's power as commander in chief has grown in response to three major developments. First, the President acquired the responsibility to protect American life and property abroad. He has invoked that vague prerogative on numerous occasions to satisfy much larger objectives of the executive branch. Second, the time boundaries of the 'war period' have become increasingly elastic. The President may initiate military operations before congressional action, and he retains wartime powers long after hostilities have ceased. Third, the postwar period, which has been marked by nuclear weapons, the cold war, intercontinental missiles, military alliances, and greater U.S. world responsibilities, has accelerated the growth of presidential power."[71]

Concluded C. Herman Pritchett, in *The American Constitution:* Presidential powers are of "tremendous impact—so great in fact that to a considerable degree they cancel out the most important grant of external authority to Congress, the power to declare war."[72] Throughout the nation's history, only two major conflicts—the War of 1812 and the Spanish-American War—were clearly the product of congressional policy.

Declared and Undeclared War

Beginning in 1950, a new dimension was injected into the question of congressional and presidential war powers: presidential commitments of American forces to combat without a declaration of war. U.S. combat troops were involved in full-scale war in Korea from 1950 to 1953 and in Indochina from 1965-73 without declarations of war. In two other instances, Lebanon in 1958 and the Dominican Republic in 1965, U.S. combat troops were used to help maintain conditions of political stability in countries threatened by or undergoing civil strife.

Justifying the absence of a declaration of war, administration spokesmen have pointed to numerous historical "precedents" which involved U.S. forces abroad without such declaration. Indeed, Congress has declared war in only five conflicts: the War of 1812, the Mexican War, the Spanish-American War, World War I and World War II. No declaration was made or requested in the Naval War with France (1798-1800), the First Barbary War (1801-05), the Second Barbary War (1815), or the various Mexican-American clashes of 1814-17.[73]

A 1966 State Department memorandum noted "at least 125 instances in which the President has ordered the armed forces to take action or maintain positions abroad without obtaining prior congressional authorization."[74] A 1970 Library of Congress study cited 160 instances in which U.S. armed forces were used abroad; most of the actions were taken in the name of protecting life and property.[75]

Both Berger and historian Arthur M. Schlesinger Jr. (in his book, *The Imperial Presidency*), have contended, however, that these incidents were relatively minor and could not be used as "precedents" for Korea or Vietnam, as claimed.[76] They have also noted that categorizing the war with France as "undeclared" may be disputed because President Adams took no independent action before Congress passed a series of acts which amounted, according to the Supreme Court, to a declaration of "imperfect war."[77]

The nineteenth century, noted Berger, offers no example of a President who plunged the nation into war in order to repel an attack on some *foreign* nation. Indeed, this did not occur until the Korean War, as both Wilson and Roosevelt obtained a declaration of war before sending troops to engage in hostilities on foreign soil.[78]

During debate on presidential war powers in the 1960s and 1970s, it was contended that declarations of war were outmoded, given the existence of nuclear weapons and the need to commit troops overseas in emergencies on a limited-war basis. Testifying before the Senate Foreign Relations Committee in 1971, Professor Alpheus T. Mason of Princeton University, commented: "The Framers, with deliberate care, made war-making a joint enterprise. Congress is authorized to 'declare war'; the President is designated 'commander in chief.' Technology has expanded the President's role and correspondingly curtailed the power of the Congress. Unchanged are the joint responsibilities of the President and the Congress. The fact that a congressional declaration of war is no longer practical does not deprive Congress of constitutionally imposed authority in war-making. On the contrary, it is under obligation to readjust its power position."[79]

Congress attempted to do just that in enacting the 1973 war powers bill.

Congress and the World Wars

Once Congress has declared war and voted the necessary funds, Presidents have vastly enlarged the scope of their authority, both in domestic and foreign affairs. During the Civil War, Congress delegated sweeping power to Lincoln to enable him to prosecute the war. Several months after he issued proclamations calling up the state militias and ordering the blockade, Congress passed an act "approving, legalizing, and making valid all the acts, proclamations, and orders of the President, etc., as if they had been issued and done under the previous express authority and direction of the Congress of the United States."[80]

By the turn of the century, the government had become increasingly active in regulating the economy, and when the United States entered World War I, Congress delegated extensive and far-reaching powers to President Wilson over the economy and domestic affairs.

The powers exercised by President Roosevelt during World War II were even more considerable, as the concept of a national emergency expanded. As Edward S. Corwin noted in his book, *The President: Office and Powers* (1787-1957), "In the First World War, as in the Civil War, the emergency that constitutional interpretation set itself to meet was a *war* emergency in the narrow, palpable sense. In the Second World War the emergency preceded the war and continued beyond it—a fact of special significance when it is considered in relation to the effect of wartime practices on the constitutional law of peacetime."[81]

After Congress declared war, mobilization authority was extended to the control of facilities and the operation of plants closed by strikes. Under the Emergency Price Control Act of 1942, the President appointed a price administrator who was authorized to set maximum rents.[82] According to Corwin, by April 1942, 42 new agencies had been created to oversee the war effort, 35 of which were of "purely presidential creation." and whose constitutional and legal status became a source of controversy.[83]

Both world wars, as well as the Civil War, highlighted the problems of ending the "national emergency." Commented Fisher: "The change-over from emergency war powers to normal executive responsibilities is by no means a rapid process. Long after hostilities have ended, many economic controls remain in force."[84]

On July 25, 1947, Congress terminated certain temporary emergency and war powers, involving about 175 statutory provisions some of which dated back to World War I. Nonetheless, 103 war or emergency statutes remained in effect.[85]

Congressional concern with the continuing existence of national emergencies and concomitant delegation of power to the President led to creation of a Special Senate Committee on the Termination of the National Emergency in 1973. At the outset of the study it was thought that the state of national emergency dated back to President Truman's December 1950 proclamation of an emergency in response to China's invasion of Korea. However, research by the committee showed that the United States had been living in a state of declared national emergency since March

1933, when Congress ratified President Roosevelt's declaration of an emergency resulting from the Depression.

The discovery pointed up the lack of knowledge in the area of emergency powers. In a Sept. 30, 1973, report, the committee stated, "Because Congress and the public are unaware of the extent of emergency powers, there has never been any notable congressional or public objection made to this state of affairs. Nor have the courts imposed significant limitations."[86] The committee listed four existing states of national emergency that should be ended and released a catalogue of some 470 existing emergency statutes which remained "a potential source of virtually unlimited power for a president should he choose to activate them."[87]

Congress and Undeclared War

In his book, *President and Congress*, Louis Fisher noted: "The President's warmaking powers were drawn originally from (1) his responsibilities as commander-in-chief, (2) his oath to preserve, protect and defend the Constitution, (3) his duty to protect the nation from sudden attack, and (4) the inherent powers derived from the general heading 'executive power.' " However, "in recent decades, the definition of inherent and implied powers has become increasingly generous because of treaty commitments, vaguely worded congressional resolutions, and an accumulation of emergency statutes. Moreover, the President's constitutional responsibility for repelling sudden attacks and waging defensive war has expanded in scope until it is now used to justify involvement in full-scale wars without legislative approval."[88]

The Korean experience, wrote historian Arthur M. Schlesinger Jr., "beguiled the American government first into an unprecedented claim for inherent presidential power to go to war and then into ill-advised resentment against those who dared bring up the constitutional issue.... By insisting that the presidential prerogative alone sufficed to meet the requirements of the Constitution, Truman did a good deal more than pass on his sacred trust unimpaired. He dramatically and dangerously enlarged the power of future Presidents to take the nation into major war."[89]

The constitutional system of checks and balances in the war power was further eroded with the steady increase of

U.S. involvement in Indochina, starting in the mid-1960s. Both Johnson and Nixon substantially enlarged the theory that actions undertaken by the President in defensive wars need not be accompanied by prior approval by the legislative branch. "The role of Congress under the Johnson theory of the war-making power," commented Schlesinger, "was not to sanction but to support the war"—and for the most part, the majority of members of Congress acquiesced in this role.[90] "Johnson and Nixon had surpassed all their predecessors in claiming that inherent and exclusive presidential authority, unaccompanied by emergencies threatening the life of the nation, unaccompanied by the authorization of Congress or the blessing of an international organization, permitted a President to order troops into battle at his unilateral pleasure."[91]

Korea. The war in Korea began with a massive attack on South Korea by North Koreans on June 25 (Korean time), 1950, and continued for three years at a cost of more than 150,000 U.S. casualties. Late on June 26 (U.S. time) President Truman ordered American air and sea forces in the Far East to aid South Korea, a day before the UN Security Council called on U.N. members for help in repelling the attack. The President on June 30 ordered ground troops into Korea and sent the 7th Fleet to act as a buffer between China and Formosa.[92]

Secretary of State Dean Acheson recommended to Truman that he " should not ask [Congress] for a resolution of approval, but rest on his constitutional authority as commander-in-chief."[93] In fact, Truman never asked Congress for a declaration of war in Korea, and he waited until Dec. 16, 1950—six months after the outbreak of hostilities—to proclaim the existence of a national emergency. In defense of this course, it was argued that the Russians or Chinese or both had violated post-World War II agreements on Korea and that emergency powers authorized during World War II could still be applied.

Provisions in the United Nations Charter were also used to justify Truman's action. A legal memorandum by the State Department in 1950 offered this defense: "Both traditional international law and article 39 of the UN Charter and the resolution pursuant thereto authorize the United States to repel the armed aggression against the

Republic of Korea."[94] However, the legality of this argument was questioned, on the ground that U.S. armed forces were ordered to Korea before the U.N. Security Council authorized the action.[95]

Although there was never a formal declaration of war or congressional resolution supporting Truman's decision, Congress implicitly ratified the action by consistently appropriating the requested funds for the war.

Congress did not mount a serious challenge to Truman's war powers until 1951. At issue then was the President's authority to dispatch troops to Korea and to Western Europe. Sen. Robert A. Taft (R Ohio) opened a three-month-long "great debate" on Jan. 5, 1951, by asserting that Truman had "no authority whatever to commit American troops to Korea without consulting Congress and without congressional approval." Moreover, Taft said, the President had "no power to agree to send American troops to fight in Europe in a war between the members of the Atlantic Pact and Soviet Russia."[96]

The debate revolved principally around the troops-to-Europe issue. It came to an end on April 4, when the Senate adopted two resolutions approving the dispatch of four divisions to Europe. One of the resolutions stated that it was the sense of the Senate that "no ground troops in addition to such four divisions should be sent to Western Europe...without further congressional approval."

President Truman hailed the action as a "clear endorsement" of his troop plans, saying "there has never been any real question" about the United States doing its part in the defense of Europe. But he ignored the Senate's claim to a voice in future troop commitments; neither resolution had the force of law.

In essence, the "great debate" had confirmed both the President's power to commit U.S. forces without prior congressional approval and the decision to defend Western Europe on the ground.

Testifying in 1951 on the plan to station American soldiers in Europe, Acheson asserted: "Not only has the President the authority to use the armed forces in carrying out the broad foreign policy of the United States and implementing treaties, but it is equally clear that this authority may not be interfered with by Congress in the exercise of powers which it has under the Constitution."[97]

Truman overstepped his powers as commander-in-chief when he relied on them, April 8, 1952, to take possession and control of all facilities, plants and properties of 86 steel companies involved in a dispute with the United Steelworkers. Congress ignored the President's request to approve the seizure order. Then on June 2, the Supreme Court ruled *(Youngstown Sheet & Tube Co. v. Sawyer,* 343 U.S. 579) that his action was without statutory authority and that it violated the concept of separation of powers by usurping functions of Congress.

Indochina. U.S. military aid to Vietnam was initiated by the Truman administration. By 1951 military aid to that country amounted to more than $500-million. Although President Eisenhower barred a U.S. combat role in Vietnam, in 1954 the United States sent 200 Air Force technicians to aid the French in their fight against the Viet Minh. The Senate Foreign Relations Committee subsequently expressed concern at the lack of congressional approval for this action, and the State Department pledged to consult with Congress before taking any additional steps in Vietnam.[98]

In March 1954—at the beginning of the 56-day battle at Dienbienphu that was disastrous for the French—the White House tentatively approved a plan for immediate U.S. air intervention, but Sens. Lyndon B. Johnson (D Texas), minority leader, and Richard B. Russell (D Ga.), ranking Democrat on the Armed Services Committee, and others rejected the proposal.

As U.S. involvement increased in Indochina during the Kennedy administration—there were about 15,000 advisers in Vietnam in early 1964—criticism intensified. On March 10, 1964, Sens. Wayne Morse (D Ore.) and Ernest Gruening (D Alaska) demanded total U.S. withdrawal.

Despite the growing criticism of the war, however, Congress during the period spanning the Tonkin Gulf resolution of 1964 and the 1973 Vietnam ceasefire agreement was never united or successful in its attempts to bring U.S. involvement to an end.

This was particularly true in the House, where many members consistently were unwilling to challenge the President's pre-eminence in the conduct of the war or related diplomacy, despite their complaints about aggrandizement of presidential war powers.

At the peak of anti-war strength in Congress only one out of three House members voted to back end-the-war proposals. Of 94 recorded votes on the war between 1966 and 1972, only a few were taken by the House, and House conferees almost invariably were responsible for deleting or emasculating Senate anti-war amendments.

The attitude in the Senate was different, but the result was similar. There was a great deal of complicated legislative action in the Senate on proposals to control or end the war, but most of the plans were deleted in conference or did not carry the force of law. Those restrictions that did become law were largely moot because they affected military activity the executive branch no longer intended to pursue.

Thirteen days before the Jan. 27, 1973, signing of the Vietnam peace agreement, Senate Majority Leader Mike Mansfield (D Mont.) insisted that Congress "can't end the war." "It's really up to the President," Mansfield said. "We shouldn't fool ourselves in that respect."

A revealing picture of congressional impotence on the war was provided by the adoption of the 1964 Tonkin Gulf resolution. The resolution affirmed congressional support for "all necessary measures to repeal any armed attack against the forces of the United States...[and] to assist any member or protocol state of the Southeast Asia Collective Defense Treaty requesting assistance...."

Initially approved overwhelmingly on the basis of what later emerged as a distorted account of a minor naval engagement, the resolution became the primary legal justification for the Johnson administration's prosecution of the war.

Congress learned subsequently that the naval incident had been misrepresented; it repealed the resolution in 1970. But the Nixon administration already had shifted to another legal rationale for its Vietnam policies. Nixon maintained that his authority to pursue policies and military actions in Vietnam derived from his constitutional prerogatives and obligations as commander-in-chief.

Following adoption of the Tonkin Gulf resolution, neither the Johnson nor Nixon administrations returned to Congress to seek specific legislative consent or additional authority for stepped-up military activity. President Nixon ordered U.S. troops into Cambodia in 1970, provided air support for South Vietnam's 1971 invasion of Laos, ordered Haiphong harbor mined in 1972 and launched the heaviest bombing of North Vietnam in December 1972—all without seeking congressional consent.

Anti-war Proposals. President Nixon's 1970 decision to send U.S. forces into Cambodia to clean out Communist sanctuaries provoked a six-week Senate debate in May and June on an amendment sponsored by Sens. John Sherman Cooper (R Ky.) and Frank Church (D Idaho) that would bar use of U.S. funds for military operations in Cambodia.[99] A weakened version of the amendment—barring use of ground forces but not aircraft—was passed in December.

Other action on anti-war proposals in 1970 included repeal of the 1964 Tonkin Gulf resolution and defeat of two "end-the-war" amendments sponsored by Sens. Mark O. Hatfield (R Ore.) and George McGovern (D S.D.).

In 1971, the Senate adopted amendments to three bills introduced by Mansfield calling for withdrawal of troops from Indochina by a certain deadline. Two of these survived House-Senate conference with the withdrawal deadline deleted—the first time the House had gone on record urging an end to the war. The President, however, said the provision was not binding and that he would not follow it. A new Cooper-Church amendment, limiting use of U.S. military funds in Indochina to troop withdrawal, was defeated on the Senate floor in a series of close votes.

Congress in 1972 enacted no legislation restricting U.S. military involvement in Southeast Asia, although the Senate took its toughest stand on terminating U.S. involvement. But continued House support for the President's policies forestalled congressional action to set a date for withdrawal.

The Senate Aug. 2 posed its most serious challenge to the President's Vietnam policy by adopting on a 49-47 roll-call vote an amendment cutting off funds for U.S. participation in the war. The amendment barred use of funds for U.S. participation in the war four months after enactment. All U.S. ground, naval and air forces would have to be out of Indochina by that date if North Vietnam and its allies had released all American prisoners of war. House conferees refused to accept the amendment.

Funding the War. The picture of the Johnson and Nixon administrations carrying on military activities in Indochina without congressional consent often has been overdrawn by critics of the war. They tended to overlook the frequent votes in Congress for appropriations to support the war. And while they often spoke of a constitutional crisis over war powers, they usually did not consider that throughout the war there was never a constitutional confrontation between a President determined to pursue the war and a Congress unwilling to appropriate the necessary funds.

Yet, from another viewpoint, the increasing number of anti-war votes in Congress—from five roll-call votes in 1969 to 35 in 1972—may well have served to reinforce President Nixon's decision to continue the policy of troop withdrawals from Indochina. The roll-call votes were a constant signal to the administration that slowing down—or even reversing—the troop withdrawal program would carry heavy political costs.

Vietnam Postscript. In the spring of 1973, there was an important postscript to the congressional action on the Vietnam War. Although it had pulled out of Vietnam two months after the Jan. 27 peace agreement, the United States had continued bombing in Cambodia and Laos in support of anti-Communist activities there. In action on a supplemental appropriations bill in May, the House for the first time voted to cut off funds for military activity in Laos and Cambodia. Final language adopted by both chambers and signed by President Nixon barred the use of any past or existing appropriations for financing directly or indirectly U.S. combat activities in, over or off the shores of North Vietnam, South Vietnam, Laos or Cambodia.

Congress did not stop with a Cambodia bombing ban in its challenge to presidential power, however. In July, Congress passed a tough war powers measure that set a 60-day limit on any presidential commitment of U.S. troops to hostilities abroad or to situations where hostilities might be imminent unless Congress declared war, specifically authorized continuation of that commitment or was unable to meet the requirements because of an armed attack upon the United States.

Policy Resolutions as War Authority

Since 1945, Congress on five occasions has passed a joint resolution authorizing or approving the President's determination to use such armed forces as he deemed necessary to repel armed attacks or threats against the nations or geographical areas covered by the resolution. Four of the resolutions were initiated by the President, who sought congressional approval for military actions either contemplated or already undertaken. The five resolutions are:

1. **Formosa** resolution (H J Res 159), signed into law Jan. 29, 1955, authorizing the President to use U.S. forces to protect Formosa (Nationalist China) and the Pescadores Islands against "armed attack" from Communist China.

2. **Middle East** resolution (H J Res 117), signed into law March 9, 1957, proclaiming U.S. policy to defend Middle East countries "against aggression from any country controlled by international communism."

3. **Cuban** resolution (S J Res 230), signed into law Oct. 3, 1962, authorizing the President to take whatever steps were necessary to defend Latin America against Cuban aggression or subversion and to oppose the deployment of Soviet weapons in Cuba capable of endangering U.S. security.

4. **Berlin** resolution (H Con Res 570), adopted by the House and Senate in October 1962, reaffirming U.S. determination to use armed force, if necessary, to defend West Berlin and the access rights of the Western powers to West Berlin.

5. Vietnam resolution (H J Res 1145), signed into law Aug. 10, 1964, known as the **Tonkin Gulf** resolution, authorizing the President to use armed forces to repel attacks against U.S. forces and affirming U.S. determination to defend any SEATO treaty member or protocol state (this included Vietnam) requesting assistance.

The most controversial of the resolutions was the Tonkin Gulf resolution of 1964—repealed by Congress in 1970—which gave rise to criticism that such resolutions in effect have acted as blank checks to support presidential war-making. In its 1967 report on the "national commitments resolution," the Senate Foreign Relations Committee concluded that the "Gulf of Tonkin resolution represents the extreme point in the process of constitutional erosion."[100]

Adoption of the Tonkin resolution and the subsequent expansion of U.S. involvement in Indochina gave rise to heated debate over whether the measure was in fact what Under Secretary of State Nicholas deB. Katzenbach claimed in 1967 to be the "functional equivalent" of a declaration of war. On the one hand, administration spokesmen cited the resolution as providing authority for executive actions; but at the same time, both Presidents Johnson and Nixon claimed they did not really need congressional approval because in any case the authority to act rested on their constitutional powers as commander-in-chief.

1973 War Powers Act

Increasingly frustrated with its ineffectual influence on American involvement in Indochina and on the scope of U.S. military commitments abroad, Congress in 1973 reacted by passing—over President Nixon's veto—a bill designed to limit the President's powers to commit U.S. forces abroad without congressional approval.[101]

The legislation, which came to be known as the "war powers bill" (H J Res 542—PL 93-148), was the product of three years of effort by most liberals and many conservatives in both chambers. The basic and most controversial of the legislation's provisions were those delineating the situations under which the President could commit troops, requiring the President to terminate any troop commitment within 60 days unless Congress specifically authorized its continuation and permitting Congress at any time by concurrent resolution to direct the President to disengage troops involved in an undeclared war.

Passage of the bill was heralded by its supporters as a major step in reasserting Congress' war-making powers. Said Jacob K. Javits (R N.Y.), chief architect of the Senate version of the legislation: "With the war powers resolution's passage, after 200 years, at last something will have been done about codifying the implementation of the most awesome power in the possession of any sovereignty and giving the broad representation of the people in Congress a voice in it. This is critically important, for we have just learned the hard lesson that wars cannot be successfully fought except with the consent of the people and with their support."

In vetoing the legislation, President Nixon declared that the resolution would impose restrictions on the authority of the President that would be "both unconstitutional and dangerous to the best interests of our nation." The major provision of the bill, he contended, would "purport to take away, by a mere legislative act, authorities which the President has properly exercised under the Constitution for almost 200 years." They were unconstitutional, he asserted, because "the only way in which the constitutional powers of a branch of the government can be altered is by amending the Constitution—and any attempt to make such alterations by legislation alone is clearly without force."

The President's position was argued by some conservatives and administration supporters during debate on the bill in both chambers. In their assertions that the bill was unconstitutional they were joined by a small group of liberals who agreed that the measure was unconstitutional, but for different reasons. Thus Thomas F. Eagleton (D Mo.), an author of the Senate's original war powers bill, branded the final version as "the most dangerous piece of legislation" he had seen in his five years in the Senate. Eagleton warned his colleagues: "We are going to give him (Nixon) more authority, and legalize it, than perhaps he ever dreamed he had. Not only President Nixon, but every President of the United States will have at least the color of legal authority, the advance blessing of Congress, given on an open, blank-check basis, to take us to war. It is a horrible mistake."

The war powers bill was put to a test in 1975, when President Ford ordered the use of U.S. troops to free the American merchant ship *Mayaguez* and its crew of 39, seized May 12 by Cambodian Communist troops off the disputed island of Poulo Wai in the Gulf of Siam. In this case, there was general agreement that the President had the authority to commit U.S. troops without regard to the war powers law, even though the President complied with it by issuing a report on his action to Congress May 15 in accordance with the bill's 48-hour reporting requirement.

Congressional reaction to Ford's use of force was generally favorable, but some members were critical of the way Congress had been consulted. Senate Majority Leader Mike Mansfield (D Mont.) said, "I did not give my approval or disapproval because the decision had already been made." He said he had questions about the whole affair and called for greater consultation, as did other congressional leaders.

Problems of Secrecy

"A popular government without popular information, or the means of acquiring it, is but a prologue to a farce or a tragedy; or, perhaps, both," wrote Madison in 1822. "Knowledge will forever govern ignorance; and a people who mean to be their own governors must arm themselves with the power which knowledge gives."[102]

In the post-war period, the executive branch secrecy system has become a major obstacle to Congress'—and the public's—ability to share a role in foreign policy-making. This has been particularly true of the activities of the intelligence community; many of its activities—some of which were illegal—were only brought to light before Congress and the public in 1975 and 1976 as a result of committee investigations.

In his discussion of "the secrecy system," Arthur M. Schlesinger Jr. notes that during the 19th century, information concerning government diplomatic activities generally was made available to Congress and the public. "Even the Civil War was fought to a remarkable degree in the open...there was no effective censorship, no Sedition Act, no Espionage Act."[103] World War I saw the growth of the system of classifying documents; the system was considerably strengthened during World War II. On March 22, 1940, President Roosevelt by executive order conferred presidential recognition for the first time on the military classification system.[104] The system rapidly spread to the State Department and other executive branch agencies until, in Schlesinger's words, "a legitimate system of restriction grew...into an extravagant and indefensible system of denial."[105]

At the start of the post-war period, the secrecy system was still relatively unsophisticated. Nonetheless, Sen. Robert A. Taft (R Ohio) told the Senate in 1951, "The result of a general practice of secrecy...has been to deprive the

Senate and Congress of the substance of the powers conferred on them by the Constitution."[106]

By the 1970s, Congress and the public had begun to lose confidence in the integrity of the secrecy system. "Illegitimate secrecy," said Schlesinger, "had corrupted the conduct of foreign affairs and had on occasion deprived voters of information necessary for democratic control of foreign policy."[107] In Congress, committees in both chambers held hearings on government secrecy.[108] In August 1972, the Senate established a special 10-member Committee to Study Questions Related to Secret and Confidential Government Documents, co-chaired by the majority and minority leaders. In its report, filed in Oct. 1973, the committee stated that Congress should take a second look at the broad grant of power it had given Presidents to classify government documents and thus put them beyond the reach even of members of Congress.[109]

The secrecy issue was dramatically highlighted with publication of the Pentagon Papers by *The New York Times* in June 1971—two years after the administration had denied them to the Senate Foreign Relations Committee—and the reading of the classified documents by Sen. Mike Gravel (D Alaska) during a special subcommittee meeting June 29.

The issue not only involved the propriety of the *Times'* publication and Gravel's action; disclosures in the Pentagon Papers raised serious questions about the propriety of the secrecy system itself.

Commenting on the revelations concerning the administration's Vietnam policy contained in the Pentagon Papers, Prof. Raoul Berger wrote: "We can only conjecture whether the course of events would have been changed had the...facts [disclosed in the papers] been spread before Congress and the people. But undeniably they were deprived of the choice which was theirs to make."[110]

"However the impact on the national interest of disclosure to the *public* may be viewed," Berger continued, "withholdings of the Pentagon Papers from the Senate Foreign Relations Committee and from Congress is something else again. Congress...was intended to be the senior partner in the new federal government, the chief agent in waging, continuing and terminating war. It was therefore entitled to be advised of all the relevant facts.... It is a measure of executive arrogance that refusal of this study to Congress was made in the name of the 'national interest.' Nowhere in the Constitution...does it appear that the Founders looked to the President to protect the 'national interest' against the Congress."[111]

Testifying before the Senate Foreign Relations Committee during its 1971 hearings on war powers legislation, historian Henry Steele Commager said: "If the executive branch is going to conduct foreign relations under cover of secrecy, it is, of course, quite likely that it can obtain from the Congress what it asks for at a time of alleged emergency.... What is needed...is a far fuller disclosure of the facts of the case.... Had the Senate been in possession of everything we now know about the situation in Southeast Asia in 1964, I think it is highly questionable whether they would have passed the Tonkin resolution, and highly doubtful whether you could have gotten a sufficient vote for a declaration of war."[112]

In his book, *Congress, the Executive, and Foreign Policy,* Francis O. Wilcox discusses the "crucial" need for Congress to obtain adequate information—much of which is available only from the executive—if it is to have a voice in foreign policy-making. "Intelligence was crucial to the policy-making process in both the Cuban missile crisis and the Dominican intervention. In the former case, the intelligence was clear and unambiguous; in the latter, almost everything depended on how it was interpreted. What was initially given to Congress and the public was the administration's interpretation.... It was not until the press and Congress examined what lay behind this interpretation that it appeared to some critics to be exaggerated and unjustified.... The executive branch has...traditionally been reluctant to give Congress access to its policy-planning documents at an early enough stage to be significant.... The result is virtually to deny Congress effective access to the policy-making process until it has been completed."[113]

Use of its own professional staff is one method whereby Congress can obtain information. In 1969 and 1970, the newly created Senate Foreign Relations Subcommittee on U.S. Security Agreements and Commitments Abroad sent a two-man team on fact-finding missions to 25 countries. The staff investigations, followed by detailed, closed-door hearings, revealed a host of U.S. commitments—some express, some implied, some secret, some not—which might lead, in Wilcox's words, to U.S. involvement "in a thousand ways in countries around the world."[114] The committee's probe revealed that the Johnson administration had agreed to special payments for Filipino, Thai and Korean troops in Vietnam. There also were secret military contingency plans with Thailand and previously undisclosed U.S. participation in the war in Laos.[115] (The hearings on Laos were published in heavily censored form.)

Concluding his discussion of "the cost of secrecy," Berger commented: "With all its shortcomings...Congress yet has one great redeeming feature: it is the national forum of debate.... Whether the people will be swayed is not so important as that they should have the opportunity to hear opposition views, to have an informed choice of options, to be alerted to possible consequences of massive commitments rather than to have commitments saddled on them by secret one-man decisions."[116]

"Restraining the secrecy system would not automatically restore a congressional voice in foreign policy," wrote Schlesinger. "But it would at least deprive Congress of a favorite alibi: that, because it did not have the facts, it had no choice but to let Presidents make the decisions."[117]

PART III

Commerce Power

Chapter 9

History of Commerce Clause

"The Congress shall have Power...To regulate Commerce with foreign Nations, and among the several States, and with the Indian Tribes." (Article I, Section 8, Clause 3)

With this simple grant of authority the Constitution attempted to remedy one of the basic weaknesses of the federal government under the Articles of Confederation. The lack of a national power over commerce had been in large part responsible for the drafting of a new Constitution, and the need for such a power was widely accepted.

The constitutional formula is a broad and general one: the positive grant of power to Congress is not coupled with a statement of the powers, if any, reserved to the states, and no definition of terms is offered. Four express limitations on the commerce power are contained in Article I, Section 9, but only one—forbidding Congress to lay a tax or duty on articles exported from any state—has had much practical significance. Thus the extent of federal power over commerce has been established largely by experience and judicial determination.

The basic Supreme Court decision involving the scope of the commerce clause was *Gibbons v. Ogden* in 1824. In a landmark opinion, Chief Justice John Marshall opted for a broad construction of the term "commerce" and emphatically asserted the supremacy of the federal power over it.[1] But he rejected the argument—advanced by Daniel Webster, counsel for Gibbons—that the congressional power over commerce was "complete and entire," holding instead that "the completely internal commerce of a state...may be considered as reserved for the state itself."[2] From this acceptance of a divided authority over commerce has stemmed the concept of interstate as opposed to intrastate commerce, with movement across state lines as the basic test of the distinction. *(Footnotes, p. 316)*

Although Congress exercised its authority over foreign commerce from its earliest days, for nearly a century it failed to exploit its powers over commerce among the states. Thus most early Supreme Court decisions in the field dealt with state regulations that were challenged as infringements on the constitutional powers of Congress. The limits of state regulatory authority are still a problem for the courts today.

With enactment of the Interstate Commerce Act in 1887, Congress moved decisively into the domestic regulatory field, and in the 20th century the scope of the commerce clause has expanded steadily. For years the Supreme Court held to the view that manufacturing and production were not a part of commerce and that the commerce power extended only to activities that affected commerce directly. Eventually, however, the court came round to the view that the commerce power embraced activities that had an "effect upon commerce," however indirectly. Application of this doctrine led to a substantial expansion of congressional authority, and in 1946 the court concluded that "the federal commerce power is as broad as the economic needs of the nation."[3]

The necessity for national control over interstate and foreign commerce was the immediate occasion for the calling of the Constitutional Convention in 1787. "Most of our political evils," Madison had written to Jefferson the previous year, "may be traced to our commercial ones."[4] Under the Articles of Confederation, adopted during the Revolutionary War, Congress had power to regulate trade only with the Indians, the control of interstate and foreign commerce having been left to the states. This defect in the Articles was universally recognized. Even those who, like Samuel Adams and Patrick Henry, feared that a federal government would be tyrannical, favored more comprehensive regulation of commerce by Congress.

The conditions under which commerce was carried on became increasingly chaotic after the Revolutionary War. Each state attempted to build up its own prosperity at the expense of its neighbors. Justice William Johnson, in a concurring opinion in *Gibbons v. Ogden,* thus described the situation that had developed:

"For a century the states had submitted, with murmurs, to the commercial restrictions imposed by the parent state; and now, finding themselves in the unlimited possession of those powers over their own commerce, which they had so long been deprived of and so earnestly coveted, that selfish principle which, well controlled, is so salutary, and which, unrestricted, is so unjust and tyrannical, guided by inexperience and jealousy, began to show itself in iniquitous laws and impolitic measures, from which grew up a conflict of commercial regulations, destructive to the harmony of the states, and fatal to their commercial interests abroad."[5]

State legislatures imposed tariffs upon goods coming in from other states as well as from foreign countries. Thus, New York levied duties on firewood from Connecticut and cabbages from New Jersey. "The commerce which Massachusetts found it to her interest to encourage," says J. B. McMaster, "Virginia found it to hers to restrict. New York would not protect the trade in indigo and pitch. South Carolina cared nothing for the success of the fur interests."[6]

Seaport states financed their governments through imposts on European goods passing through their harbors but destined for consumption in neighboring states. Madison described the plight of those states not having seaports: "New Jersey placed between Philadelphia and New York was likened to a cask tapped at both ends; and North Carolina, between Virginia and South Carolina, to a patient bleeding at both arms."[7]

Different currencies in each of the 13 states likewise hampered commercial intercourse. And if a merchant were able to carry on an interstate business in spite of tariff and currency difficulties, he often had trouble in collecting his bills. Local courts and juries were less zealous in protecting the rights of distant creditors than those of their neighbors and friends.

The chaotic condition of interstate trade prompted the General Assembly of Virginia, in 1786, to adopt a resolution proposing a joint meeting of commissioners appointed by each of the states "to take into consideration the trade of the United States; to examine the relative situations and trade of the said states; (and) to consider how far a uniform system in their commercial regulations may be necessary to their common interest and their permanent harmony." The action of the Virginia Assembly led to a meeting at Annapolis later in the year of commissioners from five states: Delaware, New Jersey, New York, Pennsylvania and Virginia.[8]

The members of the Annapolis convention, however, "did not conceive it advisable to proceed on the business of their mission, under the circumstance of so partial and defective a representation." They recommended a general meeting of all the states at Philadelphia in 1787 "for the same, and such other purposes, as the situation may be found to require."

It was the judgment of the convention that "the power of regulating trade is of such comprehensive extent and will enter so far into the general system of the federal government, that to give it efficacy and to obviate questions and doubts concerning its precise nature and limits, may require a correspondent adjustment of other parts of the federal system."

Adoption of the Commerce Clause

The desirability of uniform regulation of interstate and foreign commerce was so generally recognized that the proposal to give Congress blanket authority in this field occasioned comparatively little discussion at the Philadelphia convention. Some controversy did arise over an attempt by the South to limit the power of a congressional majority in regulating commerce. The southern states feared that the North might seek to dominate their commerce. Charles Pinckney of South Carolina proposed, therefore, that "all laws regulating commerce shall require the assent of two-thirds of the members present in each house," but this proposal was defeated by a vote of seven states to four, Maryland, Virginia, North Carolina and Georgia voting in the affirmative.

"Had Pinckney's proposal been adopted," says Charles Warren, "the course of American history would have been vitally changed. Enactment of protective tariffs might have been practically impossible. The whole political relations between the South and North growing out of commercial legislation would have been changed. The Nullification movement in the 1830s, which arose out of opposition to a northern tariff, might not have occurred."[9]

In return for the South's acceptance of the unlimited power of the majority in regulation of commerce, the northern states agreed to a ban on export taxes and to a provision that importation of slaves would not be prohibited before the year 1808. This was one of the important compromises reached at Philadelphia.

Many persons consider it remarkable that so important a part of the Constitution as the commerce clause should be so briefly expressed and should leave so much to future determination. "At that time, at least," Warren remarks, "there seems to have been no doubt as to its meaning. The violent differences of opinion which arose during the first half of the 19th century as to what the term 'commerce' included, and as to whether the power to 'regulate' was exclusive in Congress or exercisable by the states until Congress should act, were apparently not in the least foreseen by the members of the Convention." It is generally agreed that nothing more was immediately intended than that Congress should be empowered to prevent commercial wars among the states. Yet it is not to be doubted that the framers were aware of the scope of the power granted to Congress. Monroe pointed out that the commerce clause involved "a radical change in the whole system of our government."[10]

Other Federal Commerce Powers

In addition to general regulatory power over interstate commerce, the convention reposed in the federal government the admiralty jurisdiction and the powers to coin money, establish uniform laws of bankruptcy, establish post offices and post roads, regulate weights and measures and grant patents and copyrights. That the taxing power was recognized as an instrument of commercial regulation is indicated by the clause of the Constitution (Article I, Section

9) which forbids the federal government to give preference to the ports of one state over those of another "by any regulation of commerce or revenue." The importance of these federal powers was enhanced by provisions expressly forbidding the states to coin money, enact laws impairing the obligation of contracts, lay duties of tonnage or tax exports or imports.

Other specific grants of commercial power were discussed in the convention. Benjamin Franklin proposed that Congress be given power "to provide for cutting canals," and James Wilson expressed the belief that such power was necessary in order to prevent a single state from obstructing the general welfare. But Franklin's motion was lost because of the sentiment of the convention that the expense thereby incurred would be a general burden, while the benefit would be local. It was proposed also to give Congress power to grant charters of incorporation in cases where the public good might require them, and where the authority of a single state might be incompetent; to regulate stages on the post roads; to establish institutions for the promotion of agriculture, commerce, trade and manufactures; to make internal improvements, and to charter a national bank. All motions to make these grants in express terms were lost.[11]

Supreme Court Interpretation

Although the federal government's power over interstate commerce now appears as one of the most important and conspicuous it possesses, no case involving the extent of this power arose in the Supreme Court until 1824, 35 years after the adoption of the Constitution. By 1840, only five cases involving the commerce clause had reached the court, and only 30 had been settled by 1870. Moreover, these cases for the most part did not concern the affirmative power of Congress to regulate interstate commerce, but rather the question whether state laws infringed upon the federal power.

After about 1870, however, the commerce clause began to be used as the constitutional basis for the extension of federal authority over constantly larger areas of American economic life, and, as the federal commercial power was transformed from a negative into a positive one, the amount of litigation increased rapidly. During the period 1870-1900, about 185 cases involving the commerce clause were decided by the court.

The first case involving the scope of the commerce power to reach the Supreme Court was *Gibbons v. Ogden,* 9 Wheat. 1 (1824).[12] In this case, a New York law granting an exclusive privilege of navigation by steamboat on all waters within the state was held void as repugnant to the commerce clause, so far as the law prohibited vessels licensed by the United States from navigating the same waters. The court's decision, written by Chief Justice John Marshall, assumed great importance both because of the broad construction of the term "commerce" and because of the court's assertion of the supremacy of the federal power in this field.

"The subject to be regulated is commerce," Marshall said. "To ascertain the extent of the power, it becomes necessary to settle the meaning of the word.

"The counsel for the appellee would limit it to traffic, to buying and selling, or the interchange of commodities, and do not admit that it comprehends navigation. This would restrict a general term, applicable to many objects, to one of its significations. Commerce, undoubtedly, is traffic, but it is something more—it is intercourse. It describes the commercial intercourse between nations, and parts of nations, in all its branches.... All America understands...the word 'commerce' to comprehend navigation....

"The subject to which the power is next applied," Marshall continued, "is to commerce 'among the several states.' The word 'among' means intermingled with.... Commerce among the states cannot stop at the external boundary lines of each state, but may be introduced into the interior. It is not intended to say that these words comprehend that commerce which is completely internal, which is carried on between man and man in a state, or between different parts of the same state and which does not extend to or affect other states. Such a power would be inconvenient and is certainly unnecessary. Comprehensive as the word 'among' is, it may very properly be restricted to that commerce which concerns more states than one.... The completely internal commerce of a state, then, may be considered as reserved for the state itself."

On the supremacy of the federal power, Marshall said: "This power, like all others vested in Congress, is complete in itself, may be exercised to its utmost extent and acknowledges no limitations other than are prescribed in the Constitution.... If, as has always been understood, the sovereignty of Congress, though limited to specified objects, is plenary as to those objects, the power over commerce with foreign nations and among the several states is vested in Congress as absolutely as it would be in a single government, having in its constitution the same restrictions on the exercise of the power as are found in the Constitution of the United States."

The decision in *Gibbons v. Ogden* was popular. "At the time of its delivery," according to Albert J. Beveridge, "nobody complained of Marshall's opinion except the agents of the steamboat monopoly, the theorists of localism and the slave autocracy. All these influences beheld, in Marshall's statesmanship, their inevitable extinction." Jefferson was "horrified." In 1825, at the age of 82, he wrote that he viewed "with the deepest affliction, the rapid strides with which the federal branch of our government is advancing towards the usurpation of all the rights reserved to the states."[13]

Political scientists, Ogg and Ray, wrote: "Marshall not only affirmed full authority of Congress to maintain the free flow of interstate and foreign commerce within the individual states, but declared commerce to consist not only of *traffic* (buying, selling and transporting commodities), but of *intercourse* as well, thereby giving it an entirely new content and meaning.... Immediately, the carrying of persons (not simply goods) from one state to another, or to a foreign country, became 'commerce,' subject to congressional regulation; and as forms and methods of intercourse later multiplied, the field for control correspondingly expanded. In time came the steamboat; then the railroad; then the telegraph; then the telephone; then the motor vehicle; then 'wireless'; then radio-broadcasting; then the airplane; finally television.... And to all of these the regulative authority of Congress was progressively extended, with the Supreme Court coming close behind with decisions validating most of the powers asserted and sometimes hinting at even broader ones that might be assumed."[14]

Chapter 10

Interstate and Foreign Commerce

In its first century, Congress made little use of its power to regulate interstate commerce. Before the Civil War, it did so in only two classes of subjects—construction of interstate bridges and extension of the admiralty jurisdiction. But with the passage of the Interstate Commerce Act of 1887, Congress moved into regulation of the domestic economy.

Both before and after the Civil War, the states attempted in various ways to curb increasing abuses by the railroads. These efforts were generally ineffective. Then, in 1886, the Supreme Court ruled in *Wabash, St. Louis & Pacific Ry. Co. v. Illinois* (118 U.S. 557) that any enterprise engaged in interstate commerce could not be regulated by the states through which it passed. Such regulation, the court held, was barred by the commerce clause of the Constitution. The scope of the decision not only nullified state regulation of railroads but also precluded state action in such fields as the curbing of monopolies.[15]

Interstate Commerce Act. Inability of the states to regulate the railroads led directly to the passage in 1887 of the Interstate Commerce Act, which established the Interstate Commerce Commission (ICC). In 1894, the Supreme Court upheld the act as a necessary and proper means of enforcing congressional authority.[16] The ICC has served as the prototype for the other regulatory commissions created by Congress.

Under the original law, the ICC did not have power to make or revise rates; ultimately, however, the necessity of conferring extensive rate-making power was brought home to the national mind; and under the transportation acts of 1906 and 1920, the ICC (as an agent of Congress for the purpose) was authorized, on complaint and after hearing, not only to fix "just and reasonable" rates, regulations and practices, but also to prescribe definite maximum or minimum (or both) charges.[17] In time the ICC's jurisdiction was broadened to include all interstate commerce carried on by railroads, trucking companies, bus lines, freight forwarders, water carriers, oil pipelines, transportation brokers and express agencies.

Antitrust Legislation. In 1890, Congress moved into federal regulation of commercial enterprise with enactment of the Sherman Antitrust Act, "to protect commerce against unlawful restraints and monopolies." The act imposed a general prohibition upon "every contract, combination in the form of trust or otherwise, or conspiracy in restraint of trade or commerce." Federal regulation of commerce was further strengthened in 1914 by passage of the Clayton Act and the Federal Trade Commission Act.[18]

Areas Related to Commerce. An activity which does not itself involve movement across state lines may be regarded as interstate commerce because of the use of the instrumentalities of such commerce. The classic case is that of the correspondence schools which are interstate commerce because of their reliance on the U.S. mails. Regulation of public utility holding companies under the federal act of 1935 was upheld on the ground that their subsidiaries usually operate on an interstate basis, and that the services which the holding company performs for its subsidiaries involve continuous and extensive use of the mails and other facilities of interstate commerce.[19]

Police Power. Congress entered still another field of regulation in 1895 when it enacted a law prohibiting transportation of lottery tickets in interstate commerce. The Supreme Court upheld this law in 1903 with a decision that, in the words of Charles Warren, "disclosed the existence of a hitherto unsuspected field of national power." Warren said: "The practical result of the case was the creation of a federal police power—the right to regulate the manner of production, manufacture, sale and transportation of articles and the transportation of persons, through the medium of legislation professing to regulate commerce between the states. Congress took very swift advantage of the new field thus opened to it."[20]

Between 1903 and 1917, Congress enacted laws prohibiting the interstate transportation of explosives, diseased livestock, insect pests, falsely stamped gold and silver articles, narcotics, prostitutes and adulterated or misbranded foods and drugs. Interstate transportation of stolen automobiles was made unlawful in 1925, under the Dyer Act, and the so-called "Lindbergh law" of 1932 made interstate transportation of abducted persons a federal offense.

The 1910 Mann Act, forbidding the transportation of women in interstate commerce for the purpose of prostitution and debauchery, was upheld by the Supreme Court in 1913. The court held "that Congress has power over transportation 'among the several States'; that the power is complete in itself, and that Congress, as an incident to it, may adopt not only means necessary but convenient to its exercise, and the means may have the quality of police regulations."

In 1925 *(Brooks v. United States,* 267 U.S. 432), the Supreme Court laid down the following principle: "Congress can certainly regulate interstate commerce to the extent of forbidding and punishing the use of such commerce as an agency to promote immorality, dishonesty, or the spread of any evil or harm to the people of other states from the state of origin. In doing this, it is merely exercising the police power, for the benefit of the public, within the field of interstate commerce."[21]

Child Labor Decision. The same technique of closing the channels of interstate commerce was employed by Congress in enacting the Federal Child Labor Act of 1916. The 1916 act prohibited the shipment in interstate commerce of the products of factories, mines or quarries employing children below specified ages. In a historic 5-4 decision in *Hammer v. Dagenhart* (247 U.S. 251) the court ruled in 1918 that Congress had the power "to control the means by which commerce is carried on," but not the power "to forbid commerce from moving."[22]

Speaking for the majority, Justice William R. Day said: "The thing intended to be accomplished by this statute is the denial of the facilities of interstate commerce to those manufacturers in the states who employ children within the prohibited ages. The act in its effect does not regulate transportation among the states, but aims to standardize the ages at which children may be employed in mining and manufacturing within the states. The goods shipped are of themselves harmless.... Over interstate transportation, or its incidents, the regulatory power of Congress is ample, but the production of articles, intended for interstate commerce, is a matter of local regulation."[23]

In a classic dissent, Justice Holmes challenged the majority view. Congress clearly had the express power under the commerce clause, he said, to forbid the transportation of goods in interstate commerce. Therefore, if the law was to be declared unconstitutional, it would have to be because of its indirect effects on the states. "But if an act is within the powers specifically conferred upon Congress, it seems to me that it is not made any less constitutional because of the indirect effects that it may have, however obvious it may be that it will have those effects, and that we are not at liberty upon such grounds to hold it void."[24]

The court overruled the *Hammer* decision in 1941 as "a departure from the principles which have prevailed in the interpretation of the commerce clause both before and since" the 1918 decision.

"Influential as it may have been," wrote scholar C. Herman Pritchett, the 1918 decision "was never anything but an exception to the general rule, which as stated by Harlan in The Lottery Case (1903) is that the power to regulate commerce 'is plenary, is complete in itself, and is subject to no limitations except such as may be found in the Constitution.' It was the general rule, not the exception, which the court followed in upholding the power of Congress over interstate commerce in stolen motor vehicles in 1925 and kidnapped persons in 1936."[25]

Expansion of Power after 1900

Since 1900, Congress has expanded its regulatory authority over commerce into almost every area of the commercial and industrial life of the nation. For the most part, the Supreme Court has gone along with this expansion and even on occasion, hinted at broader federal powers than Congress itself claimed.

Many of the New Deal economic recovery programs were launched under the commerce clause. Until 1937, the Supreme Court tended to view the authorizing laws as unconstitutional, either because the programs were considered to range beyond the bounds of the commerce power or because they were thought to involve too broad a delegation of congressional authority. Resentment caused by these decisions led to President Roosevelt's plan to enlarge the court.

Two months after the President sent his court-packing plan to Congress, the court altered its stance. In a 5-4 decision in 1937, it upheld the constitutionality of the National Labor Relations (Wagner) Act of 1935 and at the same time clarified the scope of the commerce power. The 1935 act had established the National Labor Relations Board and given it authority to forbid any person from engaging in any unfair labor practice "affecting commerce." The case involved charges of unfair labor practices in one of the Pennsylvania plants of the Jones & Laughlin Corporation, a major steel producer with operations in several states.

Speaking for the court, Chief Justice Hughes said: "Although activities may be intrastate in character when separately considered, if they have such a close and substantial relation to interstate commerce that their control is essential or appropriate to protect that commerce from burdens and obstructions, Congress cannot be denied the power to exercise that control.... When industries organize themselves on a national scale, making their relation to interstate commerce the dominant factor in their activities, how can it be maintained that their industrial relations constitute a forbidden field into which Congress may not enter when it is necessary to protect interstate commerce from the paralyzing consequences of industrial war?" *(National Labor Relations Board v. Jones & Laughlin Corp.*, 301 U.S. 1).

In a 1941 decision upholding the Fair Labor Standards (Wages and Hours) Act of 1938, the court reversed its earlier decision in the *Hammer* case. The 1938 act banned the shipment in interstate commerce of goods produced in violation of the wage-and-hour standards set by the legislation, which included restrictions on child labor. The law was applicable to employees "engaged in commerce or in the production of goods for commerce." Justice Stone, delivering the opinion of the court, said: "The power of Congress under the commerce clause is plenary to exclude any article from interstate commerce subject only to the specific prohibitions of the Constitution." *(U.S. v. Darby Lumber Co.,* 312 U.S. 100).

In other decisions the court upheld application of the commerce clause to such matters as agricultural marketing controls, regulation of the insurance industry and control over navigable waters (including irrigation and flood control) and the hydroelectric power derived from them. In a decision in 1946 upholding the "death sentence" provision of the Public Utility Holding Company Act, the court concluded: "The federal commerce power is as broad as the economic needs of the nation." *(American Power & Light Co. v. SEC,* 329 U.S. 90).

More recently, the scope of the commerce clause has been enlarged to include civil rights. In the Civil Rights Act of 1964, Congress found sanction in the commerce clause and the "equal protection" clause of the Fourteenth Amendment for a ban on racial disccrimination in most public accommodations, such as hotels, motels, restaurants and places of amusement. In two test cases in 1964, the Supreme Court unanimously upheld the law under the commerce power alone.[26]

In 1968, Congress used the commerce clause as the basis for legislation making it a federal crime to travel in interstate commerce or use the facilities of interstate commerce to incite or participate in a riot. The measure, prompted by rioting in black ghettos, was later used to prosecute some of the participants in demonstrations against the Vietnam War.[27]

Federal Regulatory Agencies

Since the establishment of the Interstate Commerce Commission in 1887, federal regulatory agencies have come to play a major role in the American economy.[28]

Although the *United States Government Organization Manual* lists almost 50 independent federal agencies, many of which perform regulatory functions, discussion of federal regulation usually centers on activities of the so-called "Big Seven". In addition to the ICC, these are the Federal Trade Commission, organized in 1915; the Federal Power Commission, established in 1920; and four agencies established during the administration of President Franklin D. Roosevelt—the Federal Communications Commission (1934), the Securities and Exchange Commission (1934), the National Labor Relations Board (1935) and the Civil Aeronautics Board (1938).

Members of all seven agencies are appointed by the President for fixed terms. Membership ranges from five to 11, and no political party may have more than a one-member majority on any of the Big Seven.

The agencies derive their powers from acts of Congress that delegate to them certain regulatory functions that have become too complex for Congress to handle by means of ordinary legislation. Thus they are sometimes described as "arms" of Congress.

They also have quasi-judicial functions. When the Civil Aeronautics Board promulgates a rule asserting its primary jurisdiction over airspace for both civil and military purposes, it is exercising its quasi-legislative (or rule-making) power. When it decides which of several commercial airlines shall be awarded a specific airline route, it is exercising quasi-judicial (or adjudicatory) power. Similarly, the FCC is making rules when it sets up criteria for evaluating competing claims for a television license, adjudicating when it awards a license.

Regulatory commissions, therefore, exercise a blend of the legislative, executive and judicial powers. They were established by Congress to make the bulk of complicated regulations for industry that Congress had neither the time nor the expertise to do itself. They then enforce the rules they promulgate (although court review of their actions is possible). The President appoints commission members and reviews their budgets. The Senate approves the nominees, and Congress appropriates operative funds and defines in legislation the agencies' responsibilities.

"Big Seven" Powers

The powers and influence of the Big Seven regulatory agencies, reaching into virtually every corner of the

American economy, give some indication of the scope of the federal commerce power. The principal functions of these agencies are as follows:

Interstate Commerce Commission. Jurisdiction covers railroads and related carriers, common and contract motor carriers, certain domestic water carriers, pipelines and freight forwarders. ICC fixes rates; sets standards for reasonable service; issues permits or certificates required to engage in interstate transportation; controls consolidations and mergers of carriers, issuance of securities and the accounting systems and records kept by carriers; regulates safety devices and standards.

Federal Trade Commission. FTC may act to prevent practices leading to monopoly or restraint of trade, such as unfair methods of competition (e.g., false and misleading advertising), stock acquisitions of competing enterprises and price discrimination. It has power also to investigate and to issue cease-and-desist orders, and it shares antimonopoly responsibility with the Justice Department.

Federal Power Commission. FPC grants licenses to private power projects on navigable waters subject to federal jurisdiction; fixes rates on interstate sale of electric energy; prescribes uniform accounting methods; and regulates (1) mergers and security issues of electric utilities, (2) most federal power projects and (3) interstate sales of natural gas.

Federal Communications Commission. FCC regulates telephone and telegraph common carriers, including their interstate rates; allocates radio frequencies; licenses radio and television stations; licenses radio operators; monitors broadcasts; administers international communications treaties.

Securities and Exchange Commission. SEC regulates security issues; supervises the stock exchanges; regulates holding companies and investment companies.

National Labor Relations Board. NLRB adjudicates charges of unfair labor practices on the part of employers or unions; enforces requirements for collective bargaining; supervises election of bargaining representatives; decides jurisdictional disputes.

Civil Aeronautics Board. CAB licenses domestic air carriers; issues permits to foreign air carriers landing in the

United States; fixes passenger, freight and mail rates; controls mergers, pooling and other arrangements between carriers.

Delegation of Power

All of the commissions exercise, to greater or lesser degree, some executive, legislative and judicial power. By the same token, control over the commissions is shared by the President, Congress and the courts, in a system of checks and balances. The President's power to control the regulatory agencies rests largely in his appointive power, while that of Congress rests in its responsibility for appropriations.

Members of the legislative branch nevertheless have insisted periodically that the power of Congress has been delegated, not abdicated, and that in the last analysis the commissions are "creatures of Congress." The classic view of the commissions held by federal legislators was expressed in 1931 by the late Speaker of the House, Sam Rayburn (D Texas):

"Far from undermining the constitutional authority of Congress, delegation of authority to administrative agencies is one of the surest safeguards to effective legislative action. It is a procedure which conserves the vital power of Congress for vital matters.... (A commission) does not perform any act that Congress has not the authority to perform itself.... Congress...delegated responsibility to a commission of...trained experts to work out the details for them."[29]

This view has not gone unchallenged. C. Herman Pritchett, a member of the Hoover Commission, wrote in the *American Political Science Review* in October 1949 that "The spurious nature of this 'arm of Congress' claim has long been evident." Pritchett added: "The fact is that Congress has not a single control over any of the regulatory commissions that it does not possess over executive agencies generally.... [The Hoover Commission] wanted to have non-political regulation and at the same time provide for presidential control."[30]

It has been asserted that every President of the United States from Woodrow Wilson on has tried in one way or another to influence commission activity and has succeeded in doing so. For example, "President Hoover made public statements indicating how he thought the Interstate Commerce Commission ought to exercise certain of its powers, and the commission somewhat reluctantly yielded," wrote Robert E. Cushman.[31] President Roosevelt obtained the resignation of Hoover's chairman of the Federal Power Commission and added two appointees of his own. Four days after his inauguration, President Nixon recalled from the Civil Aeronautics Board "for further review and decision" the awards of new Pacific routes which President Johnson had made to five airlines on Dec. 18, 1968. (Although CAB makes final decisions in domestic route cases, the President has statutory authority to approve or reject CAB recommendations on foreign routes.)

1961 Reorganization Proposal

Regulatory commissions have found it difficult to please simultaneously the executive branch, the legislative branch and the regulated industry. Commission actions often are criticized as restrictive or permissive, and commission procedures frequently are attacked.

Numerous plans for improving the performance of federal regulatory agencies have been put forward since World War II, yet few have been adopted. Most reform proposals have foundered because of opposition in Congress. The legislative branch tends to be suspicious of any reorganization that might weaken its influence on regulatory agencies. Moreover, the regulated industries evidently prefer a sometimes uncomfortable status quo to a new regulatory environment that might be less to their liking.

The most ambitious attempt to reshape the regulatory agencies took place shortly after John F. Kennedy became President in 1961. Kennedy had asked James M. Landis, a former chairman of the Securities and Exchange Commission, to study the agencies and submit proposals for improving them. Landis' report, which noted the familiar problems of delay, ethical conduct and quality of personnel, made 16 broad recommendations. Among other things, he called for:

● Extensive reorganization of most of the agencies.
● Establishment of special offices in the White House to develop national transportation policy, telecommunications policy and energy resources policy.

● Establishment by executive order of a federal employee code of ethics and limitation of off-the-record presentation in regulatory agency cases.

● Creation of a special Office for the Oversight of Regulatory Agencies.

In a special message to Congress on regulatory agencies, April 13, 1961, Kennedy proposed to give agency chairmen "broad managerial powers" to correct the existing, diffused authority of the commissions; provide that all agency chairmen serve in that capacity at the President's pleasure; and authorize delegation of a large proportion of agency responsibilities to inter-agency boards and hearing examiners to eliminate needless work on "unimportant details" at the top level. Congress responded by reviving the Reorganization Act of 1949, which had expired two years earlier, so that the President could submit reorganization plans for the agencies.

Seven such plans were submitted, all of which had the basic aim of speeding up and streamlining agency procedures. The first four plans—those for the SEC, FCC, CAB and FTC—contained three basically identical steps. They authorized the agency to delegate some of its functions to certain employees; they empowered the chairman to assign the delegated functions; and they made review of certain lower-level decisions discretionary.

The plan for the National Labor Relations Board was the same as the first four but omitted the chairman's power of assignment; the plan for the Federal Home Loan Bank Board (FHLBB) only restored some hiring and firing powers formerly held by the chairman; and in the seventh plan, the Federal Maritime Board (FMB) was abolished and its functions assigned to other agencies.

Jealous as ever of its authority over the agencies, Congress charged that the administration planned to create a White House "czar" and establish a "direct chain of political command" over the regulatory agencies. When the smoke of battle cleared, the final score stood: three plans killed, with one replaced by a more limited version; four plans approved. Congress vetoed the reorganization plans for FCC, SEC and NLRB. It upheld those for CAB, FTC, FMB and FHLBB.

A scaled-down reorganization bill for FCC allowed the commission to delegate minor functions to employees, but it did not provide the authority requested by the administration to enable the chairman to make specific work assignments to employees and commissioners. The bill also expedited action by putting oral arguments on exceptions to agency decisions on a discretionary instead of required basis and by giving the commission authority to either accept or deny appeals for overall review without giving a reason.

Challenge in the 1970s

Fearing that the agencies were becoming increasingly more responsive to the White House and industry, Congress in 1973 took several steps to free the commissions from some executive branch controls and moved more forcefully to scrutinize the composition of commission membership.

For the first time since 1950,[32] the Senate refused to confirm a presidential nomination to a regulatory agency. And, refusing to buckle under strong pressure from the Nixon administration, Congress took two steps to free the agencies from executive branch dependence: agencies no longer had to submit information questionnaires to the Office of Management and Budget (the power was transferred to the General Accounting Office from OMB), and the Federal Trade Commission would argue its own civil cases.

The implementation of tougher standards for commission nominees was the product of the Senate Commerce Committee, which approves nominees for the FCC, FTC, ICC, CAB, Federal Maritime Commission, FPC, National Transportation Safety Board and Consumer Product Safety Commission. The first test of the committee's new policy came in January 1973, when President Nixon named Robert H. Morris, a San Francisco lawyer, to a seat on the Federal Power Commission. During his confirmation hearings, Morris acknowledged that from 1956 to 1971, approximately half of his legal work involved representation of the Standard Oil Company of California, a company whose activities are regulated by FPC.

During floor debate on the nomination in June, Commerce Committee Chairman Warren G. Magnuson (D Wash.) said, "The opposition to Mr. Morris stems from the fact that the Senate is again asked to accept, for an independent regulatory agency with vast powers over an industry which affects vital national interest, yet one more nominee whose professional career has been dedicated to the furtherance of the private interests of that industry." Magnuson also warned the White House: "The Senate should serve notice on the President that it expects revision of his criteria for the selection of nominees to all regulatory agencies. Now, more than ever, the Senate should not be asked to confirm appointments...which appear to have been designed as rewards for politically supportive industries or other special interests. Instead, the Senate should be asked to confirm nominees who have demonstrated competence and commitment to the public interest."

The Senate voted, 50-42, to recommit Morris' nomination to the Commerce Committee.

Magnuson's message was apparently not lost on the President. On Nov. 2, he nominated to what would have been Morris' FPC seat, Don S. Smith, a member of the Arkansas Public Service Commission with good marks from the state's consumer organizations. In contrast to the delays that marked Morris' confirmation proceedings, the Commerce Committee approved Smith's nomination Nov. 28. The full Senate followed suit later in the same day, confirming Smith by voice vote.

In May 1974, however, Nixon nominated Daniel T. Kingsley, of the White House staff, to another seat on the FPC—but a committee investigation uncovered Kingsley's involvement in the administration's "responsiveness program" designed to make the supposedly nonpolitical Civil Service more responsive to White House wishes. The committee refused to act on the selection, and the name was withdrawn six months later.[33]

Regulation of Foreign Commerce

The power to regulate commerce with foreign nations extends to all transportation or communication that crosses the national boundaries. It is inextricably tied to the powers over foreign relations and fiscal affairs. The commerce power may be used to promote, inhibit or simply make rules for trade with other nations. It may be implemented by treaty or international agreement, as well as by acts of Congress. Such is the breadth of this power that only a suggestion of it can be offered here.[34]

Promotion of Trade. Encouragement of foreign trade may take the form of opening up new markets for American goods in other countries or of securing favorable conditions for American traders abroad. The earliest actions in this field were efforts to replace markets lost when the nation won its independence from England. Modern laws have ranged from antitrust exemptions for exporters to use of tariff reductions to stimulate trade.

Efforts to encourage American shipping have ranged from preferential duties for goods imported in American ships (first enacted in 1789) to federal subsidies for the construction and operation of merchant ships, designed to equalize competition with foreign shipping (since 1936).

Trade Restrictions. The authority to limit or even prohibit foreign trade rests with Congress, although the legislative branch frequently delegates this power to the President or executive agencies.

Tariffs. Historically, the predominant mechanism to restrict foreign trade has been the protective tariff. The first major business of the House of Representatives in 1789 was to devise a tariff schedule; unlike many later tariff laws, this one had as its chief object the raising of revenue to finance the new government. But Congress was only four days old when a Philadelphia representative offered an amendment proposing additional duties on manufactured articles "to encourage the productions of our country and to protect our infant manufactures." Congress continued to legislate tariffs until 1930, and the pleas of special interests were frequently reflected in the tariff schedules.

The system also had other pitfalls. Members of Congress could hardly hope to master the intricacies of complicated tariff schedules, and tariffs embodied in statutes could not readily be adapted to changing conditions. A measure of flexibility was introduced in 1922, when the Fordney-McCumber Tariff Act gave the President authority to adjust tariff rates on the basis of recommendations by the U.S. Tariff Commission, which previously had had only investigative authority.

Reciprocal Trade Agreements Act. Finally, in 1934, the Roosevelt administration—hoping to assist economic recovery at home by expanding American exports—proposed that Congress delegate some of its constitutional power to the President by authorizing him to negotiate trade agreements with other nations. The administration asked authority to cut tariffs by as much as 50 per cent in return for equivalent concessions from other nations. Prodded and persuaded by Secretary of State Cordell Hull, the Democratic-controlled 73rd Congress—over the nearly unanimous opposition of Republicans—made this grant of authority in the Trade Agreements Act of 1934. Thereafter, no serious effort was made to restore congressional tariff-making in place of the method of presidential negotiation of bilateral and, after World War II, multilateral trade agreements.

Non-tariff Barriers. Non-tariff barriers to the free flow of trade range from import quotas to embargoes. Although export taxes are forbidden under the Constitution, Congress can control export trade through licensing or other means. Thus it may bar shipment of strategic materials to hostile countries or restrict exports that would deplete essential domestic supplies. Congress has curbed imports that would interfere with domestic regulatory programs (such as agricultural commodities under production-control and price-support programs). It has also enacted "Anti-Dumping," "Buy American" and "Ship American" legislation.

The ultimate restraint on foreign commerce is the embargo, which suspends commerce completely with all or with specified countries. The United States has used the embargo on a number of occasions, beginning in 1794. Trade with mainland China was completely embargoed after that country entered the Korean War. Exports of strategic goods to other Communist countries have long been subject to embargoes of varying severity.

Other Trade Laws. Laws relating to navigation and ship inspection go back to the First Congress. Since 1798, Congress has assumed responsibility for the health care of American merchant seamen; in the La Follette Seamen's Act of 1915, it undertook to safeguard their rights on shipboard as well. Congress also imposes safety regulations on ships using American ports and requires ship owners to prove financial responsibility as a means of protecting passengers from losses.

PART IV
Impeachment

Chapter 11

Constitutional Background

Impeachment is perhaps the most awesome though the least used power of Congress. In essence, it is a political action, couched in legal terminology, directed against a ranking official of the federal government. The House of Representatives is the prosecutor. The Senate chamber is the courtroom; and the Senate is the judge and jury. The final penalty is removal from office and disqualification from further office. There is no appeal.

Impeachment proceedings have been initiated in the House more than 60 times since 1789, but only 13 officers have been impeached: one President, one Cabinet officer, one senator and 10 federal judges.[1] Of these 13, 12 cases reached the Senate where two were dismissed before trial after the person impeached left office, six resulted in acquittal and four ended in conviction. (In the 13th case, federal Judge Mark H. Delahay was impeached in 1873, but resigned prior to any Senate action.[2] *(Footnotes, p. 317)*

All of the convictions involved federal judges: John Pickering of the district court for New Hampshire, in 1804; West H. Humphreys of the eastern, middle and western districts of Tennessee, in 1862; Robert W. Archbald of the Commerce Court, in 1913; and Halsted L. Ritter of the southern district of Florida, in 1936.

Two of the impeachments traditionally have stood out from all the rest. They involved Justice Samuel Chase of the

Supreme Court in 1805 and President Andrew Johnson in 1868, the two most powerful and important federal officials ever subjected to the process. Both were impeached by the House—Chase for partisan conduct on the bench; Johnson for violating the Tenure of Office Act—and both were acquitted by the Senate after sensational trials. Behind both impeachments lay intensely partisan politics. Chase, a Federalist, was a victim of attacks on the Supreme Court by Jeffersonian Democrats, who had planned to impeach Chief Justice John Marshall if Chase was convicted. President Johnson was a victim of Radical Republicans opposed to his reconstruction policies after the Civil War. *(p. 145)*

The power of the impeachment process was dramatically demonstrated in 1974 when the House of Representatives initiated an inquiry into the conduct of President Richard Nixon as a result of charges arising out of a 1972 break-in at Democratic National Headquarters in the Watergate Office Building in Washington. The House Judiciary Committee adopted three articles of impeachment against Nixon late in July 1974. The articles charged him with abuse of his presidential powers, obstruction of justice and contempt of Congress. Before the full House voted on these articles, Nixon resigned on Aug. 9—after being told by Republican House and Senate leaders that the evidence against him virtually assured that he would be impeached, convicted and removed from office.[3] *(p. 148)*

Purpose of Impeachment

Based on specific constitutional authority, the impeachment process was designed "as a method of national inquest into the conduct of public men," according to Alexander Hamilton in *Federalist* No. 65.[4] The Constitution declares that impeachment proceedings may be brought against "the President, Vice President and all civil officers of the United States," without explaining who is, or is not, a "civil officer." In practice, however, the overwhelming majority of impeachment proceedings have been directed against federal judges, who hold lifetime appointments "during good behavior," and cannot be removed by any other method. Nine of the 12 impeachment cases that have reached the Senate have involved federal judges. Federal judges have also been the subject of most of the resolutions and investigations in the House that have failed to result in impeachment.[5]

The House Judiciary Committee twice has ruled that certain federal officials were not subject to impeachment. In 1833, the committee determined that a territorial judge was not a civil officer within the meaning of the Constitution because he held office for only four years and could be removed at any time by the President. In 1926, the committee said that a commissioner of the District of Columbia was immune from impeachment because he was an officer of the District and not a civil officer of the United States.[6]

History: Curbing the Executive

Impeachment as a constitutional process dates from 14th century England when the fledgling Parliament sought to make the King's advisers accountable. The monarch, who was considered incapable of wrongdoing, was immune. Impeachment was used against ministers and judges whom the legislature believed guilty of breaking the law or carrying out the unpopular orders of the King. The system was based on the common law and the House of Lords could inflict the death penalty on those it found guilty.

Grounds for impeachment included both criminal and noncriminal activity. Joseph Story, in his *Commentaries on the Constitution of the United States* (1905), wrote: "Lord chancellors and judges and other magistrates have not only been impeached for bribery and acting grossly contrary to the duties of their office, but for misleading their sovereign by unconstitutional opinions and for attempts to subvert the fundamental laws and introduce arbitrary power."[7]

In the mid-15th century, after the conviction of the Duke of Suffolk, impeachment fell into disuse. This was in large measure due to the ability of the Tudor monarchs to force Parliament to remove unwanted officials by bills of attainder or pains and penalties. In the early 17th century, the excesses and absolutist tendencies of the Stuart kings prompted Parliament to revive its impeachment power to curb the monarch by removing his favorite aides.

The struggle between the King and the Commons came to a head with the impeachment of Charles the First's minister, the Earl of Strafford, in 1642. The Earl was impeached by the House of Commons for subverting the fundamental law and introducing an arbitrary and tyrannical government. While the charge was changed to a bill of attainder in the House of Lords, Raoul Berger wrote that "his impeachment may be regarded as the opening gun in the struggle whereby the Long Parliament 'prevented the English monarchy from hardening into an absolutism of the type then becoming general in Europe.' "[8]

More than 50 impeachments were brought to the House of Lords for trial between 1620 and 1787 when the American Constitution was being written. As the framers toiled in Philadelphia, the long impeachment and trial of Warren Hastings was in progress in London. Hastings was charged with oppression, cruelty, bribery and fraud as colonial administrator and first governor general in India. The trial before the House of Lords lasted from Feb. 13, 1788, to April 23, 1795. Hastings was acquitted, but by that time, impeachment was widely regarded as unnecessary—because of ministerial responsibility to Parliament—and overly cumbersome. The last impeachment trial in Britain occurred in 1806.

Debate in Constitutional Convention

Under the English system, an impeachment (indictment) was preferred by the House of Commons and decided by the House of Lords. In America, colonial governments and early state constitutions followed the British pattern of trial before the upper legislative body on charges brought by the lower house.

Despite these precedents, a major controversy arose over the impeachment process in the Constitutional Convention. The issue was whether the Senate should try impeachments. Opposing that role for the Senate, Madison and Pinckney asserted that it would make the President too dependent on the legislative branch. Suggested alternative trial bodies included the "national judiciary," the Supreme Court or the assembled chief justices of state supreme courts. It was argued, however, that such bodies would be too small and perhaps even susceptible to corruption. In the end, the Senate was agreed to. Hamilton (a Senate opponent during the Convention) asked later in *The Federalist:* "Where else than in the Senate could have been found a tribunal sufficiently dignified, or sufficiently independent?"[9]

A lesser issue was the definition of impeachable crimes. In the original proposals, the President was to be removed on impeachment and conviction "for mal or corrupt conduct," or for "malpractice or neglect of duty." Later, the wording was changed to "treason, bribery or corruption," and then to "treason or bribery" alone. Contending that "treason and bribery" were too narrow, George Mason proposed adding "mal-administration," but switched to "other high crimes and misdemeanors against the state" when Madison said that "mal-administration" was too broad. A final revision made impeachable crimes "treason, bribery or other high crimes and misdemeanors."[10] Debate over the meaning of this phrase resumes during every serious impeachment inquiry.

The provisions of the Constitution on impeachment are scattered through the first three articles. To the House is given the "sole power of impeachment." The Senate is given "the sole power to try all impeachments." Impeachments may be brought against "the President, Vice President, and all civil officers of the United States" for "treason, bribery or other high crimes or misdemeanors." Conviction means "removal from office and disqualification to hold" further public office. *(Article I, Section 2, 3; Article II, Section 2, 4; Article III, Section 2, pp. 285, 293, 294)*

The first attempt to use the impeachment power was made in 1796. A petition from residents of the Northwest Territory, submitted to the House on April 25, accused Judge George Turner of the territorial supreme court of arbitrary conduct. The petition was referred briefly to a special House committee and then was referred to Attorney General Charles Lee. Impeachment proceedings were dropped after Lee said, May 9, that the territorial government would prosecute Turner in the territorial courts.[11]

Procedures in Impeachment

The first impeachment proceedings, against Turner, provided no precedents for later impeachments. In fact, the process has been used so infrequently and under such widely varying circumstances that no uniform practice has emerged.

Impeachment

The House has no standing rules dealing with its role in the impeachment process, a role which the Constitution describes in fewer than a dozen words.

At various times impeachment proceedings have been initiated by the introduction of a resolution by a member, by a letter or message from the President, by a grand jury action forwarded to the House from a territorial legislature, by a memorial setting forth charges, by a resolution authorizing a general investigation, or by a resolution reported by the House Judiciary Committee. The five cases to reach the Senate since 1900 were based on Judiciary Committee resolutions.[12]

Before creation of the Judiciary Committee in 1813, the matter was referred to a special committee created for that purpose. This was the case in the first three impeachments which moved to the Senate, those of Sen. William Blount, Judge John Pickering and Justice Samuel Chase. The impeachment of Judge James H. Peck in 1830 was the first referred to the Judiciary Committee.[13]

After submission of the charges, a committee investigation is begun. The committee decides in each case whether the subject of the inquiry has the right to be present at committee proceedings, to be represented by counsel, to present and question witnesses.[14]

If the charges are supported by the investigation, the committee reports an impeachment resolution. Since 1912, articles of impeachment have been reported by the committee simultaneously with the resolution. Before that time, the articles were drawn up after the House had approved the resolution of impeachment.[15]

The House is no more bound by a committee's recommendation on impeachment than it is by a committee recommendation and action on any legislative matter. In 1933, the House Judiciary Committee found insufficient grounds to recommend impeachment of Judge Harold Louderback, but the House impeached the judge anyway.[16] The target of an impeachment resolution is impeached if the House adopts a resolution of impeachment by majority vote. The articles of impeachment may be approved by a simple majority, and may be amended on the House floor. When the articles of impeachment against President Andrew Johnson were considered by the full House in 1868, two additional articles were adopted along with those recommended by the committee.[17]

After the resolution and the articles have been adopted by the House, the House managers are selected to present the case for impeachment to the Senate, acting as prosecutors in the Senate trial. An odd number—ranging from five to 11—has traditionally been selected, including members from both parties who voted in favor of impeachment. They have been selected in various ways—by ballot, with a majority vote necessary for election; by resolution naming the slate; or by the Speaker.[18] The full House may attend the trial, but the House managers are its official representatives in the Senate proceedings.

The Senate. In 1868, for the impeachment trial of President Johnson, the Senate adopted a set of 25 rules for those proceedings. One new rule was added in 1935.

The trial is conducted in a fashion similar to a criminal trial. Both sides may present witnesses and evidence, and the defendant is allowed counsel, the right to testify in his own behalf and the right of cross-examination. If the President or the Vice President is on trial, the Constitution requires the Chief Justice of the Supreme Court to preside. The Constitution is silent on a presiding officer for lesser defendants, but Senate practice has been for the Vice President or the president pro tempore to preside.

The presiding officer can issue all orders needed to compel witnesses to appear or to enforce obedience to Senate orders. The presiding officer administers the oath to all the senators before they take part in the trial. The presiding officer rules on all questions of evidence and his ruling stands unless he decides to submit the question to a vote of the Senate or unless a Senator requests such a vote. Custom dictates that most questions concerning the admissibility of evidence are submitted to the Senate for decision. The presiding officer questions witnesses, and asks questions submitted to him in writing by various senators, who do not directly question witnesses themselves.

All of the Senate's orders and decisions during an impeachment trial are made by roll-call vote, and without debate—unless in secret session. On the final question—guilt or innocence—each senator is limited to 15 minutes of debate in secret session. The Senate votes separately on each article of impeachment; the Constitution requires a two-thirds vote for conviction. If no article is approved by two-thirds of the senators present, the impeached official is acquitted. If any article receives two-thirds approval, he is convicted. The Constitution then requires that the Senate vote to remove him from office. If desired, the Senate may also vote to disqualify him from holding future federal offices. Disqualification is not mandatory; only two of the four convictions have been accompanied by disqualification, which is decided by a majority vote.

Records, Resignations and Recesses. The shortest time from House impeachment to Senate verdict was one month—in the impeachment of federal Judge Halsted Ritter in 1936. The longest time was one year—in the early impeachments of Pickering and Chase. The impeachment of Andrew Johnson took three months from House action to Senate judgment.

The shortest Senate trial on record is that of Judge West H. Humphreys—which took only one day; the longest was the two months consumed in the Senate trial of President Johnson.

In general, the resignation of the official about to be impeached puts an end to impeachment proceedings since the primary objective, removal from office, has been accomplished. This was the case in the impeachment proceedings begun against two federal judges—Mark H. Delahay, impeached by voice vote Feb. 28, 1873, and George W. English, impeached by a 306-62 vote April 1, 1926—and in the case of President Nixon.[19]

However, resignation is not a foolproof way of precluding impeachment. Secretary of War William W. Belknap, aware of the findings of a congressional committee implicating him in the acceptance of bribes, resigned at 10 o'clock on the morning of March 2, 1876. Sometime after 3 o'clock that afternoon, the House impeached him by voice vote. The Senate debated the question of its jurisdiction, in light of his resignation, and decided by a vote of 37-29 that he could be impeached and tried despite his no longer being in office. He was found not guilty of the charges.[20]

Historical precedent indicates that an impeachment proceeding does not die with adjournment. In 1890-91 the Judiciary Committee investigated the conduct of a federal judge and decided that he should be impeached; a resolution to that effect was reported in 1891 and the House began debate, but did not conclude it before adjournment. In the new Congress in 1892, the evidence taken in the first investigation was referred to the committee again, a second investigation was conducted and the committee decided against impeachment.[21]

In the case of the impeachment of Judge Pickering, the House impeached him, but adjourned before drawing up articles of impeachment, which a committee appointed in the next Congress did do.[22]

Whether impeachment would have to begin again if the House impeached a man in one Congress, but the Senate trial could not begin until the next is unclear—although the view of the Senate as a continuing body according to custom, would indicate that the trial could begin in the new Congress without a repetition of the House procedures. The Senate did decide in 1876 that a trial of impeachment could proceed only when Congress was in session. The vote was 21-19.[23]

Controversial Questions

Three major questions have dominated the history of impeachment in the United States:
- What is an impeachable offense?
- Can senators serve as impartial jurors?
- Are there ways other than impeachment to remove a federal judge from office?

Impeachable Offenses

"Treason" and "bribery," as constitutionally designated impeachable crimes, have raised little debate, for treason is defined elsewhere in the Constitution and bribery is a well-defined act. "High crimes and misdemeanors," however, have been anything that the prosecution has wanted to make them. (In the 1970 attempt to impeach Supreme Court Justice William O. Douglas, then Rep. Gerald R. Ford (R Mich.) declared: "An impeachable offense is whatever a majority of the House of Representatives considers it to be at a given moment in history.")[24]An endless debate has surrounded the phrase, pitting broad constructionists, who have viewed impeachment as a political weapon, against narrow constructionists, who have regarded impeachment as being limited to offenses indictable at common law.

The constitutional debates seemed to indicate that impeachment was to be regarded as a political weapon. Narrow constructionists quickly won a major victory when Supreme Court Justice Samuel Chase was acquitted, using as a defense the argument that the charges against him were not an indictable offense. President Johnson also won acquittal using a similar defense. His lawyers argued that conviction could result only from commission of high criminal offenses against the United States.[25]

The only two convictions to date in the 20th century suggest that the arguments of the broad constructionists still carry considerable weight. The 20th century convictions removed Robert W. Archbald, associate judge of the U.S. Commerce Court, in 1913, and Halsted L. Ritter, U.S. judge for the southern district of Florida, in 1936. Archbald was convicted of soliciting for himself and for friends valuable favors from railroad companies, some of which were litigants in his court. It was conceded, however, that he had committed no indictable offense.[26] Ritter was convicted for conduct in a receivership case which raised serious doubts about his integrity.[27]

This debate resumed in 1974 with the impeachment inquiry into the conduct of President Nixon. The impeachment inquiry staff of the House Judiciary Committee argued for a broad view of "high crimes and misdemeanors" while Nixon's defense attorneys argued for a narrow view.

As adopted by the House Judiciary Committee, Article I charged the President with obstruction of justice, a charge falling within the narrow view of impeachable offenses. Articles II and III reflected the broader interpretation, charging Nixon with abuse of his presidential powers and contempt of Congress.

Conflicts of Interest

An equally controversial issue, particularly in earlier impeachment trials, concerned the partisan political interests of senators, which raised serious doubt about their ability to sit as impartial jurors.

President Johnson's potential successor, for example, was the president pro tempore of the Senate, since there was a vacancy in the vice presidency. Sen. Benjamin F. Wade (R Ohio), president pro tempore, took part in the trial and voted—for conviction. On the other hand, Andrew Johnson's son-in-law, Sen. David T. Patterson (D Tenn.), also took part in the trial and voted—for acquittal.

In the Johnson trial and in others, senators have been outspoken critics or supporters of the defendant, yet have participated in the trial and have voted on the articles. Some senators who had held seats in the House when the articles of impeachment first came up, and had voted on them there, have failed to disqualify themselves during the trial. On occasion, intense outside lobbying for, and against, the defendant has been aimed at senators. Senators have testified as witnesses at some trials and then voted on the articles.

Senators may request to be excused from the trial, and in recent cases senators have disqualified themselves when possible conflicts of interest arose.

Removal of Judges

Two forces have encouraged a continuing search for an alternative method of removing federal judges. One force has been led by members of Congress anxious to free the Senate, faced by an enormous legislative workload, from the time consuming process of sitting as a court of impeachment. The other force has been led by members anxious to restrict judicial power by providing a simpler and swifter means of removal than the cumbersome and unwieldy impeachment process.

The search to date has been unsuccessful. Efforts to revise and accelerate the impeachment process have failed. So, too, have attempts to amend the Constitution to limit the tenure of federal judges to a definite term of years. A more recent approach has been to seek legislation providing for a judicial trial and judgment of removal for federal judges violating "good-behavior" standards. The House passed such a bill on Oct. 22, 1941, by a 124-122 vote, but it died in the Senate.

Chapter 12

History of Impeachments

Several proposed impeachments have failed to come to a vote in the House because the defendant died or because he resigned or received another appointment, removing him from the disputed office. Among the unsuccessful impeachment attempts have been moves against two Presidents, a Vice President, two Cabinet officers, and a Supreme Court justice.[28]

Tyler. The House on Jan. 10, 1843, rejected by an 84-127 vote a resolution by Rep. John M. Botts to investigate the possibility of initiating impeachment proceedings against President Tyler. Tyler had become a political outcast, ostracized by both Democrats and Whigs, but impeachment apparently was too strong a measure to take.

Colfax. A move developed in 1873 to impeach Vice President Schuyler Colfax because of his involvement in the Credit Mobilier scandal. The matter was dropped when the Judiciary Committee recommended against impeachment on the ground that Colfax had purchased his Credit Mobilier stock before becoming Vice President.

Daugherty. A similar move to impeach Attorney General Harry M. Daugherty in 1922 on account of his action, or lack of action, in the Teapot Dome affair was dropped in 1923 when a congressional investigation of the scandal got under way. Daugherty was forced by President Coolidge to tender his resignation, March 28, 1924.

Mellon. A running fight between Rep. Wright Patman (D Texas) and Secretary of the Treasury Andrew W. Mellon over federal economic policy in the Depression came to a head in 1932. Patman on Jan. 6 demanded Mellon's impeachment on the ground of conflicting financial interests. To put an end to that move, President Hoover on Feb. 5 nominated Mellon to be ambassador to Great Britain and the Senate confirmed the nomination the same day. Mellon resigned his Treasury post a week later to take on his new duties.

Hoover. Two Depression-era attempts by Rep. Louis T. McFadden (R Pa.) to impeach President Hoover on general charges of usurping legislative powers and violating constitutional and statutory law were rejected by the House. The first attempt was tabled Dec. 13, 1932, by a 361-8 vote; the second was tabled Jan. 17, 1933, by a 344-11 vote.

Douglas. Associate Justice William O. Douglas of the Supreme Court was subjected to several impeachment attempts. The day after Douglas granted a stay of execution to Soviet spies Julius and Ethel Rosenberg in June 1953, Rep. W. M. Wheeler (D Ga.) introduced a resolution to impeach the justice. The resolution was unanimously tabled by the Judiciary Committee in July, after a one-day hearing at which Wheeler had been the sole witness. In April 1970 two resolutions for Douglas' impeachment were introduced in the midst of a bitter conflict between President Nixon and the Senate over Senate rejection of two Supreme Court nominations. Among the charges cited were possible financial conflicts similar to those that had led to Senate rejection of the Nixon nominees for the Court. A special House Judiciary Subcommittee on Dec. 3 voted 3-1 that no grounds existed for impeachment.

Officials Impeached

The House has impeached 13 federal officers.[29]

1. Name: William Blount (1797-99). **Position:** Senator. **Charge:** Conspiring to carry on a military expedition for the purpose of conquering Spanish territory for Great Britain. **Decision:** Senate dismissed impeachment proceedings after voting to expel Blount.

On July 3, 1797, President John Adams sent to the House and Senate a letter from Sen. William Blount

(Tenn.) to James Carey, a U.S. interpreter to the Cherokee Nation of Indians. The letter told of Blount's plans to launch an attack by Indians and frontiersmen, aided by a British fleet, against Louisiana and Spanish Florida to achieve their transfer to British control. Adams' action initiated the first proceedings to result in impeachment by the House and consideration by the Senate.

In the Senate, Blount's letter was referred to a select committee, which recommended his expulsion for "a high misdemeanor, entirely inconsistent with his public trust and duty as a Senator." The Senate expelled Blount on July 8 by a 25-1 vote.

The House, meanwhile, July 7 adopted a committee resolution impeaching Blount, and on the same day it appointed a committee to prepare articles of impeachment. On Jan. 29, 1798, the House adopted five articles accusing Blount of attempting to influence the Indians for the benefit of the British.

Senate proceedings did not begin until Dec. 17, 1798. Blount challenged the proceedings, contending that they violated his right to a trial by jury, that he was not a civil officer within the meaning of the Constitution, that he was not charged with a crime committed while a civil officer, and that courts of common law were competent to try him on the charges. On Jan. 11, 1799, the Senate by a 14-11 vote dismissed the charges for lack of jurisdiction. Citing the Senate vote, Vice President Thomas Jefferson ruled Jan. 14, that the Senate was without jurisdiction in the case, thus ending the proceedings.

2. Name: John Pickering (1803-04). **Position:** Federal judge. **Charge:** Misconduct in a trial and being intoxicated. **Decision:** Removal from office.

In a partisan move to oust a Federalist judge, President Jefferson on Feb. 4, 1803, sent a complaint to the House citing John Pickering, U.S. judge for the district of New Hampshire. The complaint was referred to a special committee, and on March 2 the House adopted a committee resolution impeaching the judge. A committee was appointed Oct. 20 to prepare articles of impeachment, and the House on Dec. 30 by voice vote agreed to four articles charging Pickering with irregular judicial procedures, loose morals and drunkenness. The judge, who was known to be insane at the time, did not attend the Senate trial, which began March 8, 1804, and ended March 12, with votes of 19-7 for conviction on each of the four articles. The Senate then voted 20-6 to remove Pickering from office, but it declined to consider disqualifying him from further office.

3. Name: Samuel Chase (1804-05). **Position:** Associate Justice of the Supreme Court. **Charge:** Misconduct in trials impairing the court's respect. **Decision:** Acquitted.

In an equally partisan attack on another Federalist judge, the House on Jan. 7, 1804, by an 81-40 vote adopted a resolution for an investigation of Chase and of Richard Peters, a U.S. district court judge in Pennsylvania. Ostensibly, the investigation was to study their conduct during a recent treason trial. The House dropped further action against Peters by voice vote on March 12. On the same day, by a 73-32 vote, it adopted a committee resolution to impeach Chase. A committee was appointed to draw up articles, and the House in a series of votes on Dec. 4, 1804, agreed to the eight articles, charging Chase with harsh and partisan conduct on the bench and with unfairness to litigants.

The trial began Feb. 9, 1805; Chase appeared in person. The Senate voting on March 1 failed to produce the two-thirds majority required for conviction on any of the eight articles; "not guilty" votes outnumbered the "guilty" votes on five of the articles.

4. Name: James H. Peck (1830-31). **Position:** Federal judge. **Charge:** Misconduct in office by misuse of contempt power. **Decision:** Acquitted.

On Jan. 7, 1830, the House adopted a resolution authorizing an investigation of Peck's conduct. On April 24, the House by a 123-49 vote adopted a Judiciary Committee resolution impeaching Peck, and later the same day it appointed a committee to prepare articles of impeachment. A single article was adopted May 1 by voice vote charging Peck with setting an unreasonable and oppressive penalty for contempt of court. The trial stretched from Dec. 20, 1830, to Jan. 31, 1831, when 21 senators voted for conviction and 22 for acquittal.

5. Name: West H. Humphreys (1862). **Position:** Federal judge. **Charge:** Supported secession and held Confederate office. **Decision:** Removed from office.

During the Civil War, Humphreys, a U.S. judge for the east, middle and west districts of Tennessee, accepted an appointment as a Confederate judge, without resigning from his Union judicial assignment. Aware of the situation the House on Jan. 8, 1862, by voice vote adopted a resolution authorizing an inquiry. On May 6, the House, also by voice vote, adopted a Judiciary Committee resolution impeaching Humphreys. On May 19, seven articles of impeachment were adopted. Humphreys could not be personally served with the impeachment summons because he had fled Union territory. He neither appeared at the trial nor contested the charges. In a one-day trial June 26, the Senate convicted Humphreys on all except one charge, removed him from office by a 38-0 vote and disqualified him from further office on a 36-0 vote.

6. Name: Andrew Johnson (1867-68). **Position:** President of the United States. **Charge:** That he removed the Secretary of War contrary to an act of Congress and criticized Congress. **Decision:** Acquitted.

The House adopted a resolution in 1867 authorizing the Judiciary Committee to inquire into the conduct of President Johnson. A majority of the committee recommended impeachment, but the House voted against the resolution 57-108. In January 1868, however, the House authorized an inquiry by the Committee on Reconstruction, which on Feb. 22 reported an impeachment resolution the day after President Johnson had removed Secretary of War Edwin M. Stanton from office. The House Feb. 24 voted to impeach Johnson, 126-47.

Nine of the 11 articles drawn by a select committee and adopted by the House on March 2 and 3 related solely to the President's removal of Stanton; articles 10 and 11 were broader in scope. The trial began March 30, 1868. When voting began in mid-May, the Senate voted only on three of the articles. Johnson was acquitted on each, 35 "guilty" to 19 "not guilty," one vote short of the two-thirds required to convict. *(Details, p. 145)*

7. Name: Mark H. Delahay (1873). **Position:** Federal judge. **Charge:** Misconduct in office, unsuitable personal habits, including intoxication. **Decision:** Resigned before articles of impeachment prepared, hence no Senate action.

In 1872 the House adopted a resolution authorizing an investigation of district court Judge Delahay. The Judiciary

Committee in 1873 proposed a resolution of impeachment, which the House adopted. Delahay resigned before the articles of impeachment were prepared, and the matter was not pursued further by the House.

8. Name: William W. Belknap (1876). **Position:** Secretary of War (resigned). **Charge:** That he received money for appointing and continuing in office a post trader at Ft. Sill, Okla. **Decision:** Acquitted.

Faced with widespread corruption and incompetence among high officers of the Grant administration, the House in 1876 initiated a number of general investigations of government departments. On March 2, 1876, the House adopted a resolution from the Committee on Expenditures in the War Department impeaching Belknap. Belknap resigned, but the Judiciary Committee continued work on impeachment articles, and the House April 3 agreed to five articles of impeachment.

As pre-trial manuevering proceeded, the Senate on May 29 declared by a vote of 37-29 that it had jurisdiction over Belknap regardless of his resignation. The trial, which ran from July 6 to Aug. 1, 1876, ended in acquittal, with a substantial number of senators indicating that they had voted against conviction on the ground that the Senate lacked jurisdiction.

9. Name: Charles Swayne (1903-05). **Position:** Federal judge. **Charge:** Padding expense accounts; using railroad property in receivership for his personal benefit; misusing contempt power. **Decision:** Acquitted.

On Dec. 10, 1903, the House adopted a resolution for a Judiciary Committee investigation of Swayne, U.S. judge for the northern district of Florida. Months later, the committee recommended impeachment, and the House adopted the resolution by voice vote on Dec. 13, 1904. After the vote to impeach, 13 articles were drafted and approved by the House in 1905; however, only the first 12 articles were presented to the Senate. The Senate trial opened Feb. 10 and ended Feb. 27, when the Senate voted acquittal on all 12 articles.

10. Name: Robert W. Archbald (1912-13). **Position:** Associate judge, U.S. Commerce Court. **Charge:** Misconduct including personal profits, free trips to Europe, improper appointment of jury commissioner. **Decision:** Removed from office.

Impeachment

On May 4, 1912, the House adopted a Judiciary Committee resolution authorizing an investigation of Archbald, associate judge of the U.S. Commerce Court. A committee resolution impeaching Archbald and setting forth 13 articles of impeachment was adopted by the House July 11 by a 223-1 vote. The trial, which began Dec. 3, ended Jan. 13, 1913, with Archbald convicted on five of the 13 articles. The Senate on the same day removed him from office by voice vote and, by a 39-35 vote, disqualified him from further office.

11. Name: George W. English (1925-26). **Position:** Federal judge. **Charge:** Partiality, tyranny and oppression. **Decision:** Senate dismissed charges at request of House managers following judge's resignation.

A resolution asking for an investigation of English, U.S. judge for the eastern district of Illinois, was introduced Jan. 13, 1925. The House on April 1, 1926, adopted by a 306-62 vote a Judiciary Committee resolution to impeach English. The resolution also set forth five articles of impeachment. The trial was set to begin Nov. 10, but on Nov. 4 English resigned, and, at the request of House managers the Senate dismissed the charges Dec. 13 by a vote of 70 to 9.

12. Name: Harold Louderback (1932-33). **Position:** Federal judge. **Charge:** Appointing incompetent receivers and allowing them excessive fees. **Decision:** Acquitted.

On June 9, 1932, the House by voice vote adopted a resolution for an investigation of Louderback, U.S. judge for the northern district of California. The Judiciary Committee's study produced mixed results. The majority recommended censuring but not impeaching Louderback. However, the House on Feb. 24, 1933, by a 183-142 vote adopted a minority resolution impeaching the judge and specifying five articles. They accused Louderback of favoritism and conspiracy in the appointment of bankruptcy receivers. A trial that lasted from May 15 to May 24 ended in acquittal, with the "not guilty" votes outnumbering the "guilty" votes on all except one of the five articles.

13. Name: Halsted L. Ritter (1933-36). **Position:** Federal judge. **Charge:** A variety of judicial improprieties, including receiving corrupt payments; practicing law while serving as a federal judge; preparing and filing false income tax returns. **Decision:** Removed from office.

On June 1, 1933, the House by voice vote adopted a resolution for an investigation of Ritter, U.S. judge for the southern district of Florida. A long delay followed. Then on March 2, 1936, the House by a 181-146 vote adopted a Judiciary Committee impeachment resolution, with four articles of impeachment (the four original articles were subsequently replaced with seven amended ones). The trial lasted from April 6 to April 17. Although there were more "guilty" than "not guilty" votes on all except one of the first six articles, the majorities fell short of the two-thirds required for conviction. However, on the seventh article, with 56 votes necessary for conviction, the vote was 56 guilty and 28 not guilty. Thus, Ritter was convicted. He was ordered removed from office by voice vote. An order to disqualify him from further office was defeated, 0-76.

Impeachment of Andrew Johnson

Impeachment is the ultimate limitation on the power of the President. The only presidential impeachment occurred in 1868. President Andrew Johnson was charged with violation of a federal statute, the Tenure of Office Act. But, in addition, the procedure was a profoundly political struggle.

Questions such as control of the Republican Party, how to deal with the South in a state of chaos following the Civil War, and monetary and economic policy all had an effect on the process.

Johnson as President was an anomaly. Lincoln's running mate in 1864, he was a southerner at a time when the South was out of the Union; a Jacksonian Democrat who believed in states' rights, hard money, and minimal federal government activity running with an administration pursuing a policy of expansion both in the money supply and the role of government.

Johnson had been the only member of the U.S. Senate from a seceding southern state (Tennessee) to remain loyal to the Union in 1861. Lincoln later made him military governor of Tennessee and chose him as his running mate in 1864.

On Lincoln's death in 1865, this outsider without allies or connections in the Republican Party succeeded to the presidency. Johnson's ideas on what should have been done to reconstruct and readmit the southern states to representation clashed with the wishes of a majority of Congress, overwhelmingly controlled by the Republicans.

Congress was divided into roughly three groups. The small minority of Democrats supported the President. About half the Republicans were known as "radicals" because they favored strong action to revolutionize southern society, by harsh military means if necessary. The other half of the Republicans were more conservative; while unwilling to go as far as the radicals, they wanted to make sure the South did not return to the unquestioned control of those who ruled it before the Civil War.

Upon taking office, Johnson began to pursue Lincoln's mild and tolerant reconstruction plans. The new President felt that a few basics were all that needed to be secured: abolition of slavery; ratification of the Thirteenth Amendment, which abolished slavery in all states; repudiation of all state debts contracted by the Confederate governments; nullification of secession. When the southern states had done these things, Johnson felt they should be readmitted.

But Republicans wanted more: a Freedmen's Bureau, to protect and provide services for the ex-slaves, a civil rights bill guaranteeing the Negroes their rights, and an overall plan of reconstruction providing for temporary military governments in the South. Throughout 1866, Johnson and Congress battled over these issues.

The Tenure of Office Act, the violation of which was to be the legal basis for Johnson's impeachment, was passed over his veto March 2, 1867. The act forbade the President to remove civil officers (appointed with the consent of the Senate) without the approval of the Senate. Its purpose was to protect incumbent Republican officeholders from executive retaliation if they did not support the President.

Unsuccessful Ashley Resolution. About the time the Tenure of Office Act was being debated, the first moves toward impeachment began. On Jan. 7, 1867, Rep. James M. Ashley (R Ohio 1859-69) rose on a question of privilege and formally charged the President with high crimes and misdemeanors.

Ashley made general charges, and no specific violations of law were mentioned. Most members recognized the charges as basically political grievances rather than illegal acts. The matter was referred to the House Judiciary Committee, which reported on March 2, 1867, two days before the expiration of the 39th Congress, that the committee had reached no conclusion.

On March 7, 1867, the third day of the 40th Congress, Ashley again introduced his resolution, and it was referred to the Judiciary Committee for further investigation. The committee studied the matter throughout the year and on Nov. 25, 1867, reported an impeachment resolution. When the House voted on the matter on Dec. 7, the radicals suffered a crushing defeat. The resolution calling for impeachment was turned down 57 to 108.

Successful Second Try. Johnson had long wanted to rid himself of Secretary of War Edwin M. Stanton. Stanton was a close ally of the radical Republicans. After repeatedly trying to get him to resign, Johnson suspended him on Dec. 12, 1867. On Jan. 13, 1868, the Senate refused to concur, thus, under the terms of the Tenure of Office Act, reinstating Stanton.

Apparently flushed by his recent victory on the impeachment issue in the House, Johnson decided to force the issue. He dismissed Stanton on Feb. 21, citing the power and authority vested in him by the Constitution.

This action enraged Congress, driving conservative Republicans into alliance with the radicals on impeachment. A House resolution on impeachment was immediately offered and was referred to the Committee on Reconstruction, headed by Rep. Thaddeus Stevens of Pennsylvania, one of the radical Republican leaders. The next day, Feb. 22, the committee reported a resolution favoring impeachment. The House vote, taken two days later, was 126 to 47 in favor, on a strict party-line basis.

Trial in the Senate. The House March 2-3 approved specific articles of impeachment and appointed managers to present and argue the charges before the Senate. There were 11 articles in all, the main one concerning Johnson's removal of Stanton in contravention of the Tenure of Office Act.

Between the time of the House action and the beginning of the trial in the Senate, the conservative Republicans had time to reflect. One of the main objects of their reflection was fiery Ben Wade of Ohio. Wade was president pro tempore of the Senate and, under the succession law then in effect, was next in line for the presidency. He was also one of the most radical of the radical Republicans, a hard-liner on southern reconstruction and a monetary expansionist.

The impeachment trial opened March 30, 1868. The managers for the House were John A. Bingham (R Ohio), George S. Boutwell (R Mass.), James F. Wilson (R Iowa), Benjamin F. Butler (R Mass.), Thomas Williams (R Pa.), John A. Logan (R Ill.) and Stevens. The President did not appear at the trial. He was represented by a team of lawyers headed by Henry Stanbery, who had resigned as Attorney General to lead the defense. Associated with Stanbery were Benjamin R. Curtis, Jeremiah S. Black, William M. Evarts, Thomas A. R. Nelson and William S. Groesbeck.

After weeks of argument and testimony, the Senate on May 16 took a test vote on Article XI, a general, catch-all charge, thought by the House managers most likely to produce a vote for conviction. The drama of the vote has become legendary. With 36 "guiltys" needed for conviction, the final count was guilty, 35, not guilty, 19.

Seven Republicans joined the 12 Democrats in supporting Johnson. Stunned by the setback, Senate opponents of the President postponed further voting until May 26. Votes were taken then on Article II and Article III. By identical 35-19 votes Johnson was acquitted also on these articles. To head off further defeats for Johnson opponents, Sen. George H. Williams (Union Republican Ore.) moved to adjourn *sine die,* and the motion was adopted 34-16, abruptly ending the trial.

The Tenure of Office Act was virtually repealed early in Grant's administration, once the Republicans had control of the appointing power, and was entirely repealed in 1887. And in 1926, the Supreme Court declared, "The power to remove...executive officers...is an incident of the power to appoint them, and is in its nature an executive power" *(Myers v. United States,* 272 U.S. 52). The opinion, written by Chief Justice William Howard Taft, himself a former President, referred to the Tenure of Office Act and declared that it had been unconstitutional.

President Nixon's Resignation

In the case of President Richard Nixon, the process of impeachment did not move beyond its first stage—and yet it realized its purpose. Ten days after the House Judiciary Committee recommended that Nixon be impeached for obstruction of justice, abuse of power and contempt of Congress, Nixon resigned. In the face of certain impeachment by the House and removal by the Senate, he chose to leave the White House voluntarily.

The impeachment inquiry was but one in the chain of events which brought about Nixon's premature departure from the presidency—a chain which began on June 17, 1972, with a burglary at Democratic National Headquarters in the Watergate Office Building in Washington, D.C.

But the work of the House Judiciary Committee and its dramatic conclusion—a televised debate involving all 38 members—were crucial in preparing the nation to accept the resignation, in disgrace, of the man elected President by an overwhelming vote less than two years earlier.

Nixon precipitated the inquiry with the "Saturday night massacre"—his firing on Oct. 20, 1973, of the first Watergate Special Prosecutor, Archibald Cox. Cox was persisting in his effort to force Nixon to release tapes of certain of his conversations following—and, Cox suspected, concerning—the Watergate break-in.

On the Monday following the Cox firing a flurry of impeachment resolutions were introduced in the House and referred to the House Judiciary Committee. On Feb. 6, 1974, the House formally authorized the committee "to investigate fully and completely whether sufficient grounds exist for the House of Representatives to exercise its constitutional power to impeach Richard M. Nixon, President of the United States of America...." The vote was 410-4.

"We cannot turn away, out of partisanship or convenience, from problems that are now...our inescapable responsibility to consider," said Judiciary Committee Chairman Peter W. Rodino Jr. (D N.J.). "It would be a violation of our own public trust if we...chose not to inquire, not to consult, not even to deliberate...."

Aware of the import of their task, the committee approached it deliberately. From February to May, the staff, led by former Assistant Attorney General John M. Doar, assembled evidence related to the various charges against the President, which ranged from Watergate-related matters to questions of his personal finances. The committee subpoenaed the President for additional material.

Nixon refused to comply, although he did release edited transcripts of a number of the tapes of the conversations the committee sought.

On May 9, the committee began considering the evidence in executive session, a process which continued until mid-July. President Nixon was represented at the proceedings by James D. St. Clair, his chief defense counsel and a noted Boston trial attorney.

On July 18-19, the committee heard Doar and St. Clair summarize the arguments for and against impeachment.

Doar advocated impeachment, telling the committee that "reasonable men acting reasonably would find the President guilty" of abusing his presidential powers. Defending the President, St. Clair argued that there was a "complete absence of any conclusive evidence demonstrating Presidential wrongdoing sufficient to justify the grave action of impeachment."

Until mid-July, the committee was assumed to be divided precisely along party lines on impeachment. The Democrats with the possible exception of three conservative southern members were thought to be solidly in favor; the Republicans, equally united in opposition.

But on July 23, Rep. Lawrence J. Hogan (R Md.) became the first of the Republicans to break ranks, speaking out publicly for impeachment.

The next morning, a unanimous Supreme Court rejected Nixon's claim of executive privilege to withhold evidence sought by the Watergate Special Prosecutor. Nixon, the court ruled, must comply with subpoenas for the tapes of certain of his conversations.

Hours later, on the evening of July 24, before blazing lights and whirring television cameras, the Judiciary Committee began the final phase of its inquiry. For the first time, each of its 38 members spoke publicly to the nation and to his or her constituents to give his views on the evidence.

By the end of the evening the outcome was clear. Seven of the 17 Republicans indicated that they would support impeachment. All of the Democrats agreed. The vote would be clearcut and bipartisan—recommending impeachment.

Paramount in the minds of some who spoke was the question of the historical impact of a decision against impeachment. "What if we fail to impeach?" asked Rep.

Walter Flowers (D Ala.). "Do we ingrain forever in the very fabric of our Constitution a standard of conduct in our highest office that in the least is deplorable, and at worst is impeachable?"

Four days after the debate began, on the evening of Saturday, July 27, the decisive roll-call came. By a vote of 27-11, the committee approved the first article of impeachment, charging Nixon with obstructing justice, primarily in the Watergate investigation. Six Republicans joined all 21 Democrats to approve the charge.

The second article, charging abuse of power, was approved July 29, by the even wider margin of 28-10. The third, charging contempt of Congress, was approved July 30, 21-17. Two other proposed articles were rejected. Its work completed, the committee adjourned late on the evening of July 30.

House debate on impeachment was to begin Aug. 19; the outcome was considered a certainty. The Senate began preparing for a trial. Public opinion swung heavily in favor of impeachment and, for the first time, polls showed a majority of the American people in favor of conviction and removal as well.

But the process of impeachment would not continue. On Aug. 5, Nixon released transcripts of three of the taped conversations that the Supreme Court ruling forced him to turn over to the special prosecutor. These made clear his knowing participation in the coverup of White House involvement in the Watergate burglary.

Faced with this new evidence, even the members of the Judiciary Committee who had continued to defend Nixon called for his resignation or impeachment. On Aug. 7 Republican leaders told the President that he had no more than 10 supporters left in the House and 15 in the Senate.

On Aug. 8, Nixon told the nation he would resign. He made no mention of impeachment. On Aug. 9, his resignation effective, he left the White House. The House Aug. 20 accepted the report of the committee inquiry, 412-3, formally taking note of the recommendation of impeachment and concluding the matter.

PART V

Investigations

Chapter 13

Origins of Investigations

The first congressional investigation, a House inquiry into an Army disaster in Indian territory, was conducted in 1792. The hearings staked out a major new area of activity that was to become one of the most controversial and highly publicized powers of Congress.

Since 1792, investigating committees of the House and the Senate have left an erratic trail, marked by some of the brightest and darkest moments in congressional annals. Investigations have led Congress into repeated confrontations with the executive and judicial branches over the constitutional separation of powers. They have elevated comparatively minor political figures to presidential status, broken the careers of important public men and captured the attention of millions of newspaper readers and, in later years, radio listeners and television viewers.

Based on the constitutional assignment of "all legislative powers herein granted" to Congress, investigations have served as the eyes and ears of the two chambers. Investigations have gathered information on the need for possible future legislation, tested the effectiveness of past legislative action, inquired into the qualifications and performance of members and laid the groundwork for impeachment proceedings. The congressional power of investigation has long been regarded as one of the essential functions of the national legislature. The practices of some committees, however, have led critics to brand investigations as political vehicles for personal publicity and as an extravagant waste of time and money, producing few, if any useful legislative results. *(Box on definition of investigations, p. 157)*

Woodrow Wilson, writing on congressional government as a Johns Hopkins University graduate student in 1884, asserted that "The informing function of Congress should be preferred even to its legislative function."[1] President Truman, who achieved national fame as chairman of the World War II Senate Special Committee to Investigate the National Defense Program said in the Senate in 1944: "In my opinion, the power of investigation is one of the most important powers of Congress. The manner in which that power is exercised will largely determine the position and prestige of the Congress in the future."[2] *(Footnotes, p. 319)*

Others, however, have disagreed with this assessment of the value of congressional investigations. Walter Lippmann once spoke of "that legalized atrocity, the congressional investigation, in which congressmen, starved of their legitimate food for thought, go on a wild and feverish manhunt, and do not stop at cannibalism."[3]

No period of American history has been without investigations. Only the Spanish-American War in 1898, of all major U.S. military engagements, escaped congressional scrutiny. President McKinley forestalled legislative inquiry into that conflict by appointing the Dodge commission.[4]

Many early investigations involved traditional legislative privileges, such as charges against a senator or representative or trials of members accused of libels, assaults or bribery attempts. Until toward the end of the 19th century, however, most of the investigations concerned the civil and military activities of the executive branch. For example, the Post Office Department was the target of probes in 1820, 1822 and 1830, the Bank of the United States in 1832 and 1834, the Smithsonian Institution in 1855 and the General Land Office in 1897.[5]

By 1880 a new field for congressional investigation was emerging—economic and social problems across the nation. There were studies of black migration from South to North (1880), strikebreaking by the railroads (1892) and the concentration of wealth in the "money trust" (1912-13).[6]

Definition of Investigations

For purposes of this book, "investigation" has been defined as an inquiry by any congressional committee or subcommittee that used investigative procedures (examining records, summoning and questioning witnesses) for one or more of the following reasons:

● Fact-finding for possible special and remedial legislation.

● Fulfilling Congress' function as a "watchdog" over government operations and programs.

● Informing the public.

● Resolving questions concerning membership or procedure such as conduct of elections or fitness of members of Congress.

Among committee activities not included in the definition: inquiries conducted by staff members without participation by members of Congress in formal hearings; routine hearings; and action on bills and resolutions.

Government operations and social conditions served as the principal subjects of congressional investigation until the period between World Wars I and II, when the fear of subversion from foreign ideologies led to inquiries of a different sort. Investigations of social conditions and government operations continued but for a time lost much of their former glamor. Meanwhile, probes into possible subversion expanded rapidly, developing new and harsh methods of inquiry. Hearings involved broadscale intrusions into the thoughts, actions and associations of all manner of persons and institutions, and raised searching legal and moral questions about the power and procedures of congressional inquiry.

The expanded use of investigations made Congress' investigating power itself a major political issue. To some, the threat to national security posed by Communist subversion was so great as to justify exceptional procedures. To others, the threat to individual liberties from the behavior and authority of some committees appeared a more real danger than that of communism. The conflict over the powers of the committees and the rights of witnesses continued, with shifting results and varying intensity, throughout the pre-World-War-II and the postwar period. It was waged in Congress, in the courts, in the executive branch, in the councils of both parties and in public debates and election campaigns.

Power of Congress to Investigate

Congress received its power to investigate from the Constitution.[7] The investigative power of a legislative body had been established as early as the 16th century by the British House of Commons. The Commons first used its investigative power in determining its membership. It then made increasing use of investigations to assist it in performing its lawmaking functions and in overseeing officials responsible for executing laws and spending the funds made available by Parliament. Investigating committees of the House of Commons had authority to summon witnesses and to examine documents, and the Commons could support its committees by punishing uncooperative witnesses for contempt. American colonial legislatures, the Continental Congress and state legislatures relied on these parliamentary precedents in carrying out their own investigations.

Uncertainty arose, despite the precedents, because of the constitutional assignment to Congress of "all legislative powers herein granted." Strict constructionists asserted that limitation of the authority of Congress to specifically granted powers restricted investigations to clearly defined judicial functions, such as election disputes, impeachment proceedings or cases involving congressional privileges. Broad constructionists argued that the precedents supported an inherent investigative power in the legislative function. The broad constructionists prevailed, and won approval of the Army investigation in 1792. That first investigation served as a precedent for others. Since then, no serious challenge of the basic authority of Congress to investigate has ever been mounted. However, specific investigations have been challenged, with mixed results; opposition has arisen mainly in the case of investigations that have pried into private affairs, infringed on personal liberties or conflicted with executive branch prerogatives.

Power to Punish for Contempt

Like the investigative power which it reinforced, the congressional power to punish for contempt was based on parliamentary precedents dating from Elizabethan times.[8] No express power to punish for contempt, except in the case of a member, was granted Congress in the Constitution. But Congress assumed that it had inherent power to send persons in contempt to jail without a court order because it regarded such power as necessary for its own protection and for the integrity of its proceedings.[9]

The first use of the congressional power to punish a non-member for contempt was on Dec. 28, 1795, when Robert Randall was summoned to the bar of the House on a charge of having tried to bribe a member. Following debate, the House on Jan. 4, 1796, voted 78-17 to jail Randall for a week. Both chambers drew on precedents established in the Randall case to punish other non-members for contemptuous acts. The first committee witness cited for contempt was Nathaniel Rounsavell, editor of the Alexandria, Va., *Herald,* who refused in 1812 to answer questions before a House committee investigating a breach in the security of a secret House session. After a day's confinement in the custody of the House sergeant at arms, Rounsavell apologized for his behavior and was discharged.[10]

The Senate first voted a contempt of Congress citation on March 20, 1800, when William Duane was ordered arrested for libeling a member. On May 14, the Senate by a 13-4 vote sentenced him to 30 days in jail and ordered him to pay costs. The first Senate committee witness to be cited was Thaddeus Hyatt, who had refused a summons by a committee investigating John Brown's raid on Harpers Ferry in 1859. The Senate March 12, 1860, by a 44-10 vote ordered Hyatt jailed. He was released June 15.[11]

Constitutionality of the Power. In 1821 *(Anderson v. Dunn,* 6 Wheat. 204), the Supreme Court upheld the constitutionality of summary use of the contempt power by Congress. The court declared that the power to punish contempts was assumed to be inherent in each chamber because without it, Congress would be "exposed to every indignity and interruption that rudeness, caprice, or even conspiracy may mediate against it." The power was limited, however, by the court "to the least possible power adequate to the end proposed," and imprisonment could not extend beyond the adjournment of Congress.[12]

Passage of Criminal Statute. Considering the limitation of imprisonment only to the end of a legislative session inadequate, Congress in 1857 passed a law, still in effect in amended form (2 U.S.C. 192), making it a criminal offense to refuse information demanded by either chamber.[13] Even after passage of the 1857 law, Congress preferred to punish persons in contempt itself, reasoning that a few days of confinement might induce a witness to cooperate, while turning him over to a court would put him out of reach of the inquiring committee. Later, however, as the press of legislative business mounted and as court review of summary congressional punishment became more frequent, Congress increasingly relied on criminal prosecution for contempt under the 1857 law. Since 1945, all contempt citations have been prosecuted under the criminal statute.

The congressional power of investigation was further strengthened in 1862 by an amendment to the 1857 law providing that no witness could refuse to testify or to produce documents on the ground that doing so would "tend to disgrace him or otherwise render him infamous."

Use of Contempt Power. Between 1789 and 1976, Congress voted 384 contempt citations in cases where a witness refused to appear before a committee, refused to answer questions before a committee, or refused to produce documents for a committee. Most of these citations have occurred since 1945, primarily as the result of activities by the House Un-American Activities Committee. As Ronald L. Goldfarb and Carl Beck have noted in their studies of the contempt power, in the period from 1792 until 1942, there were only 600 congressional investigations and only 108 contempt citations.[14]

Moreover, until 1945, Congress frequently overruled the recommendations of its committees on contempt citations. From 1796 to 1945, the House or Senate reversed the actions of committees in 34 cases.[15] But after 1945, when Congress ended the tradition of deciding both guilt and punishment in contempt cases and began referring its contempt citations to the Justice Department for prosecution, the record was drastically altered.

According to Beck, of 226 contempt citations presented to both houses by 14 committees between 1945 and 1957, few cases were debated, few were discussed and none was defeated. After 1945, Beck wrote, the courts determined guilt or innocence, and approval of a committee's contempt citation by the full House or Senate was "almost automatic."[16]

One exception to the general rule that the House and Senate normally support a committee's contempt citation resolution occurred on July 13, 1971. On that day, the House, by a 226-181 roll-call vote, recommitted—and thus killed—a House Interstate and Foreign Commerce Committee resolution (H Res 534) recommending that the Columbia Broadcasting System (CBS) and its president, Frank Stanton, be cited for contempt of Congress.

On June 24, Stanton had refused to comply with a subpoena issued by the committee's Investigations Subcommittee for film and sound recordings prepared for but not used in the network's controversial documentary, "The Selling of the Pentagon."

Use of the contempt power in congressional cases has fallen into two general classes: (1) those involving positive acts, such as bribery or libel, which directly or indirectly obstruct the legislature in carrying out its functions, and (2) those involving refusal to perform acts which the legislature claims authority to compel, such as testifying or producing documents. Few cases of the first type have occurred in recent years, and the courts have had little opportunity to define positive acts of contempt. The second type, while giving rise to much more extensive judicial interpretation, continues to raise many legal questions because of its greater complexity.

Resorting to the inherent power of Congress to punish for contempt, a committee may introduce a resolution directing the presiding officer of the chamber to issue a warrant for arrest of the witness in contempt by the chamber's sergeant at arms. The witness is brought before the bar of the House, or Senate, and questioned. Subsequently, the full chamber may adopt a resolution ordering the confinement of the witness or his discharge, or the witness simply may be reprimanded by the chamber's presiding officer.

When a committee in either chamber wishes to institute criminal proceedings against a contumacious witness, it introduces a resolution in the parent body citing him for contempt. Only a simple majority vote is necessary for approval; there seldom is opposition to such a resolution. The matter is then referred to a U.S. attorney for presentation to a grand jury.

A recent case of contempt of Congress occurred in 1973 as a result of the Watergate and related probes. The House Sept. 10, 1972, voted 334-11 to cite Watergate conspirator G. Gordon Liddy for contempt of Congress. The case was turned over to the U.S. Attorney in the District of Columbia for presentation to a grand jury.

Liddy, a former member of the "plumbers" special investigative unit at the White House, was cited for his refusal to be sworn in to testify before the House Armed Services Committee's Special Intelligence Subcommittee July 20. The subcommittee and then the full committee approved the resolution citing him for contempt.

Liddy was found guilty of contempt of Congress May 10, 1974. U.S. District Court Judge John H. Pratt, who heard the case without a jury in Washington, gave Liddy a suspended six-month sentence.[17]

Chapter 14

Investigative Procedures

From the beginning, Congress has delegated its power to investigate to committees.

Prior to passage of the Legislative Reorganization Act of 1946 (PL 79-601), the majority of investigations were carried out by special or select committees, with subpoena power, established to conduct the inquiry. When an investigation was concluded, the committee went out of existence and the subpoena power ended. The first attempt to give subpoena power to a standing committee—the House Committee on Manufactures, for tariff investigation—was strongly opposed but was approved Dec. 31, 1827, by a 102-88 vote. Opponents said the proposal was unheard of because subpoena power previously had been used only by committees acting as judicial bodies.[18]

At first, House committees dominated congressional investigations. The House, for example, conducted 27 of the 30 inquiries between 1789 and 1814. But as time passed, the Senate pulled in front of the House, conducting about 40 of the 60 investigations between 1900 and 1925.[19] (The Senate first granted subpoena power to a special investigating committee during an 1818 study of the Seminole war.)[20]

In the meantime, as the number of standing committees increased in both chambers, it became common practice for them to conduct investigations on their own initiative, withoug a special authorizing resolution, although specific House or Senate approval was still required to compel testimony and to provide funds. Of the 146 investigations between 1929 and 1938, 89 were made by standing committees and 57 by select committees.[21]

The spectacular growth of the executive branch during the New Deal and World War II years led to a proliferation of congressional investigating committees as Congress struggled to fulfill its traditional function of overseeing the administration of laws and the spending of appropriations. By 1945, the House had a total of 111 committees and the Senate, a total of 75; between 1945 and passage of the Reorganization Act in 1946, at least 50 investigations had been voted.[22]

Subpoena Powers in Senate

The 1946 Act attempted to restore the balance by strengthening the congressional investigative procedures and expanding committee staffs. The act reduced the number of standing committees from 48 to 19 in the House and from 33 to 15 in the Senate. It authorized standing committees of both chambers to "exercise continuous watchfulness of the execution by the administrative agencies concerned of any laws, the subject matter of which is within the jurisdiction" of the respective committees. Further, the act extended permanent subpoena power to all standing committees of the Senate and authorized $10,000 in investigating funds for each committee during each Congress. The act also authorized professional staff members for all standing committees.

Subpoena Powers in House

General subpoena power for House committees was blocked for many years by the leadership of Speaker Sam Rayburn (D Texas) and Minority Leader Joseph W. Martin (R Mass.), who feared that such power would make the committees uncontrollable and lead to sensational inquiries motivated by political ambitions. (It was granted in 1974. *See p. 165.)* The only exception was the Un-American Activities Committee, which was authorized to issue subpoenas. Subsequently, general subpoena power was granted to the House Committee on Expenditures in the Executive Departments (Government Operations) in 1947 and to the

House Appropriations Committee in 1953. When the Un-American Activities Committee was re-named the House Committee on Internal Security, on Feb. 18, 1969, the new committee also was given subpoena power. As a result of Rayburn's and Martin's opposition to general subpoena power for House committees, the panels had to seek specific House approval for authority to compel testimony and documents. In practice, the House normally authorized broad committee investigatory power and use of the subpoena. When the 93rd Congress began in 1973, for example, the House on one day adopted resolutions authorizing eight standing committees to investigate subjects within their legislative jurisdictions and to issue subpoenas.

General Subpoena Power Granted. The House in 1974 gave its committees and subcommittees general subpoena power to compel the attendance and testimony of witnesses and the production of books, records and any other documents considered necessary to an investigation. Specific subpoena authority no longer had to be given to each committee. However, the 1974 change required that a majority of a committee or subcommittee approve a subpoena before it is issued. In addition, compliance with a subpoena may be enforced only by action of the full House.

The general subpoena power was given in a House resolution (H Res 988) dealing with committee jurisdictions, procedures and activities (known informally as the Hansen committee proposals). The provisions granting the authority became part of the House rules.

Watergate Subpoenas. The Senate Select Committee on Presidential Campaign Activities (Watergate committee) construed its subpoena power more broadly, many thought, when it sought a large but unspecified number of White House tapes and documents Dec. 18, 1973. (The committee had issued earlier subpoenas in July.)[23]

The House Banking and Currency Committee was the first congressional committee to attempt to use its subpoena power to investigate the Watergate break-in. On Oct. 3, 1972, the committee rejected, 20-15, a resolution backed by Chairman Wright Patman (D Texas) to call 40 individuals and organizations to testify about possible violations of banking laws and irregularities in Republican campaign financing suggested by the break-in.[24]

Impeachment Investigation. The House Judiciary Committee, responsible for conducting the inquiry into charges against President Nixon, was one of the standing committees granted general subpoena power by resolution at the beginning of the 93rd Congress in 1973. At that time, however, the official list of subjects under the committee's jurisdiction did not include impeachment.

But on Feb. 6, 1974, with only four members voting "nay," the House formally granted the committee power to investigate the conduct of President Nixon to determine whether there were grounds for his impeachment.[25] The resolution gave explicit authorization for the committee to conduct the investigation—already under way—and granted it special subpoena power during the inquiry.

The committee's issuance of subpoenas to Nixon in the spring and summer of 1974 was an unprecedented action. In the only other impeachment proceedings against a President—Andrew Johnson in 1867-68—Johnson himself was not subpoenaed.[26]

Before Nixon was served with subpoenas for tapes and documents July 23, 1973—two from the Senate Watergate investigating committee and one from the Watergate special prosecutor—the only President in office to be subpoenaed was Thomas Jefferson in 1807, when former Vice President Aaron Burr was on trial for treason. Burr asked Chief Justice John Marshall, who was presiding over the trial at the circuit level, to subpoena the President, contending that he had a letter which would contradict testimony that had been given against Burr.

Marshall found that without doubt the court could issue a subpoena to the President. He said the only question was whether or not the subpoena could require the President to produce the letter referred to. Eventually, Marshall ruled that the subpoena requiring the letter from the President could be issued. Jefferson did not testify in person, but he said he would—and in fact did—produce the letter without the compulsion of a subpoena.[27]

Cost of Investigation

The combined effect of the 1946 Legislative Reorganization Act and executive branch expansion beginning with the New Deal period in the 1930s was an explosion of investigative activity following World War II. Compared to approximately 500 investigations in almost 150 years from 1789 to 1938, the 90th Congress (1967-68) alone authorized 496 investigations. The cost of investigations paralleled the rising number of inquiries. From 1910 to 1919 the Senate spent approximately $330,000 on investigative activities, compared to $2.9-million in the two years 1951 and 1952.[28] In the two years of the 90th Congress the Senate and House together spent $21,994,843 on investigations. The number and cost of the studies rapidly outdistanced the $10,000 per committee authorized in the 1946 Act, and the committees were again required to seek special funds.

In 1975, the Senate authorized an investigative budget of $19.4-million for 22 standing committees, and the House authorized $21.2-million for 21 committees.[29]

In 1973, the Senate Watergate investigating committee alone was authorized $2-million to conduct its inquiry.[30]

Although Congress continued to establish special investigating committees in postwar years, most major investigations were carried on by a handful of standing committees or their subcommittees: the House and Senate Committees on Government Operations, the Internal Security Subcommittee of the Senate Judiciary Committee, the Senate Government Operations Permanent Investigations Subcommittee and the (now-defunct) House Internal Security Committee.

Procedural Stages

Congressional investigations undergo three stages of development: authorization, staff preparation and public hearings.[31]

Authorization. Many reasons may cause a senator or representative to propose an investigation. Whatever the reason, the authority and scope of the inquiry are incorporated in a resolution for introduction in the House or Senate. Once introduced, the resolution is referred to a committee. In the Senate, resolutions to authorize and fund investigations are considered by the Rules and Administration Committee and by the standing legislative committee having jurisdiction over the subject to be studied. In the House, the Administration Committee considers the funding of investigations. Prior to January 1975, House resolutions for investigations also had to be considered by the Rules Committee before being sent to the floor. However, this requirement has been eliminated, and in 1975 all standing committees were given direct authority to conduct investigations.

After being reported by the committees, a resolution is voted on by the full chamber. Joint House-Senate investigating committees are authorized by a concurrent resolution adopted by both chambers.

Many resolutions to authorize investigations, like bills and resolutions on other matters, are never acted upon by a committee and die. But if a resolution authorizing an investigation is approved by a committee and adopted on the floor, an investigation almost always follows. One exception occurred in 1933 when an authorized investigation of the Reconstruction Finance Corporation by the Senate Banking and Currency Committee did not occur; the committee reported later that it had had no specific inquiry in mind and had asked for the investigatory power only as a precautionary step.[32]

It has long been a matter of courtesy in both House and Senate that the sponsor of the resolution for an investigation shall preside over the inquiry. When the study is to be made by a standing committee, a subcommittee generally is appointed by the chairman of the full committee, with the sponsor of the resolution being named subcommittee chairman. When a select committee is authorized, the members are chosen by consultation between the Vice President, or the Speaker, and the majority and minority leaders.

The life of a special House investigation committee expires with a Congress, but that of a Senate committee depends upon its authorization.

Staff Preparation. Early congressional investigative committees had no staff and inquiries were undertaken informally. The investigating committee frequently knew little about the subject under study and simply struck out blindly, asking questions and considering evidence, hoping that something might be found that would be useful to the investigation.[33]

Committee staffs first came into use by investigating committees in the late 1800s and early 1900s. By the 1920s and 1930s the practice of relying on staff members to gather information was firmly established. Trained investigators, poring over files and records before the start of public hearings, generally have accumulated most of the information produced by investigations. Occasionally an investigating committee has been authorized access to income tax returns, customarily by executive order.

The Nye committee's staff investigating the munitions industry in the 1930s consisted of three lawyers, two accountants, a specialist in international law, a financial writer, two free-lance newspapermen, and five persons who were doing or had done graduate work in the social sciences.[34] On the staff of the Truman committee during World War II were a chief counsel, an associate counsel, an assistant counsel, a chief investigator, 12-18 investigators, a committee clerk, an editor and clerical personnel.[35] In 1975, the staff of the Senate Government Operations Permanent Investigations Subcommittee included a chief counsel, a minority chief counsel, a special counsel, a professional staff director, two assistant counsels, seven professional staff members, two research assistants, one executive assistant, seven investigators, a staff editor, a chief clerk and 11 clerical assistants.[36]

At its peak in 1973, the Senate Watergate committee had a total staff of 64, including 17 attorneys; the House Judiciary Committee's impeachment inquiry staff in 1974 numbered close to 100 and included 43 attorneys.[37]

Hearing. Public hearings have been the most visible and controversial element of investigations, but as a rule they have brought forth little material not already uncovered or suggested by staff work.[38] Hearings have helped to act as a check on staff investigators by giving the investigated person a chance to present his case. A witness usually has been allowed to present a prepared statement and to be accompanied by and to consult with a lawyer. Questioning of witnesses has been conducted by members of the committee, frequently the chairman, and by the committee's staff. In some instances, galley proofs of the testimony have been sent to the witness for corrections; this was the practice of the Truman committee. Public hearings have provided a method of presenting facts dramatically to the public and a means of influencing public opinion. Public opinion, in turn, has been affected by methods used in the hearings, particularly when the procedures appeared to infringe on the rights of witnesses.

Chapter 15

Witnesses' Rights

Not until the late 1930s did the rights of a witness in a congressional investigation become a serious issue.

The potential conflict between the right of Congress to seek information and the right of a witness to protect his privacy always was present; but early legislative investigations were conducted in a comparatively low-key atmosphere, free from the instant mass publicity of television. Witnesses often were allowed to call their own witnesses and to cross-examine hostile witnesses.[39]

The advent in the 1930s of the inquisitorial congressional panel, typified by the House Special Committee to Investigate Un-American Activities (Dies committee) aroused new concern. The low-key atmosphere had vanished, replaced by relentless probing questions before massed newsmen and newsreel cameras. Complaints mounted that the procedures of congressional investigators were exceeding their powers and violating the rights of witnesses.

In fact, as witnesses—and the courts—discovered, investigating committees had virtually free rein to determine their procedures. Challenges of the legality of committee procedures raised sensitive questions. They loomed as a potentially divisive force between two co-equal branches of the government, the legislative and the judicial, and the courts studiously sought to avoid the issue. They attempted to rule on narrow points of law rather than on the central point, which was the power of a committee to set its own procedures.

The result of the courts' evasiveness was that a witness in essence was at the mercy of the investigating committee, protected only by the general constitutional limitations on congressional authority and by the Bill of Rights. A 1954 study of congressional investigative power by the Legislative Reference Service of the Library of Congress concluded: "There are few safeguards for the protection of a witness before a congressional committee.... In committee, his treatment usually depends upon the skill and attitude of the chairman and the members."[40] That conclusion was foreshadowed clearly by a 1948 comment by House Un-American Activities Committee Chairman J. Parnell Thomas (R N.J.): "The rights you have are the rights given you by this committee. We will determine what rights you have and what rights you have not got before the committee."[41]

During the postwar era, the rights of witnesses before congressional investigating committees became a bitter issue. The growing number and broadened scope of investigations, and the increasing use of committee hearings for the purpose of edifying the public rather than informing the legislature, led to pressure for more precise definitions of committee powers. The advent of television coverage of hearings, first used spectacularly during House Un-American Activities Committee investigations of communism in 1948, exposed witnesses to vast publicity.

In search of protection, witnesses turned repeatedly to the Constitution. Despite the constitutional assignment of only specified powers to Congress, the courts repeatedly had shown reluctance to limit congressional investigating power. The new search for safeguards led to tests of the effectiveness of the Bill of Rights in protecting the rights of witnesses.

Most frequently cited were the First, Fourth and Fifth Amendments. Efforts by witnesses to invoke the First Amendment in refusing to provide committees with information, on the ground that Congress had no right to probe their private convictions or their political views or propaganda activities, had mixed results. The Fourth

Amendment guarantee against unreasonable search and seizure likewise offered uncertain protection. The arbitrary power of committees to demand the production of documents was the most used—and disputed—authority through the history of congressional investigations.

Once the courts upheld the right of congressional committee witnesses to invoke the Fifth Amendment's protection against self-incrimination, use of the amendment to avoid answering questions became highly controversial. The Fifth Amendment generally stood up as a defense against prosecution for contempt of Congress. However, witnesses could not invoke the privilege partially, answering as to incriminating facts and then refusing further explanation. For this reason, some witnesses repeatedly pleaded the Fifth Amendment in refusing to answer apparently innocuous questions.

Because of the uncertainty and delay in attempting to establish constitutional safeguards for witnesses, pressures mounted both in and out of Congress for reform of committee procedures to protect the rights of witnesses and to give greater assurance that the purposes for which the investigations were instituted would be accomplished.

Rules Reforms

Proposals for "fair play" rules for investigations were numerous in the 83rd Congress.[42] Both the House Rules Committee and the Senate Rules and Administration Committee in 1954 held hearings on a variety of proposed codes of committee procedure sponsored by both parties.

House. The House March 23, 1955, adopted by voice vote a resolution (H Res 151) amending House Rules to establish a minimum standard of conduct for House committees. The resolution:

● Required a quorum of at least two members when committees take testimony and receive evidence.

● Allowed witnesses at investigations to be accompanied by counsel.

● Required a committee, if it found that evidence "may tend to defame, degrade, or incriminate any person," to receive the evidence in secret session and to allow the person injured to appear as a witness and to request subpoenas of other witnesses.

● Required committee consent for release of evidence taken in secret session.

Senate. The Senate prescribed no "fair play" code for its committees. However, the Senate Republican Policy Committee on March 10, 1954, offered as "suggestions" a set of rules for investigations and sent the proposals to all Senate committee chairmen. The Republican proposals would have allowed counsel for witnesses, prohibited release of executive testimony except by majority vote, and strengthened the control of investigations by the majority of the committee.

The Rules Subcommittee of the Senate Rules and Administration Committee on Jan. 6, 1955, issued a unanimous report recommending 12 rules to protect witnesses and to ensure greater majority control of investigations. Among the recommendations were those to:

● Allow a person who felt his reputation had been damaged by other testimony to testify in his own behalf or file a sworn statement.

● Ban public release of testimony given in closed session, except by authorization of the committee.

● Advise each witness, in advance, of the subject of the investigation.

● Allow witnesses to request that television and other cameras and lights not be directed at him during his testimony, and have committee members present at the time to rule on the request.

The report said "elaborate procedural devices" would be unnecessary if there were "courtesy and understanding on the part of committee members and staff," and ineffective if those qualities were lacking. The subcommittee reported, "What might have been classified decades ago as private opinion of no concern to Congress, takes on a different connotation in the light of world events whose impact Congress may not disregard."

The Senate left investigative procedures to the discretion of individual committees, whose practices varied considerably. The Permanent Investigations Subcommittee of the Senate Government Operations Committee, after Sen. John L. McClellan (D Ark.) replaced McCarthy as chairman, Jan. 18, 1955, adopted rules requiring the presence of two committee members when testimony was being taken, permitted anyone who was the subject of an investigation to submit questions in writing for cross-examination of other witnesses, and allowed any person adversely affected by testimony to request an appearance or file a statement.

Not only do rules vary from one committee to another in the Senate and, except for the minimum code, in the House, but the strictness with which committees adhere to their own rules is not uniform.

Various codes and rules have been proposed for improving congressional investigatory procedures, but in the last analysis the actions of committees are determined by its members. For as Sen. J.W. Fulbright (D Ark.) pointed out in 1951: "In order to investigate effectively, a congressional committee must have within the field of inquiry assigned to it a virtually unrestrained delegation of this vast congressional power. As a practical matter, this means that the power to investigate is wielded by individuals, not by institutions.... This is...at once both the weakness and the strength of our legislative processes."[43]

Immunity Statute

The need for immunity statutes first became apparent in the United States in the mid-19th century. In passing the federal statute providing for punishment of recalcitrant witnesses before congressional committees, Congress in 1857 added a second section that contained an automatic and sweeping grant of immunity to witnesses testifying under the compulsion of congressional power. As enacted, the law provided that "no person examined and testifying before either House of Congress or any committee of either House, shall be held to answer criminally in any court of justice, or subject to any penalty or forfeiture, for any fact or act touching which he shall be required to testify before either House of Congress or any committee of either House, as to which he shall have testified, whether before or after this act;.... Provided, that nothing in this act shall be construed to exempt any witness from prosecution and punishment for perjury committed by him in testifying as aforesaid."[44]

In 1862, however, when it was revealed that embezzlers of millions of dollars in Indian trust bonds had escaped prosecution by appearing before an investigating committee, Congress repealed the 1857 immunity law and replaced it with a provision stating: "No testimony given by a witness before either House, or before any committee of either House...shall be used as evidence in any criminal proceeding against him in any court, except in a prosecution for perjury committed in giving such testimony." Thus, although witnesses' own testimony could not be used as evidence to convict them, there was nothing to prevent its being used as a lead in discovering other evidence of crime.[45]

Congress inserted a similar provision in the 1887 act creating the Interstate Commerce Commission (ICC) and delegating investigatory powers to it. (Subsequently Congress delegated powers of investigation to other independent regulatory commissions.) The act authorized the ICC to require witnesses before it to testify despite any claim of privilege against self-incrimination, but provided that such testimony "shall not be used against such person on the trial of any criminal proceeding." (This provision was somewhat modified in 1893.) The constitutionality of the ICC's use of immunity was upheld by the Supreme Court in 1896.[46] *(Brown v. Walker,* 161 U.S. 591)

The 1862 law regarding immunity before congressional committees remained unchanged until 1954, when the Eisenhower administration proposed, and Congress adopted, the Immunity Act of 1954. The bill (PL 83-600) permitted either chamber of Congress by majority vote, or a congressional committee by two-thirds vote, to grant immunity to witnesses in national security investigations, provided an order was first obtained from a U.S. district court judge and also provided the Attorney General was notified in advance and given an opportunity to offer objections. The bill also permitted the U.S. district courts to grant immunity to witnesses before the court or grand juries. The bill was aimed at witnesses invoking the Fifth Amendment privilege against self-incrimination. Immunity would have the effect of compelling them to testify or go to jail.[47] The Supreme Court upheld the act in *Ullmann v. United States* (350 U.S. 422, 1956).

Watergate and Immunity

Congressional grants of immunity became an issue during the hearings of the Senate Select Committee on Presidential Campaign Activities (the Watergate com-

175

mittee). In one of his first moves as Watergate special prosecutor, Archibald Cox June 4, 1973, urged the committee to delay its public hearings. One of his arguments for postponement was that a grant of partial immunity for certain witnesses before the committee might prevent them from being convicted later.[48]

U.S. District Court Judge John J. Sirica heard arguments June 8 on his power to deny the Senate committee's request for immunity for John W. Dean III and Jeb Stuart Magruder. The two were known to be under consideration for indictment in connection with the Watergate scandal and were reportedly prepared to offer evidence of the involvement of top White House officials, including the President.

Sirica denied Cox's request for postponement of the hearings, ruling June 12 that the court lacked any power of intervention. The judge granted limited—or "use"—immunity to Dean and Magruder, thus clearing them to appear before the committee.[49]

Investigations and the Courts

During the greater part of the 19th century, congressional investigations were not subjected to judicial review. The Supreme Court ruling in the 1821 case of *Anderson v. Dunn* (6 Wheat. 204), that the action of the House must be "presumed" to be in accordance with law, warded off legal challenges to the power of Congress to punish for contempt.[50]

This precedent was set aside in 1881 by the court's decision in the important case of *Kilbourn v. Thompson* (103 U.S. 168), which established the principle of judicial review of the investigative activities of Congress. Other cases were to follow. Emerging from the series of judicial decisions since *Kilbourn* was a broad outline of congressional investigative power:

● The power to conduct investigations and to compel the attendance of witnesses and the production of evidence, under the threat of citation for contempt of Congress, was accepted as a necessary corollary of the power to legislate.

● The investigative power was to be connected with a legislative power authorized by the Constitution; before a committee could compel a witness to testify, it had to inform the witness of the connection between the questions and the legislative purpose for which the inquiry was undertaken.

● Investigations were subject in varying degrees to constitutional protection of individual rights and the Constitution's division of powers among three separate and equal branches of government.

● The courts had authority to review investigative activities, although committees were allowed to determine their procedures virtually without restraint.[51]

Kilbourn v. Thompson. The *Kilbourn* case originated with the refusal of a witness, Hallet Kilbourn, to produce papers demanded by the House Select Committee on the Real Estate Pool and Jay Cooke Indebtedness, which was investigating the failure of the banking firm of Jay Cooke. Kilbourn, manager of the real estate pool, said he would not acknowledge "the naked, arbitrary power of the House to investigate private business in which nobody but me and my customers have concern." The House ordered that he be jailed for contempt. Released on a writ of habeas corpus, Kilbourn sued the Speaker, members of the investigating committee and Sergeant at Arms John G. Thompson for false arrest. The Supreme Court heard the case and sustained Kilbourn's claim. In its decision, the court held that the houses of Congress did not have a general power to punish for contempt. A reluctant committee witness could be punished for contempt, the court ruled, only if the inquiry for which the witness had been called was within the "legitimate cognizance" of Congress.

The *Kilbourn* decision appeared to restrict the congressional power to investigate to "legitimate" inquiries, without specifying what they were. In deciding the case, the court declared that investigations of the private affairs of a citizen were not legitimate, but that those made in connection with some specifically granted constitutional power, such as impeachment or the election and qualification of members, were proper. Later court decisions have largely removed the limitations imposed in *Kilbourn;* its value has stemmed from the principle of judicial review of congressional contempt action, which it established.

In re Chapman. Sixteen years after *Kilbourn,* in 1897, the Supreme Court held *(In re Chapman,* 166 U.S.

661) that investigations were "legitimate" inquiries when they involved the conduct of members of Congress.[52] This unanimously upheld the constitutionality of the 1857 contempt of Congress statute.

McGrain v. Daugherty. In 1927, the court issued a landmark decision *(McGrain v. Daugherty*, 273 U.S. 135) that swept away nearly all the restrictions on the investigating power of Congress left over from the *Kilbourn* decision.[53] The effect of *McGrain* was to uphold the power of Congress to conduct legislative and oversight investigations. These two types of investigations, together with membership inquiries, have comprised the vast majority of congressional investigations since 1789. Thus, *McGrain* firmly established the investigation power.

The *McGrain* decision grew out of a refusal by Mally S. Daugherty, brother of Attorney General Harry M. Daugherty (1921-24), to testify before a Senate committee investigating the Justice Department. The Senate issued a warrant ordering Deputy Sergeant at Arms John J. McGrain to arrest Mally Daugherty, who had challenged the Senate's power to compel him to testify.

Sinclair v. United States. In 1929 *(Sinclair v. United States*, 279 U.S. 263) the Supreme Court held that a witness who refused to answer questions asked by a congressional committee could be punished if he were mistaken as to the law on which he based his refusal.[54] The fact that a witness acted in good faith on the advice of counsel was no defense, the court held. This precedent made any challenge of committee powers risky, with the possibility of a jail sentence for any witness seeking to test his rights in court.

The case grew out of an investigation in the Teapot Dome scandals. The Interior Department had leased public lands, containing oil, to the Mammoth Oil Co., the president and sole stockholder of which was Harry F. Sinclair. Sinclair had refused to answer questions of a Senate investigating committee on the ground that the whole matter was of exclusively judicial concern and therefore beyond the Senate's legitimate range of inquiry. He was convicted and sentenced under the 1857 statute. In upholding the conviction, the Supreme Court declared that the naval oil reserves and their disposition were clearly a proper matter for congressional scrutiny.

Jurney v. MacCracken. In 1935, the court ruled *(Jurney v. MacCracken,* 249 U.S. 125) that an investigating committee had authority to punish for contempt a witness who destroyed papers after the service of a subpoena for them.[55] Several letters had been removed from the office of William P. MacCracken, a Washington lawyer, during a Senate committee investigation of airmail contracts.

United States v. Rumely. Following World War II, the Supreme Court was far more protective of the rights of witnesses than of the rights of congressional committees. In the 1953 case of *United States v. Rumely,* (345 U.S. 41, 1953), the Supreme Court upheld a Court of Appeals decision reversing the conviction for contempt of Congress of Edward A. Rumely. Rumely had refused to tell the House Select Committee on Lobbying Activities the names of individuals making bulk purchases of books distributed by the Committee for Constitutional Government, an archconservative organization. He had asserted to the committee that "under the Bill of Rights, that is beyond the power of your committee to investigate."

A majority of the court avoided the constitutional questions by narrowly construing the authority granted by the resolution establishing the committee. It held that the mandate to investigate "lobbying activities" was limited to "representations made directly to the Congress, its members, or its committees," and excluded attempts to influence Congress indirectly through public dissemination of literature.

Subversive and Fifth Amendment Cases

The wartime and postwar quest to uncover subversion in the United States produced a new style of investigation. The overriding purpose of the anti-subversion hearings was exposure, as was indicated in the comments by Rep. Martin Dies (D Texas), chairman of the House Special Committee to Investigate Un-American Activities: "I am not in a position to say whether we can legislate effectively in reference to this matter, but I do know that exposure in a democracy of subversive activities is the most effective weapon that we have in our possession."[56]

Committee witnesses balked at the new investigative tactics, and the number of contempt of Congress citations grew, leading to new court tests. To meet the new legal issues raised by the anti-subversive inquiries, the courts handed down a number of decisions further defining the rights of witnesses and the powers of investigating committees. Nearly all of the cases originated in hearings by the House Un-American Activities Committee.

The Supreme Court did not consider any contempt of Congress cases in which a witness had pleaded the Fifth Amendment until 1955. That year, in two decisions decided on the same day (Emspak v. United States, 349 U.S. 190 and Quinn v. United States, 349 U.S. 155), in a spirited defense of the controversial right, the court laid down general guidelines for the use of the privilege. No special combination of words or "ritualistic formula" was required of a witness wishing to claim the privilege, the court said. If the investigating committee had been in any doubt as to the ground on which refusal to testify was based, it should have asked the witness whether he was in fact relying on the Fifth Amendment.

In the late 1950s, the court handed down a pair of decisions which attempted to establish limits to the "exposure power" of a committee. The courts declared in a 1957 case (Watkins v. United States, 345 U.S. 178), that "there is no congressional power to expose for the sake of exposure." Conceding that the public was entitled to be informed of the workings of the government, the court said: "That cannot be inflated into a general power to expose where the predominant results can only be an invasion of the private rights of individuals." The ruling was praised by many as an important restriction on the procedures of committees investigating subversion.

But two years later, in 1959 (Barenblatt v. United States, 360 U.S. 109), the court backed away from the Watkins declaration. A challenged Un-American Activities Committee hearing was not unlawful on the ground that its purpose was "exposure," the court said in the 1959 case. "So long as Congress acts in pursuance of its constitutional power, the judiciary lacks authority to intervene on the basis of the motives which spurred the exercise of that power," the court said. In addition, the court made clear that it would broadly interpret the power of Congress.

In two 1961 decisions (Wilkinson v. United States, 365 U.S. 399 and Braden v. United States, 365 U.S. 431), the court went a step beyond the *Barenblatt* decision, affirming the convictions of the defendants, who contended they had been subpoenaed simply because of their criticisms of the Un-American Activities Committee.

Although it thus appeared that the court had recognized a practically unlimited power of congressional inquiry, from 1961 to 1966, it reversed almost every contempt conviction which came before it. According to scholar C. Herman Pritchett, "These reversals were accomplished for the most part without challenging the scope of investigatory power or querying the motives of the investigators. They were achieved primarily by strict judicial enforcement of the rules on pertinency, authorization, and procedure, plus strict observance of the constitutional standards governing criminal prosecutions."[57]

Chapter 16

Investigations and the Executive

Investigations have often led Congress into conflict with the executive branch. The most frequent cause of contention has been refusal by the President to comply with congressional demands for information.

Practically every administration since 1792 has clashed with Congress over the question of "executive privilege," although the term was first used only in 1958,[58] and the issue has yet to be resolved. Some experts have asserted that executive departments, having been established by Congress and maintained by its appropriations, are the creatures of the legislature and cannot deny it information regarding their activities. Congress may seek to back up its demands by arousing public support for disclosure, especially if there is any suspicion that an administration is seeking to protect its political reputation by hiding mistakes or malfeasance. However, the long list of precedents in which Presidents have successfully defined congressional demands for information, and Congress' reluctance to settle the issue by legislation forcing it into the courts, support claims that the constitutional separation of powers permits the President, at his discretion, to withhold information sought by Congress.

A variety of reasons has been used to justify denying information to Congress. Perhaps the most common has been the need for secrecy in military and diplomatic activities.

Presidents have also sought to avoid unwarranted exposure of individuals to unfavorable publicity, especially when documents or files requested contain incomplete, distorted, inaccurate, misleading or unsubstantiated information. The need for confidential exchange of ideas between members of an administration has been cited as justifying refusal to provide records or describe conversations in the executive branch. Fears that disclosures would interfere with criminal or security investigations sometimes have prompted administrative secrecy. Critics of an administration have frequently charged that its real motive for refusing to divulge information was to escape criticism or scandal.

"Clearly, the President cannot turn over documents to Congress so that Congress can then decide whether or not they should have been turned over," wrote Telford Taylor in his 1955 study of investigations. "If there is an executive privilege to withhold information when disclosures would not be "in the public interest,' then the President must be the one to determine in any particular case whether the public interest permits disclosure or requires non-disclosure. Just as clearly, this leaves open the possibility that the President may abuse his prerogative, especially in instances where the information would reflect unfavorably on him or his administration of the nation's affairs."[59]

Taylor was writing during a period when critics of the congressional investigating power were pointing to what they considered abuses of the power by the McCarthy panel in excessive demands for information from the administration. Twenty years later, however, following clashes between President Johnson and Congress over Vietnam War information and between President Nixon and Congress over Watergate documents and testimony by members of the administration, the weight of opinion had seemed to shift against use of the "privilege." Harvard University Prof. Raoul Berger, writing in 1974, offered a detailed critique of the use of "executive privilege," terming it a "constitutional myth"[60]—"a product of the nineteenth century, fashioned by a succession of Presidents who created 'precedents' to suit the occasion.... At bottom, the issue concerns the right of Congress and the people to participate in making the fateful decisions that affect the fortunes of the nation. Claims of presidential power to bar such participation or to withhold on one ground or another the information that is indispensable for intelligent participation undermine this right and sap the very foundations of democratic government."

Presidents who refused demands from investigating committees have included Washington, Jefferson, Monroe, Jackson, Tyler, Polk, Fillmore, Lincoln, Grant, Hayes, Cleveland, Theodore Roosevelt, Coolidge, Hoover and all subsequent presidents or members of their administrations.[61] In some cases committees have accepted the President's refusal without comment. Other times, the refusal has led to a full-scale constitutional confrontation. A series of selected cases follows.

Early Refusals to Give Information

Washington. The "precedent" of executive privilege was first established in 1792 when a select House committee, conducting the first congressional inquiry, investigated an Indian victory over Maj. Gen. Arthur St. Clair and his men in the Northwest Territory. The committee wrote to War Secretary Henry Knox and asked him to turn over all the documents relating to the St. Clair expedition. Knox asked President Washington for advice; the President raised the subject at a Cabinet meeting. The Cabinet agreed that the House could conduct such an investigation and could call for such papers. It decided, according to the report of Thomas Jefferson, "that the executive ought to communicate such papers as the public good would permit, and ought to refuse those, the disclosure of which would endanger the public." As it developed, none of the St. Clair papers were regarded as confidential, and the President on April 4 directed Knox to make the papers available to the committee.[62]

(Four years later, in 1796, Washington claimed executive privilege when he refused a House request for correspondence relating to the intensely controversial Jay's Treaty with Great Britain. The House was debating a bill to implement portions of the treaty; the bill eventually was passed.)

Jackson. A House committee appointed "to examine into the conditions of the executive departments" adopted on Jan. 23, 1837, a series of resolutions that directed President Jackson and members of his Cabinet to furnish lists of federal appointments made without the concurrence of the Senate, along with information as to the salaries of the appointees and as to whether they were being paid without having taken office. Jackson, backed by a large majority in the House categorically refused, in what was to become one of the most successful efforts of a President to resist congressional investigators.[63]

After three months of fruitless questioning of some Cabinet officers and others, the committee concluded that it had overstepped its authority in submitting a blanket request for documents, and dropped the inquiry. The Jackson majority on the committee explained that it had gone along with the requests of Chairman Henry A. Wise (D Va.) to avoid charges of protecting the administration. In a report on March 3, 1837, the committee said: "The condition of the various executive departments is prosperous, and...they have been conducted with ability and industry."

Tyler. The House on May 18, 1842, adopted a resolution requesting War Secretary J. C. Spencer to make available to the Indian Affairs Committee reports on the Cherokee Indians and alleged frauds committed against them. After consulting with President Tyler, Spencer on June 3 refused, asserting that negotiations to settle claims with the Indians still were in progress. The committee persisted in its request, and on Aug. 13 the House by an 83-60 vote adopted a committee resolution requesting the information from Tyler. Tyler took no action on the request. On Dec. 30, the House adopted another resolution asking when the President was going to act.[64]

Tyler replied, Jan. 31, 1843, that the claims negotiations had been concluded in the meantime, and information dealing with the alleged frauds would be submitted. However, the President withheld portions of the reports containing personal comments about Indian negotiators and about recommendations for future action. In doing so, the President argued that the House could not demand information, even if relevant to a House debate, if the information would interfere with the discretion of the executive branch.

Cleveland. President Cleveland in 1885 was the first Democrat in the White House since Buchanan in 1861.[65] Democrats also controlled the House, but Republicans had a majority in the Senate. As the new President began replacing holdover Republican officeholders with Democrats, the Senate committees to which the nominations were referred repeatedly requested the information that had led to removal of the Republican incumbents. The standard department reply was that at the direction of the President it refused, on the ground that the public interest would not be served or that the removal had been a purely executive action.

Some 650 Republican officeholders were replaced. Finally, on Dec. 26, 1885, the Senate Judiciary Committee asked Attorney General A. H. Garland for information on the dismissal of George N. Durskin, U.S. district attorney for the southern district of Alabama. There being no response from Garland, the Senate on Jan 26, 1886, adopted a committee resolution directing the Attorney General to furnish the papers. In his reply, Feb. 1, Garland said the President had directed him to report that "the public interest would not be promoted by compliance with the resolution." The Senate responded, Feb. 18, by adopting a resolution refusing to concur in the removal of officeholders when the documents on which the removal was based were withheld.

In a message to the Senate, March 1, Cleveland disclaimed any intent to withhold official papers and asserted that the letters and reports leading to the dismissals were inherently private and confidential.

From March 9 to 26 the Senate debated the issue. It concluded by adopting a resolution citing the attorney general for being "in violation of his official duty and subversive of the fundamental principles of the government...." President Cleveland stood his ground, however, and the Senate ultimately confirmed his nominee, John D. Burnett, to replace Durskin.

Continued Insistence on Executive Privilege

Hoover. During Senate consideration of the London Naval Treaty of 1930, the Foreign Relations Committee asked for the papers relating to the London Conference at which the treaty had been negotiated. Secretary of State Henry L. Stimson submitted some of the papers but withheld others, explaining June 6, 1930, that he had been "directed by the President to say" that their production "would not in his opinion be compatible with the public interest." The committee adopted a resolution, June 12, asserting that the documents were "relevant and pertinent when the Senate is considering a treaty for the purpose of ratification." On July 10, the Senate, supporting the committee, adopted by a 53-4 vote a resolution requesting the President to submit the material, "if not incompatible with the public interest." Pleading the next day that the papers were confidential, Hoover again declined to produce them. The Senate on July 21 consented to ratification of the treaty, with "the distinct and explicit understanding" that it contained no secret agreements.[66]

Truman. President Truman in 1948 became involved in a head-on clash between the executive branch and an investigating committee of Congress. On March 1 the House Un-American Activities Special Subcommittee on National Security issued a report that called Dr. Edward U. Condon, director of the Bureau of Standards, "one of the weakest links in our national security." The subcommittee promptly subpoenaed Commerce Department records of loyalty investigations of Condon, but Secretary of Commerce W. Averell Harriman refused to release them on the ground that their publication would be "prejudicial to the public interest."[67]

President Truman took a direct hand in the controversy on March 13 when he issued a directive barring disclosure of any loyalty files to Congress.

On April 22 the House by a 302-29 vote adopted a resolution (H Res 522) demanding that Harriman surrender an FBI report on Condon. The disputed documents were transferred to the White House, and the President refused to release them—despite Condon's request that they be made public. The House on May 12 passed by a 219-152 vote a bill (H J Res 342) "directing all executive departments and agencies of the federal government to make available to any and all standing, special or select committees of the House of Representatives and the Senate, information which may be deemed necessary to enable them to properly perform the duties delegated to them by Congress." Refusal to comply was to be considered a misdemeanor, punishable by a fine of up to $1,000 or imprisonment for up to one year, or both. In the Senate, the bill was referred to the Committee on Expenditures in the Executive Departments

(Government Operations), where it died upon expiration of the 80th Congress.[68]

Eisenhower. During the Army-McCarthy hearings before the Senate Government Operations Permanent Investigations Subcommittee, President Eisenhower on May 17, 1954, forbade testimony about a Jan. 12 meeting between Attorney General Herbert Brownell Jr. and Army Counsel John Adams. Developments in the aggressively anti-Communist hearings being conducted by Subcommittee Chairman Joseph R. McCarthy (R Wis.) had been discussed at the meeting. In a letter to Defense Secretary Charles E. Wilson imposing the ban on testimony about the meeting, Eisenhower stressed the importance of candid, private communication within the executive branch and the "proper separation of power between the executive and legislative branches." When Adams cited the President's order in refusing to answer a question on May 24, McCarthy accused him of using "a type of Fifth Amendment privilege."[69]

The Democrats on the subcommittee protested McCarthy's call for informers, and Brownell on May 28, with the President's approval, issued a statement: "The executive branch...has the sole and fundamental responsibility under the Constitution for the enforcement of our laws and presidential orders...."

Kennedy Limitations. President Eisenhower's May 17, 1954, letter and accompanying memorandum soon became the basis for an extension of the claim of "executive privilege" far down the administrative line from the President. After that time, according to a 1973 report prepared by the Government and General Research Division of the Library of Congress, "the executive branch answer to nearly every question about the authority to withhold information from the Congress was 'yes,' they had the authority."[70]

The pattern of invoking the "privilege" by executive branch officials far down the administrative line from the President was somewhat altered, but not broken, by President Kennedy in 1962. The previous year, a special Senate subcommittee had opened hearings on the Pentagon's system for editing speeches of military leaders. When the panel asked the identity of the editors, the President directed the Secretary of Defense, in a Feb. 8, 1962, letter, "not to give any testimony or produce any documents which would disclose such information." He added, however: "The principle which is at stake here cannot be automatically applied to every request for information. Each case must be judged on its own merits." And on March 7, 1962, the President wrote, "Executive privilege can be invoked only by the President and will not be used without specific presidential approval."[71]

Nonetheless, after the Kennedy directive, executive branch officials in his administration refused to provide information to congressional committees three times, apparently without presidential authority.[72]

President Johnson continued this trend, despite a letter of April 2, 1965, in which he stated that "the claim of 'executive privilege' will continue to be made only by the President." Although he personally did not invoke the privilege, there were two refusals by appointees in his administration to provide information to congressional committees.

Nixon Assertions. In addition to Watergate-related information, President Nixon personally and formally invoked the claim of "executive privilege" against congressional committees four times after issuing a memorandum on March 24, 1969, stating that the privilege would not be used without specific presidential approval. Between 1969 and 1973, moreover, there were at least 15 other instances (most of them related to defense or foreign policy) in which documents or testimony were refused to congressional committees without direct presidential approval.[73] "In fact, the presidential statements [on executive privilege] have been limitations in name only," concluded the Library of Congress report.[74]

Chapter 17

Watergate and Executive Privilege

The most dramatic clash over use of executive privilege was bound up with Watergate and pitted Nixon against two congressional committees, the special prosecutor (both Archibald Cox and his successor, Leon Jaworski) and a grand jury.

The confrontation began with establishment of the Senate Watergate committee in February 1973. At first, Nixon pleaded executive privilege, refusing to allow his aides to appear before the panel. But in April he reversed himself, stating that government employees and particularly White House employees "are expected fully to cooperate in this matter. I condemn any attempts to cover up in this case, no matter who is involved."

On May 3, the White House issued new guidelines on the privilege: "The President desires that the invocation of executive privilege be held to a minimum." The privilege should be invoked only in connection with conversations with the President, conversations among aides involving communications with the President, and with regard to presidential papers and national security matters.[75]

On May 29, Nixon said he would refuse to provide information through oral or written testimony to the Watergate grand jury or to the Senate committee. For him to do so would be "constitutionally inappropriate" and a violation of the separation of powers.[76]

Nixon repeated his refusal to appear before the committee or to hand over presidential papers in a letter to Chairman Sam J. Ervin Jr. (D N.C.) July 6.[77] No President could function if the private papers of his office, prepared by his personal staff, were open to public scrutiny," he said. "Formulation of sound public policy requires that the President and his personal staff be able to communicate among themselves in complete candor.... If I were to testify before the committee, irreparable damage would be done to the constitutional principle of separation of powers."

Thus the limits of inquiry were apparently set, both for the co-equal judicial branch within which the grand jury investigation was continuing and for the co-equal legislative branch within which the Senate committee was working.

The executive privilege issue assumed new dimensions in July, however, with revelation that tape recordings had been made of many presidential conversations in the White House during the period in which the break-in occurred and the cover-up began. Immediately, a struggle for the tapes began. The legal battle would last almost exactly a year, from July 23, 1973, when the Senate committee and the Watergate grand jury subpoenaed the first group of tapes, to July 24, 1974, when the Supreme Court ruled against Nixon. But the Senate investigating committee never obtained the tapes it sought. The administration's argument against relinquishing the tapes to the Senate committee prevailed in the courts.

In refusing to relinquish the tapes, Nixon repeated his arguments that to do so would be "inconsistent with the public interest and with the constitutional position of the presidency." On Aug. 29, U.S. District Court Judge John J. Sirica ruled that the President should give him the tapes so that he could review them. On Oct. 12, the U.S. Court of Appeals for the District of Columbia Circuit upheld Sirica's decision. In a 44-page majority opinion, the court viewed executive privilege as a qualified privilege to be weighed by courts against competing public interests. On the other hand, a view of executive privilege as absolute and exercised at the sole discretion of the President marked the two lengthy dissenting opinions.[78]

Five days later, Oct. 17, Sirica ruled on the Senate Watergate committee's request for the same tapes. In this decision the judge ruled that he had no jurisdiction to consider the committee's effort to force Nixon to give up the tapes. In dismissing the case, Sirica said Congress had never enacted any law giving federal courts jurisdiction in such a case.

Moving quickly to rectify the situation, Congress by Dec. 3 had sent to the White House legislation specifically granting the federal district court in the District of Columbia jurisdiction over suits brought by the Senate Watergate committee to enforce subpoenas. The bill became law (PL 93-190) without Nixon's signature. The Senate committee Dec. 19 approved new subpoenas for nearly 500 presidential tapes and documents; Nixon Jan. 4 refused to comply.[79]

Deciding to seek enforcement of the original subpoenas before litigating Nixon's refusal to comply with the more recent demands, the committee Jan. 7, 1974, renewed its original suit and asked Sirica to reconsider it in light of PL 93-190. Sirica referred the case to federal District Court Judge Gerhard A. Gesell. Again, the White House asked the court to dismiss the suit.

On Jan. 25 Gesell issued his ruling quashing the July 23 subpoena for documents, but directing Nixon to respond more directly to the July 23 subpoena for the five tapes. The judge asked Nixon to provide a detailed statement explaining what parts of the subpoenaed tapes he considered covered by executive privilege. "This statement must be signed by the President," wrote Gesell, "for only he can invoke the (executive) privilege at issue."[80]

In quashing the broader July 23 committee request for documents, Gesell described the subpoena as too broad and too vague, disregarding "the restraints of specificity and reasonableness which derive from the Fourth Amendment," which guarantees citizens protection against unreasonable search and seizure.[81] On Feb. 6, Nixon sent Gesell a letter stating simply that disclosure of the tapes "would not be in the public interest."[82]

On Feb. 8, the Senate Watergate committee suffered another defeat in court, when Gesell refused to require the White House to turn over the five tapes to the panel, citing the risk that the committee's use of the tapes might make it difficult to obtain an unbiased jury for the trials arising out of the Watergate matter.[83]

"The committee's role as a 'grand inquest' into governmental misconduct is limited," wrote Gesell. "It may only proceed in aid of Congress' legislative function...the time has come to question whether it is in the public interest for the criminal investigative aspects of its work to go forward in the blazing atmosphere of...publicity."

The Senate Watergate committee Feb. 19 agreed to terminate its public hearings, but also decided to appeal the Feb. 8 ruling. The bid was lost May 23, when a U.S. Court of Appeals rejected the request on grounds that the committee had failed to show a pressing enough need for the tapes.[84]

Meanwhile, Cox's successor, Leon Jaworski, and the House Judiciary Committee (which was authorized to begin an impeachment inquiry in February 1974) issued their subpoenas for tapes and documents. Again, Nixon and his lawyers, arguing presidential confidentiality, refused to comply. However, Nixon modified his position and announced April 29, 1974—the day before the deadline set by the Judiciary Committee subpoena—that he would make public the transcripts of 46 tapes the next day. Still the committee was not satisfied. Divided closely along party lines, the committee voted May 1 to inform the President that "you have failed to comply with the committee's subpoena...." Jaworski—whose subpoena for evidence Nixon had also rejected—took his case to the Supreme Court late in May.

On July 24, hours before the Judiciary Committee began public debate on impeachment, the Supreme Court ruled unanimously against the President and ordered him to give up the tapes. *(United States v. Nixon)*

Thus, the Court reaffirmed its 1803 decision, *Marbury v. Madison* (1 Cranch. 137), establishing the power of the courts to review the actions of the other two branches of government.

Quickly following the Supreme Court's decision, the Judiciary Committee adopted three articles of impeachment, among them contempt of Congress for failing to comply with subpoenas authorized by the panel.

Nixon began surrendering the tapes to Sirica on July 30. On Aug. 2, Nixon made public the transcript of some of the tapes which showed his participation in a coverup after the Watergate break-in and his approval of the use of the CIA to block an FBI investigation of the event. These revelations wiped out almost all of Nixon's remaining support in Congress and led to his resignation Aug. 9.

Chapter 18

Politics of Investigations

"Large-scale investigations of alleged mismanagement or improper activities on the part of executive officers are likely to be greatly influenced by partisan considerations," Joseph P. Harris said in his book, *Congressional Control of Administration*.[85] "It is not uncommon for such an inquiry to result in reports that divide along party lines, with pro-administration members of the committee absolving the officers of blame, and anti-administration members finding the charges sustained. Partisanship is also often responsible for the initiation of investigations and greatly affects the manner in which they are conducted.... That an investigation can be conducted in a nonpartisan manner was notably proved by the Truman committee during World War II and by its successor, the Senate Preparedness Subcommittee, but it must be said that these constitute somewhat exceptional examples."

President Truman was a Democrat and the House was controlled by Republicans during the 1948 fight over the loyalty file of Dr. Edward U. Condon, director of the Bureau of Standards. Similar conflicting political forces, at countless other times, have had a profound impact on congressional investigations. By their very nature, investigating committees have become focal points of partisan strife.

As an illustration, the three most intensive periods of congressional investigative activities—the last years of the

Grant administration and the periods immediately follow-ing World Wars I and II—coincided with shifts of con-gressional majorities that transferred power to a party long in the minority. Grant, a Republican, was President from 1869 to 1877; and when the Democrats in the 1874 election recaptured control of the House for the first time since 1859, the number of investigations soared. In the 1918 election, Republicans gained control of the House and set off on a series of studies of World War I mobilization under Presi-dent Wilson, a Democrat. In similar fashion, World War II mobilization, and reported infiltration of the government by Communists during the administrations of Democratic Presidents Roosevelt and Truman, were studied closely by committees of the Republican 80th Congress, elected in 1946.

Personal motives have also figured significantly in the inauguration and conduct of congressional investigations. Hopes for favorable publicity or the desire to win popularity have frequently spurred members of Congress to propose and undertake investigations, although Senate munitions probe chairman Gerald P. Nye maintained in 1933: "I have yet to meet the member of Congress who has enjoyed the tremendous responsibility accompanying appointment to such a committee."[86] A further stimulus to inquiry is bound up in the pet hobbies or hates of individual members. A study of nine major investigations of foreign affairs between 1919 and 1940 indicated that "five...grew out of the personal predilections of certain congressmen."[87] Sen. Key Pittman (D Nev.), for example, on behalf of the silver mining in-terests, conducted an investigation in 1930 of the reduced trade between the United States and China, believing that it was due to the depreciated price of silver in relation to gold.[88]

Maneuvering for Committee Control

A subtler, and potentially far more important form of investigation politics, has taken place in the maneuvering for control of a particular inquiry. The conduct of in-vestigations has depended substantially on the attitude of the investigating committees and of their chairmen. Thus Radical Republicans, gaining control of the joint committee investigating the conduct of the Civil War, used the committee as a platform from which to criticize the moderate policies of President Lincoln and to force more vigorous prosecution of the war.

A similar example, with quite different results, occurred after World War II. The release by President Truman on Aug. 29, 1945, of Army and Navy reports on the Pearl Harbor disaster, brought numerous Republican demands for a congressional investigation. Through quick maneuvering, the Democrats initiated action. Taking advantage of his right to be recognized first, Senate Majority Leader Alben W. Barkley (D Ky.) obtained unanimous consent, Aug. 29, for consideration of a concurrent resolution to appoint a joint House-Senate committee which, with the Democrats in control of Congress, would have a Democratic majority. The resolution was adopted by both chambers without opposition, though House Republicans made an effort, defeated on a party-line vote, to gain equal membership on the committee. Barkley was named chairman, and the committee conducted hearings. The committee's final report, filed July 20, 1946, absolved President Roosevelt of blame for the Pearl Harbor disaster but held Adm. Harold B. Sark, chief of naval operations, and Maj. Gen. Walter C. Short, Army commander in Hawaii, primarily responsible. A Republican minority report laid the primary blame on Roosevelt, suggesting what might have been the majority view if Republicans had been in command of the inquiry.[89]

When controversy over the Vietnam War was building in Congress during the late 1960s, war-related investigations divided more along committee jurisdiction than party lines. The Senate Foreign Relations Committee was critical of the Vietnam policies of the administration, while House and Senate Armed Services Committee inquiries supported the policies or urged stronger war efforts. The positions of the committees reflected the opposing interests of their chairmen. Sen. J.W. Fulbright (D Ark.) of the Foreign Relations panel opposed the war. Sen. John C. Stennis (D Miss.) and Rep. L. Mendel Rivers (D S.C.) of the Armed Services groups favored strong military action.

Resort to Select Committees

Occasionally, a proposed investigation has overlapped the jurisdictions of different committees. When, in addition, the committees have held conflicting views on the subject, the impending impasse has been resolved by formation of a select committee, whose members have been drawn from the opposed standing committees. In 1957, for example, both the Labor and Public Welfare Committee and the Government Operations Permanent Investigations Subcommittee of the Senate claimed jurisdiction to investigate labor racketeering and management malpractices uncovered during a Permanent Investigations Subcommittee study of Defense Department procurement. The issue was resolved by the creation of a Select Committee on Improper Activities in the Labor or Management Field. Four members from each party and from each of the two committees were named to the newly formed group.[90]

A decade later, in 1968, a similar dispute over investigation of reports of hunger and malnutrition in the United States involved the Agriculture and Forestry Committee and the Labor and Public Welfare Committee of the Senate. Government food assistance programs were operated by the Agriculture Department but benefited welfare recipients. Once again, the dispute was resolved by creating a select committee, the Select Committee on Nutrition and Human Needs, composed of members of both committees plus other senators not on either committee.

The jurisdictional lines, however, often reflect only the surface differences between conflicting claims of committees to conduct an investigation. More fundamental is the conflicting philosophical views of committees that flow from the constituencies represented on the panels.

In the case of food assistance programs, for example, the congressional Agriculture Committees, reflecting the views of the Agriculture Department and farmers and food processors, have never been overly sympathetic to government attempts to provide food for low-income persons. These committees and the groups they represent traditionally have viewed their job as promoting the interest of agriculture—which often has meant keeping farm incomes up and preventing boom and bust in agricultural prices. Members of the committees generally have come from conservative farm states not known for their sympathy to welfare problems that tend to be concentrated in large urban-industrialized states.

The Labor and Public Welfare Committee, on the other hand, traditionally has been concerned about providing government aid to low-income workers and persons on welfare. Committee members tend to be allied with organized labor and other liberal organizations more concerned about urban than rural farm (agricultural) problems. Their preference normally is to keep food prices down in order to benefit not only welfare clients and poor people but average working persons who are their constituents, rather than to keep farm prices high.

This traditional tension between these committees had a concrete focus in the 1960s and 1970s when the food stamp program was created and grew into a multibillion-dollar government effort to provide extra food-purchasing power for low-income and impoverished Americans. The food stamp program was financed out of the Agriculture Department budget, a source of continuing annoyance to the department and to Agriculture Committee members who argued that the funds should go directly to agriculture programs and welfare (food stamp) program money should come from the government's welfare budget.

Consequently, committees with fundamentally different views of a problem, and of their responsibility for a solution, will want to control any congressional investigation that might affect the interest of their constituents. The conclusions from a study of food assistance programs, which could directly affect congressional policy, probably would be quite different depending on whether the Agriculture Committee or Labor Committee was in charge. For this reason, the tug-of-war between competing committees over investigations often is resolved by creation of a new select committee.

Watergate Committee. Controversy accompanied formation of the Senate Select Committee on Presidential Campaign Activities—the Watergate panel—established Feb. 7, 1973, as well as the creation in 1975 of House and Senate select committees to investigate operations of U.S. intelligence and law enforcement agencies, particularly the Central Intelligence Agency (CIA) and Federal Bureau of Investigation (FBI).

Since the CIA was created in 1947, detailed reports on its activities traditionally had been provided by the agency only to intelligence subcommittees of the House and Senate

Armed Services and Appropriations Committees. The sub-committees' oversight had long been criticized as inadequate, and their members were said to be too sympathetic to the military and intelligence establishments.

During debate in both chambers on resolutions creating the select committees, divisions were apparent between more conservative members who wanted the existing standing committees to retain their jurisdiction and conduct the investigation, on the one hand, and liberal critics of those panels, on the other. The composition of the select committees also was an issue, with members urging that appointment of pro- or anti-CIA "extremists" be avoided.[91]

Once established, moreover, the House Select Committee on Intelligence was torn by internal dissension, which finally caused its chairman to offer his resignation and immobilized the investigation until a new panel was formed in its place.[92]

PART VI

Confirmations

Chapter 19

Confirmation of Nominations

Senatorial confirmation of executive appointments is a distinctly American political and legislative phenomenon. The authors of the Constitution spent considerable time debating how appointments should be made before agreeing to a compromise proposal that the President appoint governmental officers with the advice and consent of the Senate.

If the Founding Fathers were alive today, one of the features of the contemporary political system that probably would much surprise them would be the nominations process. Although the mechanics of the confirmation system have remained much the same, the growth of the federal government has dramatically increased the number of nominations.

In the last 20 Congresses spanning 40 years, the number of nominations received by the Senate has grown sixfold—from 22,487 in the 74th Congress (1935-36) to 134,-384 in the 93rd (1973-74).

Routine Confirmation or Detailed Inquiry

Numbers alone do not give an accurate picture of the nominations process. The vast majority of nominations sent annually to the Senate involve the routine confirmation of appointments and promotions for military officers and officers of specialized services such as the Foreign Service and Public Health Service. These nominations are usually passed en bloc and confirmation is a formality. In his book, *The Advice and Consent of the Senate,* Joseph P. Harris placed 99 per cent of the nominations in this category.

It is the remaining 1 per cent of nominations, involving people who will occupy top policy-making positions in government, that sometimes locks the President and Senate in battle. These include nominations to Cabinet and sub-Cabinet posts, the federal judiciary, major diplomatic and military positions and top positions on independent boards and regulatory agencies. Although most nominations are confirmed by the Senate, pro forma approval is not always certain. Political considerations always have been a part of the nomination and confirmation process. But in recent years, the Senate often has carefully examined a nominee's economic views, social philosophy and personal finances.

Cabinet Nominations

By contrast, Cabinet nominations usually are confirmed with little difficulty, on the theory that the President should have great leeway in selecting the members of his official "family." Since 1789, only eight men nominated to the Cabinet have been rejected by the Senate.

Nominations to sub-Cabinet positions, which have multiplied phenomenally in the 20th century, are treated much like Cabinet nominations, although the President is expected to consult in advance with key members of Congress on appointments in which they have a particular interest, and sub-Cabinet posts frequently are used to reward various party factions. Since 1933 few such nominations have been withdrawn and none rejected.

Appointments to independent boards and commissions offer a somewhat different situation. Usually created by act of Congress and not subordinate to any executive department, they frequently are viewed as an arm of Congress rather than the executive branch, and members of Congress expect to play a larger role in the selection process. Typically, the act of Congress creating an independent agency may require a bipartisan membership or impose geographical or other limitations on the President's selection power. Contests with the Senate over these nominations have been frequent, although few nominees actually have been rejected. Independent agencies with single administrators have fewer problems—these nominations tend to be treated more like Cabinet nominations.

Diplomatic and Other Nominations

Major diplomatic nominations usually encounter little opposition. Although in the early days of the Republic the Senate attempted to exercise extensive authority over diplomatic appointments, in modern practice the President has been allowed wide discretion in his selection of ambassadors and other persons to assist him in the conduct of foreign relations.

Appointments to lower federal courts are another matter. By 1840 it had become customary for district court judges to be selected by the senators from the state in which the district was located, provided the senators were of the same party as the President. If they were not, the President was expected to consult with state party leaders before making a selection. Senatorial dictation of judicial appointments was reinforced by the institution of senatorial courtesy; under this unwritten custom, the Senate generally will refuse to confirm a nomination to an office situated within a particular state if the senators of the President's party from that state oppose it. The President has wider discretion in making appointments to circuit court judgeships because these jurisdictions embrace several states, and to other specialized courts such as the tax and customs.

Appointees in one other broad classification historically were selected by the legislative branch. Postmasters of the first, second and third classes constituted the largest group of civilian employees appointed with Senate confirmation. Although it was the Senate that gave its advice and consent, custom decreed that members of the House—if they were of the same party as the President—made the actual selection of appointees in their districts.

This patronage system survived until 1970 when Congress created an independent U.S. Postal Service. The postal reorganization set up an independent government agency, the Postal Service, to take over operations of the Post Office Department. The legislation ended congressional influence over appointment of postmasters.

U.S. attorneys and marshals continue as patronage appointments. Although appointed with Senate confirmation for four-year terms, they actually serve only at the pleasure of the President.

History of Appointments

The President "shall nominate, and by and with the Advice and Consent of the Senate, shall appoint...." U.S. Constitution, Article II, Section 2.[1] *(Footnotes, p. 322)*

The constitutional language governing the appointment power, hammered out in the final weeks of the Constitutional Convention of 1787, represented a compromise between those delegates who favored vesting in the Senate sole authority for appointing principal officers of the government and those who held that the President alone should control appointments as an executive function.

As finally adopted, the Constitution required Senate confirmation of principal officers of the government—"Ambassadors, other public Ministers and Consuls, Judges of the Supreme Court" were mentioned specifically—but provided that Congress could "by law vest the appointment of such inferior officers, as they think proper, in the President alone, in the courts of law, or in the heads of departments."

Approval of the compromise language did not, however, settle the controversy over the Senate's role in the appointment process.

To Hamilton, writing in *The Federalist* (No. 66), the Senate's function did not appear significant: "It will be the office of the President to *nominate,* and with the advice and consent of the Senate to *appoint.* There will, of course, be no exertion of *choice* on the part of the Senate. They may defeat one choice of the Executive and oblige him to make another; but they cannot themselves *choose*—they can only ratify or reject the choice he may have made."[2]

John Adams saw it differently. "Faction and distraction," he wrote, "are the sure and certain consequences of giving to the Senate a vote on the distribution of offices."[3] Looking ahead to the emergence of political parties, Adams foresaw the rise of the spoils system and the use of the appointive power as a senatorial patronage tool.

President Washington regarded the appointment power as "the most irksome part of the executive trust,"[4] but his exercise of that power was widely acclaimed and the Senate withheld its consent only five times during his administration.

Precedents Established by Washington

Methods of handling presidential nominations had to be established early in the new government. Washington established the precedent of submitting nominations to the Senate in writing, and the Senate after debate on the propriety of the secret ballot determined to take *viva voce* votes on nominations. The President rejected suggestions that he be present during Senate consideration of appointments: "It could be no pleasing thing, I conceive, for the President, on the one hand to be present and hear the propriety of his nominations questioned; nor for the Senate on the other hand to be under the smallest restraint from his presence from the fullest and freest inquiry into the character of the person nominated."[5]

Uncertainty over the extent of the Senate's powers with respect to appointments surfaced early in the administration. Could the Senate only give its consent to the person named, or could it also rule on the necessity for the post and the grade of the appointee? Washington's nominations of ministers to Paris, London and The Hague in December 1791 were blocked for weeks by Senate debate on a resolution opposing the appointment of "ministers plenipotentiary to reside permanently at foreign courts."[6] Washington's nominations finally were approved, by narrow votes on the ground of special need for representation at the three capitals.

Washington maintained high standards for selection of appointees, and although he consulted widely both with members of Congress and others, he rebuffed all attempts at encroachment on his prerogatives. Thus he refused to appoint Aaron Burr as minister to France in 1794, despite the recommendation of a caucus of Republican senators and representatives, because he questioned Burr's integrity.

Washington was not always successful in resisting senatorial pressure. Early in the First Congress, the Senate rejected his nomination of Benjamin Fishbourn to the post of naval officer (a customs official handling manifests, clearances, etc.) of the Port of Savannah as a courtesy to the two Georgia senators, who had a candidate of their own. Washington yielded; he nominated the senators' choice, and senatorial courtesy was born.

The practice of inquiring into the political views of a presidential nominee also had its beginning in the Washington Administration. John Rutledge of South Carolina, nominated in 1795 to succeed John Jay as Chief Justice of the United States, was rejected by the Senate on a 10-14 vote, primarily because of his opposition to the Jay Treaty with Great Britain. Rutledge, one of the original six Supreme Court justices (1789-91), was already serving as Chief Justice on a recess appointment.

Injection of Politics

John Adams, that vigorous critic of the appointment provisions of the Constitution, found nothing in his experience as President to make him change his views. The Federalist Senate cleared his appointments with Federalist leader Alexander Hamilton (then a private citizen), and Adams later complained that he "soon found that if I had not the previous consent of the heads of departments, and the approbation of Mr. Hamilton, I ran the utmost risk of a dead negative in the Senate."[7]

During Adams' tenure, appointments became increasingly subject to political considerations. The practice of consulting, and bowing to the wishes of, state delegations in Congress upon appointments in their states also grew.

Jefferson had far less trouble with appointments than his predecessor. He was the acknowledged leader of his party, and for most of his term that party was in control of Congress. Perhaps his most embarrassing failure was the unanimous rejection of his final nomination, that of William Short as minister to Russia. However, the opposition apparently was directed more against the establishment of the mission than against Short himself.

Unlike Jefferson, Madison soon found that he had to submit to Senate dictation in the matter of appointments. Thus a small clique of senators was able to force the appointment of Robert Smith as Secretary of State, although Madison had wanted to give the post to his Secretary of the Treasury, Albert Gallatin.

Gallatin's subsequent appointment as envoy to negotiate a peace treaty with Great Britain also met with difficulty in the Senate. Gallatin was already in Europe when the Senate adopted a resolution declaring that the duties of envoy and Secretary of the Treasury were incompatible. Subsequently, Gallatin resigned his Treasury post and was confirmed as envoy.

This nomination led to a controversy over the propriety of consultation between the President and a Senate committee on pending nominations. Although previous Presidents had so consulted with committees appointed by the party caucus or by the Senate itself, Madison decided to put an end to the practice. In a message to the Senate, he insisted that if the Senate wanted information on nominations, the correct procedure was to confer with appropriate department heads, not the President. "The appointment of a committee of the Senate to confer immediately with the executive himself," he said, "appears to lose sight of the coordinate relation between the executive and the Senate, which the Constitution has established, and which ought therefore to be maintained."[8] In spite of this message, the President received a special committee appointed by the Senate to confer with him about the Gallatin nomination, but he refused to discuss the nomination with them.

Madison in 1811 suffered the second outright rejection of a Supreme Court nomination. Alexander Wolcott was opposed by the Federalists because as collector of customs in Connecticut he had vigorously enforced the unpopular embargo acts passed prior to the War of 1812. He was rejected, 9-24, following charges by the press that he lacked the requisite legal qualifications for service on the court.

Growth of Spoils System

The administrations of James Monroe and John Quincy Adams were marked by the growth of the spoils system, as members of the Senate increasingly insisted on control of federal appointments in their states.

The "Four Years" law, enacted in 1820, greatly increased the number of appointments available. This law provided fixed four-year terms for many federal officers who previously had served at the pleasure of the President. Although its ostensible purpose was to ensure the accountability of appointees, its value as a patronage tool soon became clear. Commented Adams: "The Senate was conciliated by the permanent increase of their power, which was the principal ultimate effect of the act, and every senator was flattered by the power conferred upon himself of multiplying chances to provide for his friends and dependents....."[9]

Both Monroe and Adams resisted pressure to use the "Four Years" law as a means of introducing rotation in office; they followed the policy of renominating officers upon expiration of their terms, unless they had been guilty of misconduct. Upon taking office as President in 1825, Adams resubmitted all of Monroe's nominations on which the Senate had failed to act; by contrast, Jackson withdrew all of Adams' nominations.

One of Adams' Supreme Court nominations was blocked by the Senate. The name of John J. Crittenden, a Kentucky Whig, had been sent up shortly before Adams' administration ended in 1829. Jacksonians, who wished to allow the newly elected Democratic President to make the appointment, blocked Senate action on confirmation of Crittenden by a vote of 23-17. Jackson later filled the seat with a man of his choice.

Jackson, to whom rotation in office was a leading principle, made full use of the "Four Years" law to find places for his supporters. Although he was in constant conflict with the Senate over appointments, such was his popularity in the country that relatively few were rejected.

One of the most significant of the rejections was the appointment of Martin Van Buren as minister to England. Van Buren in 1831 resigned his post as Secretary of State in a Cabinet reorganization, and President Jackson then gave him a recess appointment to the Court of St. James. He was already in London when the Senate met in December. Clay, Webster and Calhoun, all aspirants for the presidency who looked on Van Buren as a likely opponent, led the opposition to his appointment. When the nomination came to a vote in January 1832, a tie was contrived so that Vice President Calhoun could vote against Van Buren. Although his opponents thought a Senate rejection would end Van Buren's political career, he returned home a martyr and was soon elected Vice President of the United States.

The Senate twice rejected Jackson's renomination of four incumbent directors of the Bank of the United States.

Senate opposition stemmed from reports critical of the bank that had been submitted to the President by the directors. Efforts to recommit the nominations having failed, the Senate rejected them, 20-24. Jackson renominated the same persons, and they again were rejected.

The Bank of the United States also figured in rejection of the nomination of Roger B. Taney as Secretary of the Treasury in 1834. Taney was rejected on an 18-28 vote after having served for nine months under a recess appointment. Opposition rested on his withdrawal of federal funds from the bank, an action which he had recommended as Attorney General and which he had been appointed Secretary of the Treasury to carry out. This was the first outright Senate rejection of a Cabinet appointee in U.S. history, although Madison had been prevented from appointing Gallatin as Secretary of State in 1809 because he feared Gallatin would be rejected.

Early in 1835 Jackson nominated Taney to the Supreme Court. The Senate did not take up that nomination until the closing days of its session, when it voted, 24-21, for an indefinite postponement. Undaunted, the President in December 1835 named Taney to be Chief Justice, a position made vacant by the death of John Marshall. Notwithstanding charges that the selection was an insult to the Senate, because it had twice rejected the nominee, Taney's appointment was confirmed by a vote of 29-15.

Patronage at a Peak, Civil Service Reform

The 40-year period from 1837 to 1877 marked the high point of Senate efforts to control appointments. During this period, the spoils system reached its peak and all Presidents were subject to intense pressure for patronage appointments. Senatorial courtesy—the practice of permitting senators of the President's party to control appointments to federal offices within their states—was firmly entrenched.

Senatorial ascendancy over the President in the matter of appointments and the excesses of the spoils system led, under Grant, to public pressure for civil service reform. In response to this pressure, Congress in 1871 enacted a civil service law but failed to appropriate funds to implement it.

Three of Grant's appointments to the Supreme Court failed to win Senate approval. The first was his Attorney

General, Ebenezer Rockwood Hoar, who had earned the enmity of the Senate by refusing to bow to political pressure in the filling of new judgeships created under an 1869 law. Following Hoar's rejection, 24-33, Sen. Simon Cameron of Pennsylvania exclaimed: "What could you expect for a man who has snubbed 70 senators!"[10] In 1874, Grant was forced to withdraw two successive nominations for Chief Justice, Attorney General George H. Williams and former Attorney General Caleb Cushing. Cushing had been rejected also for the post of Secretary of the Treasury in the Tyler administration.

The accession to the presidency of Rutherford B. Hayes in 1877 marked the beginning of presidential efforts to curb senatorial control over nominations. Hayes' selection of his own Cabinet members without consulting Senate leaders was viewed as presumptuous by them, and they countered with unprecedented delay in acting upon nominations. However, when public opinion came to the aid of the President, the nominations were rushed to confirmation.

Unable to obtain from Congress the civil service reform legislation he recommended, Hayes nevertheless attempted throughout his one term of office to curb patronage abuses.

The Senate did not consider Hayes' nomination of former Republican Sen. Stanley Matthews of Ohio to the Supreme Court in 1881. There was some feeling that Hayes was rewarding Matthews for his support in the Hayes-Tilden contest in 1876 and for his service as counsel before the commission which dealt with disputed returns from that election. Garfield later resubmitted Matthews' name and he was confirmed by a one-vote margin.

A protracted conflict over the corruption-ridden New York customhouse led to a showdown between Hayes and Sen. Roscoe Conkling of New York over the right of senators to control nominations. When two Conkling protégés—Chester A. Arthur, the customs collector, and Alonzo B. Cornell, the naval officer of the customhouse—refused to comply with a presidential order prohibiting federal employees from actively engaging in partisan politics, Hayes asked for their resignations. When they refused to resign, he nominated two other persons to replace them. Conkling appealed to senatorial courtesy, and the President's nominees were rejected, 25-31. After Congress adjourned, Hayes suspended Arthur and Cornell and made two more appointments to the posts. Despite Conkling's opposition, the Senate in the following session confirmed the President's choices by wide margins.

Conkling was the loser in another showdown, in 1881, with Hayes' successor, James A. Garfield. Garfield's nomination of one of his own supporters, Judge W. H. Robertson, as collector of the New York port infuriated the senator, who wanted to maintain control of all New York patronage. Conkling invoked the rule of courtesy in his effort to block Robertson's confirmation, and the Republican caucus supported him. However, the Democrats would not agree to vote against the nominee, and Conkling feared a rebuff on the floor. Asserting that they had been humiliated, he and his New York colleague, Sen. Thomas C. Platt, then took the extraordinary step of resigning from the Senate as a rebuke to the President for his presumption in making his own appointment. They expected to be re-elected by the state legislature as a vindication of their position, but they were disappointed. Conkling's political career was at an end, but Platt later returned to the Senate and to leadership of the Republican Party in New York.

Meanwhile, the heyday of the spoils system was drawing to a close. Previous efforts at meaningful civil service reform had ended in failure, but public revulsion over Garfield's assassination by a disappointed office-seeker in 1881 provided new impetus for reform. With the rather surprising endorsement of President Chester A. Arthur, a civil service system was established by the Pendleton Act of 1883.

Resistance to Patronage Demands

A test of the President's right to suspend federal officers, which occurred during Grover Cleveland's first term, was followed by repeal of the Tenure of Office Acts.

Few Cleveland nominations were rejected thereafter. However, in his second term, two conservative appointees to the Supreme Court were rejected upon appeal to the rule of courtesy by Sen. David B. Hill of New York. William B. Hornblower and Wheeler H. Peckham, respected New York attorneys but of a political faction opposed to Hill, were rejected by votes of 24-30 and 32-41, respectively. Cleveland then nominated Sen. Edward Douglas White of Louisiana, who was confirmed immediately—an example of the courtesy traditionally accorded by the Senate to one of its own members.

Theodore Roosevelt, like William McKinley before him, tried to avoid patronage fights with Congress. However, Roosevelt, an advocate of civil service reform, insisted on qualification standards for federal office. Members of Congress, he said, "may ordinarily name the man, but I shall name the standard and the men have got to come up to it."[11]

President William H. Taft recommended a massive extension of the Civil Service, to include postmasters and other field officers then subject to Senate confirmation, but Congress did not enact the necessary legislation.

Woodrow Wilson accepted William G. McAdoo's suggestion that he let his department heads handle distribution of patronage, a chore that traditionally had been undertaken by the President himself. Wilson generally tried to get along with the Senate and on occasion yielded to it in the interests of party harmony, but he suffered several notable rejections in contests over local offices.

Noteworthy Nomination Contests

The two most significant nomination contests during Wilson's administration resulted in the Senate's rejection of the appointment of George Rublee to the Federal Trade Commission and its confirmation of the nomination of Louis D. Brandeis as an associate justice of the Supreme Court.

Rublee was rejected in 1916, following a two-year fight led by Sen. Jacob H. Gallinger of New Hampshire, who opposed the nomination on the ground that it was "personally obnoxious" to him. Sen. Robert M. La Follette of Wisconsin deplored Gallinger's use of the "personally obnoxious" formula against a national appointment; it was the first such application of the rule, he said, since he had been in the Senate. Meanwhile, Rublee actually served on the FTC for a year and a half on a recess appointment.

The confirmation of Brandeis, also in 1916, ended one of the most dramatic appointment contests in the nation's history. The opposition to Brandeis, led by New England business groups that considered him a radical and a crusader because of his unpaid public activities, charged that he was untrustworthy and guilty of unethical conduct.

After four months of unusual open hearings by a Senate Judiciary subcommittee—hearings which were twice reopened—and with adjournment of Congress and the national political convention fast approaching, the full committee still had not acted on the nomination. Finally, after personal appeals by Brandeis and the President to doubtful members, the committee cleared the nomination by a 10-8 party-line vote. When the Senate voted June 1, Brandeis was confirmed, 47-22, and again the vote followed party lines.

Controversial Roosevelt Appointments

Franklin D. Roosevelt had few problems with appointments in his first years in office, but following the defeat of his court-packing plan and his unsuccessful effort to purge Democratic opponents in the 1938 primaries, difficulties increased.

The only major appointment controversy of his first term involved Rexford G. Tugwell, a member of the President's "brain trust" who was nominated in 1934 to the newly created post of under secretary of agriculture. Despite opposition based on his liberal philosophy, Tugwell was confirmed, 53-24. In Roosevelt's second term, many more appointees came under attack because of their allegedly radical views. Perhaps the most notable of the second-term contests involved Harry Hopkins, who won confirmation as Secretary of Commerce in 1939 only after a fight in which politics in the Works Progress Administration was the central issue. Hopkins was confirmed, 58-27, but a number of Democrats abstained.

Roosevelt's efforts to cut off patronage of Democratic senators who opposed his program had mixed success. He succeeded in disciplining Sens. Huey P. Long of Louisiana and Rush D. Holt of West Virginia but failed with Sens. Harry F. Byrd and Carter Glass of Virginia, Pat McCarran of Nevada and W. Lee O'Daniel of Texas—all of whom successfully invoked senatorial courtesy to defeat nominations they had not approved.

Of Roosevelt's eight nominees to the Supreme Court, only one—Hugo L. Black—faced serious opposition. Roosevelt appointed Black, a senator from Alabama who had vigorously supported New Deal programs, in 1937 following the defeat of the President's court-packing plan. Although it was traditional for the Senate to confirm one of its own members immediately without reference to committee, the Black nomination was sent to the Judiciary Committee—the first such action in 50 years. The nomination was cleared by the committee, 13-4, and the Senate, 66-15, after a debate punctuated by charges that Black had been a member of the Ku Klux Klan and had received Klan support in his 1926 election campaign. Black's confirmation did not end this controversy, and he finally made a public statement that he had once been a member of the Klan but had resigned and severed all ties with the organization.

Partisanship declined during World War II, and the President in the interests of national unity tried to avoid controversial nominations. Most of the emergency agencies were created by executive order, and their heads did not require Senate confirmation.

However, controversy erupted anew in 1945 with the appointment of Henry A. Wallace as Secretary of Commerce to succeed Jesse Jones. Wallace had been dumped from the Democratic ticket in 1944 because of conservative opposition to his "radical" economic views, but he had participated vigorously in the fall campaign and was expected to be rewarded with a Cabinet post. On Inauguration Day 1945, Roosevelt wrote to Jones asking him to step aside for Wallace. "Henry Wallace deserves almost any service which he believes he can satisfactorily perform," the letter said.[12]

Wallace's chief reason for wanting the Commerce post was that it would give him control of the vast lending powers of the Reconstruction Finance Corporation. However, before acting on the Wallace nomination, Congress passed legislation to remove the RFC from the Commerce Department and give it independent status. Jones, testifying on the bill, said the RFC should not be directed by a man who was willing to jeopardize the country's future with untried ideas and idealistic schemes."[13] Wallace, replying to charges that he was not qualified to supervise the RFC, said: "...it is not a question of my lack of experience. Rather, it is a case of not liking the experience I have."[14]

Following enactment of the RFC removal bill, the Senate on March 1 confirmed Wallace as Secretary of Commerce by a 56-32 vote. Ten Republicans joined 45

Democrats and one independent in voting for confirmation; five Democrats and 27 Republicans were opposed.

Truman's Battles With the Senate

President Harry S Truman engaged in a number of noteworthy contests with the Senate over appointments. Early in his administration he was widely criticized for appointing "cronies" to important offices. The 1946 appointments of George E. Allen to the RFC and James K. Vardaman to the Federal Reserve Board were subject to this charge, as was the 1949 appointment of Monrad C. Wallgren to the Federal Trade Commission. All three men were confirmed.

In 1946, Truman was forced, after a two-month fight, to withdraw the nomination of Edwin W. Pauley to be under secretary of the Navy. Pauley was a California oil man and former treasurer of the Democratic National Committee. In hearings before the Senate Naval Affairs Committee, the opposition, led by Sen. Charles W. Tobey of New Hampshire, presented witnesses who accused Pauley of having used political influence to protect his oil interests. Secretary of the Interior Harold L. Ickes said Pauley had told him, during the 1944 Presidential campaign, that $300,000 in campaign contributions from California oil men could be raised if the government would drop its suit to establish federal title to the tidewater oil lands. When Truman said at a press conference that Ickes might be mistaken, Ickes resigned his post, accusing the President of wanting him to commit perjury for the sake of the Democratic Party. Pauley denied categorically all the charges made against him and then asked the President to withdraw his nomination. The committee was reported to be divided 10-8 against him.

After the 1946 mid-term election, in which the Republicans won control of Congress, Truman tried to avoid controversy by nominating men who would be acceptable to the Senate. The Republican 80th Congress did not actually reject any of Truman's nominees, although 153 names were withdrawn. However, in 1948 the Senate took no action on 11,122 nominations—apparently in the expectation that a Republican President would be able to fill the vacancies with Republican nominees in 1949.

The two most explosive contests that did occur in the 80th Congress concerned nominees who had been named before the 1946 election, David E. Lilienthal and Gordon R. Clapp. In the autumn of 1946, Truman gave Lilienthal, chairman of the Tennessee Valley Authority, a recess appointment to the chairmanship of the newly created Atomic Energy Commission. He appointed Clapp, who had served under Lilienthal, to replace him as TVA chairman.

The opposition to both nominations was led by Sen. Kenneth McKellar (D) of Tennessee, who for years had been engaged in a patronage dispute with the TVA management. During the mid-1940s, McKellar had made several unsuccessful efforts to require Senate confirmation of all TVA employees earning $4,500 a year or more, and he resented TVA's insistence on a merit employment policy. Further, he had locked horns with TVA in 1941 over the location of a dam to be constructed in his state. Although he was not a member of the committees that considered the two nominations, McKellar conducted lengthy interrogations of witnesses and accused both Lilienthal and Clapp of having Communist sympathies. When the nominations finally reached the floor in April 1947, Lilienthal was confirmed, 50-31, and Clapp, 36-31. During the debate on Clapp, McKellar complained that the President had appointed him "without saying beans to me" and declared that he was "hurt beyond expression" that his colleagues should vote for nominees he opposed.[15]

In 1949, President Truman met two outright defeats at the hands of the Senate. Leland Olds, nominated to a third term as member of the Federal Power Commission, was rejected, 15-53, in the face of opposition by oil and natural gas interests. Opponents, led by Sen. Lyndon B. Johnson of Texas, cited articles Olds had written in the 1920s for the labor press as evidence of Communist leanings. As a member of the FPC, Olds had played a key role in the development of federal regulation of natural gas.

The other 1949 rejection was that of Carl A. Ilgenfritz, who refused to take the chairmanship of the Munitions Board (salary: $14,000) unless he could retain his $70,000 annual salary as a steel executive. The Senate rejected him, 28-40.

Senatorial courtesy played a role in several Truman defeats at the hands of the Senate. In 1950 the Senate rejected, 14-59, the nomination of Martin A. Hutchinson as a member of the Federal Trade Commission. Hutchinson, a foe of Virginia's Byrd machine, was opposed by Sens. Byrd and A. Willis Robertson of that state. In 1951 Sen. Paul H. Douglas of Illinois successfully appealed to the courtesy of the Senate to defeat two of President Truman's choices for federal district judgeships in Illinois. Douglas said the President should have nominated two candidates recommended by him.

One of the plums of congressional patronage came to an end in 1952. President Truman proposed, and Congress accepted, a reorganization plan putting all Internal Revenue Bureau jobs except that of commissioner under Civil Service. The action followed 1951 congressional hearings on scandals in the bureau. The Senate, however, defeated other reorganization plans to put postmasters, customs officials and U.S. marshals under Civil Service.

Eisenhower, Kennedy Appointments

At the outset of his administration in 1953, President Eisenhower was criticized by conservative Republicans who contended that his Cabinet selections failed to give appropriate recognition to the Taft wing of the party. The President also gave his department and agency heads free rein to select their own subordinates, but when Republican leaders in the Senate complained that their suggestions were being ignored and that even the customary clearances were not being obtained, the senators were invited to take their recommendations directly to the department heads. Subsequently, more appointments went to Taft supporters.

Several of Eisenhower's early nominations were opposed on conflict-of-interest grounds. The most celebrated of these cases was the nomination of Charles E. Wilson as Secretary of Defense. Wilson, former president of General Motors, was required to divest himself of all GM stock before the Senate Armed Services Committee consented to recommend his confirmation. Wilson had not planned to give up his stock. Similar issues arose with the nominations of Harold E. Talbott as secretary of the Air Force and Robert T. Stevens as secretary of the Army. From this time on, the Senate showed a continuing preoccupation with conflict-of-interest issues in the consideration of presidential nominations.

Confirmations

One of Eisenhower's subsequent Cabinet nominations was defeated in the Senate in 1959—the first such rejection since 1925. Lewis L. Strauss already was serving under a recess appointment when, after months of hearings, the Senate rejected his nomination as Secretary of Commerce by a 46-49 vote. Opponents accused Strauss of lack of integrity and criticized his conservative approach to government. Specific issues raised against him included his role in the Dixon-Yates power contract, viewed by public power advocates as an attempt to undermine the Tennessee Valley Authority; his actions in the J. Robert Oppenheimer security case; and his alleged withholding of information, while chairman of the Atomic Energy Commission, from Congress and the public.

Of President Eisenhower's five appointees to the Supreme Court, three took their seats on the Court under recess appointments before they had been confirmed by the Senate. Chief Justice Earl Warren was unanimously confirmed in 1954 after publication of a 10-point summary of charges against him, including allegations that he was at one time connected with a liquor lobbyist and that he lacked judicial experience. William J. Brennan Jr. was confirmed by voice vote in 1957 after Sen. Joseph R. McCarthy protested that Brennan had compared congressional investigations of Communists to Salem witch hunts. Potter Stewart was confirmed in 1959, on a 70-17 vote; all opponents were southern Democrats, who criticized Stewart's concurrence in the Supreme Court's 1954 school desegregation decision.

In 1960, the Senate adopted, 48-37, a Democratic resolution expressing the sense of the Senate that the President should not make recess appointments to the Supreme Court, except to prevent or end a breakdown in the administration of the court's business; and that a recess appointee should not take his seat on the court until the Senate had "advised and consented" to the nomination. Proponents claimed it was difficult to investigate the qualifications of a person already sitting on the court; opponents charged that the Democrats hoped for a victory in the 1960 presidential election and feared that a vacancy might occur on the court before January, enabling the Republican President to give a recess appointment to a Republican.

Efforts of the Democratic-controlled Congress to keep judicial appointments out of the hands of the Republican President also led to a four-year delay in enacting legislation to create an unprecedented number of new circuit and district court judgeships. Proposed by Eisenhower in 1957, the bill did not become law until after President Kennedy took office in 1961. The 73 judgeships created by this law, plus 42 judgeship vacancies created by death or resignation, gave Kennedy in his first year in office the largest number of judicial appointments ever available to a President in a single year.

Kennedy participated far more actively than Eisenhower had done in the selection of appointees. Although recruitment of candidates for federal office was carried out by a well publicized talent hunt, some care was taken to clear appointments with appropriate members of Congress.

None of Kennedy's nominations was rejected by the Senate, and few were contested. His two nominees to the Supreme Court — Byron R. White and Arthur J. Goldberg in 1962 — were confirmed without difficulty.

Racial issues figured in several confirmation contests. Despite southern opposition, Robert C. Weaver was confirmed in 1961 by voice vote as administrator of the Housing and Home Finance Agency. Weaver, a black, had been national chairman of the National Association for the Advancement of Colored People. Similarly, Spottswood W. Robinson III, dean of the Howard University Law School, and a black, was confirmed as a member of the Civil Rights Commission. (He was named a U.S. district court judge in 1964 and a member of the U.S. Court of Appeals for the District of Columbia Circuit in 1966.) But Kennedy's nomination of Thurgood Marshall, a civil rights lawyer, to the Second Circuit Court of Appeals was held up by the Senate Judiciary Committee for a year. Marshall was confirmed in 1962, 54-16, with all the dissenting votes cast by southern Democrats. (Marshall in 1967 became the first black member of the Supreme Court.)

Fight Over Fortas

Lyndon B. Johnson, with one dramatic exception, had very little trouble with the Senate over nominations. His cabinet appointees were confirmed without difficulty, and his first two Supreme Court appointments encountered only routine opposition.

The nomination of Abe Fortas to be an associate justice was confirmed by voice vote in 1965, although three Republicans raised objections on the floor that he had reportedly asked Washington newspaper editors to delay release of a story that presidential aide Walter W. Jenkins had been arrested on a morals charge shortly before the 1964 presidential election.

In 1967, President Johnson nominated Thurgood Marshall, then Solicitor General, to be the first black associate justice of the Supreme Court. Despite criticism from some senators of Marshall's stated belief in an activist judiciary, his nomination was confirmed 69-11. Ten southern Democrats and one northern Democrat voted against him.

However, in 1968 Johnson was unsuccessful in his effort to elevate Fortas to Chief Justice in place of Earl Warren who sought to retire. The Fortas nomination finally was withdrawn in the face of a Senate filibuster, and Warren agreed to remain on the court through the 1968-69 term—thus assuring that his successor would be appointed by the incoming President. Johnson's nomination of Judge Homer Thornberry of the Fifth Circuit Court of Appeals to replace Fortas as associate justice was not acted on.

The fight against Fortas was led by Sen. Robert P. Griffin of Michigan. He charged that the appointment was based on "cronyism" and that Warren had timed his retirement to assure appointment of his successor by a Democratic President. The "lame duck" charge gave way to more serious questions of propriety in the course of hearings held by the Judiciary Committee between July 11 and Sept. 16. One was the question of Fortas' continued involvement in White House affairs after he went on the court in 1965, an involvement that Fortas admitted but played down in his testimony before the committee. Toward the end of the hearings, it was disclosed that Fortas had received a fee of $15,000 for conducting a nine-week law seminar at American University in the summer of 1968. The money for the fee and other seminar expenses had come from five former business associates, one of whom had a son who was involved in a federal criminal case. During the hearings, as in the subsequent floor debate, attacks were made on the court in general and on Fortas in particular for decisions on criminal procedural law and obscenity.

By an 11-6 vote, Sept. 17, 1968, the Judiciary Committee ordered the Fortas nomination reported to the Senate with the recommendation that it be confirmed. The majority, made up of eight Democrats and three Republicans, described Fortas as "extraordinarily well qualified for the post"[16] of Chief Justice.

In the floor debate, which began Sept. 25, Sen. Griffin pressed the attack relentlessly, and as his following grew, the chances of confirmation became more remote. They virtually vanished Sept. 27 when Minority Leader Everett McKinley Dirksen reversed his position and announced that he was officially neutral. Majority Leader Mike Mansfield moved to end what was plainly a filibuster by reading to the Senate, Sept. 29, a cloture motion signed by 26 senators. The motion was rejected Oct. 1 by a roll-call vote of 45-43, which was 14 votes short of the 59 needed for cloture. The next day Fortas asked the President to withdraw his name. Terming the action of the Senate "tragic," Johnson consented. Renewed controversy over Fortas' extra-judicial activities led to his resignation from the court in 1969. He was the first justice in history to step down under threat of impeachment.

A further diminution of senatorial patronage occurred during the Johnson administration, when Congress acceded to a presidential reorganization plan placing the Customs Bureau on a career, Civil Service basis. Previously, appointments of customs collectors and other officers had been made by the President, generally on senators' recommendations. President Johnson submitted the reorganization plan in 1965, and it was allowed to go into effect. A Senate resolution disapproving the plan was rejected, 17-64.

Nixon's Appointments

Early in his first year in office, President Nixon cut off another source of congressional patronage. He said he was ending the patronage system of appointing postmasters and rural letter carriers, and that henceforth high scores on competitive examinations would be the sole criterion for filling the posts.

The system of choosing postmasters from among the three highest scorers on competitive examinations already was in effect. However, under past practice, the preferred candidate of a member of Congress or party official was allowed to repeat the test until he gained a place among the top three. Under the new system, the test would be given only once, and the postmaster general would select from among the three leading scorers. Members of Congress would still be consulted, but their recommendations would not necessarily be followed.

Nixon also sought congressional approval of legislation to end presidential appointment and senatorial confirmation of first, second and third-class postmasters. The Senate passed the bill in 1969, but the House did not act. This goal was achieved in the Postal Reorganization Act of 1970, which eliminated all political influence in the selection of postal employees, including postmasters.

President Nixon's early appointments to major policy posts were confirmed with little difficulty, although Interior Secretary Walter J. Hickel's confirmation was delayed briefly in the face of opposition from conservation groups and Deputy Defense Secretary David Packard's confirmation raised conflict-of-interest questions.

Appointments that were never made also generated controversy. Dr. John H. Knowles was slated to get the job of assistant secretary of Health, Education and Welfare for health and scientific affairs, but the proposed nomination was blocked after opposition was voiced by Senate Minority Leader Dirksen and the American Medical Association. Franklin Long was rejected for appointment to head the National Science Foundation because of his opposition to the ABM nuclear defense system.

Nixon Court Nominees

These controversies paled by comparison with the struggles that arose over President Nixon's efforts to fill one of two vacancies on the Supreme Court. His first court nomination, that of Warren E. Burger to replace retiring Chief Justice Warren, was confirmed quickly by a 74-3 vote of the Senate. Burger, a judge of the Court of Appeals for the District of Columbia Circuit, appeared to meet Nixon's standard of judicial conservatism.

It was with his next court nomination that Nixon ran into a confrontation with the Senate. In May 1969, Associate Justice Fortas resigned under fire for accepting an outside fee from the family foundation of a convicted stock manipulator. To fill the vacancy, Nixon in August nominated Clement F. Haynsworth Jr. of South Carolina, chief judge of the Fourth Circuit Court of Appeals.

Haynsworth was opposed by labor and civil rights leaders, but as in the Fortas case the debate centered on judicial ethics. Foes of the nomination, led by Democratic Sen: Birch Bayh of Indiana, repeatedly said they did not question Haynsworth's honesty or integrity. But they did question his sensitivity to the appearance of ethical impropriety and his judgment regarding participation in cases in which his financial interests could be said to be involved, if only indirectly.

During committee hearings in September, Haynsworth, his financial affairs and his judicial record were scrutinized more thoroughly and extensively than those of any other court nominee before him. The Judiciary Committee approved the nomination, Oct. 9 by a 10-7 vote. The 10-man majority asserted that Haynsworth was "extraordinarily well qualified" for the court post and that the objections raised to his nomination were without substance.[17]

Notwithstanding growing opposition, the President remained steadfast in his refusal to withdraw the nomination. Political pressure to influence the final vote was exerted by both sides. After a week's debate, the Senate on Nov. 21 rejected the Haynsworth nomination by a 45-55 roll-call vote. Republican defections played a decisive role in the outcome. Seventeen Republicans, including the three top GOP leaders in the Senate, joined 38 Democrats in voting against confirmation. Twenty-six Republicans and 19 Democrats—16 of them from the South—voted for it.

Early in 1970, President Nixon tried once more to fill the Supreme Court vacancy. This time he nominated another southerner, G. Harrold Carswell of Florida, a judge of the Fifth Circuit Court of Appeals. Few senators wanted a repetition of the Haynsworth fight, and opposition to Carswell developed slowly. However, when it came to light that Carswell in a 1948 campaign speech had pledged himself to the principle of white supremacy, resistance to the nomination began to build. Carswell repudiated the views he had expressed more than 20 years earlier, but further charges of a continuing racist attitude were raised against him. Other critics, including many within his own profession, contended that Carswell was a man of mediocre abilities who lacked the judicial competence requisite for service on the High Court.

Carswell won the Judiciary Committee's approval, Feb. 16, 1970, by a vote of 13-4. But when the nomination moved to the Senate floor in March, opponents succeeded in delaying the final vote until after the Easter recess. When the Senate returned to consideration of the nomination at the beginning of April, the opposing sides remained closely matched and the outcome was in doubt.

In this atmosphere, Nixon wrote a letter to a pro-Carswell Republican senator declaring that rejection of the nomination would impair his constitutional responsibility and the constitutional relationship of the President to Congress.

Nixon said he respected the right of any senator to differ with his selection. However, he stated: "The fact remains, under the Constitution, it is the duty of the President to appoint and of the Senate to advise and consent. But if the Senate attempts to substitute its judgment as to who should be appointed, the traditional constitutional balance is in jeopardy and the duty of the President under the Constitution impaired."[18]

By agreement, the first Senate vote on Carswell came April 6, on a motion to recommit the nomination to the Judiciary Committee. Opponents had hoped originally to defeat the appointment indirectly by burying the matter in committee, but the recommittal effort became instead a diversionary tactic, a preliminary skirmish that was won by the administration. The recommittal move was rejected, 44-52.

After two days of intensive lobbying, the final vote on Carswell was taken April 8, and the nomination was rejected 45-51. Thirteen Republicans joined 38 Democrats, five of them from the South, in opposition. Not since 1894 had a President suffered similar consecutive rejections of two nominees to a Supreme Court seat.

Nixon responded to the Senate's action with an angry statement that he had "reluctantly" decided that the Senate "as presently constituted" would not confirm a judicial conservative from the South. Thus, he said, he would go elsewhere for his next nominee.[19]

Less than a week later, on April 14, the President nominated Harry A. Blackmun of Minnesota, a judge of the Eighth Circuit Court of Appeals, to fill the Supreme Court vacancy. Blackmun had a reputation as a moderate and scholarly judge, and both liberals and conservatives praised the President's selection. The Senate Judiciary Committee unanimously reported the nomination May 9, and the Senate confirmed it May 12 by a 94-0 vote.

In 1971, President Nixon nominated and the Senate confirmed Lewis F. Powell Jr. and William H. Rehnquist as associate justices of the Supreme Court. Powell acceded to the seat left vacant by the resignation of Hugo Black. Rehnquist took the seat vacated by the resignation of John Marshall Harlan. Both men retired because of poor health. Not since Warren G. Harding had one President, in his first term, had the opportunity to appoint so many members of the Supreme Court. Nixon's four appointees put a decidedly more conservative stamp on the court.

The impact of Nixon's appointments to the courts and regulatory agencies was expected to be felt for many years after the Watergate crisis forced him to resign the presidency on Aug. 9, 1974. In addition to his Supreme Court appointments, he named 215 judges to the lower courts of the federal judicial system. Nixon appointees (or persons named by previous presidents whom he reappointed) dominated the twelve regulatory agencies.

By the day of his resignation, Nixon had nominated all members of eight regulatory agencies: the five members of the Civil Aeronautics Board, the seven members of the Federal Communications Commission, the five members of the Federal Maritime Commission, the five members of the Federal Power Commission, the five members of the National Labor Relations Board, the three members of the National Mediation Board, the five members of the Securities and Exchange Commission and the five members of the Consumer Product Safety Commission.

Ford's Appointments

President Ford encountered no opposition strong enough to lead to the rejection of his Cabinet appointees and nominee to the Supreme Court in 1975. However, three of his appointments to government boards were rejected by Senate committees within two weeks in late 1975. The rejections in two cases were based upon objections to the nominee's social philosophy and in another to a conflict-of-interest.

A number of Cabinet changes were made during President Ford's first 15 months in office until only Agriculture Secretary Earl L. Butz, Secretary of State Henry A. Kissinger and Treasury Secretary William E. Simon remained from the Nixon administration.

Only one of Ford's Cabinet nominations was highly controversial. Stanley K. Hathaway, who was appointed Secretary of the Interior, was attacked by liberal senators and environmental groups for what they considered a pro-development and anti-conservation record as governor of Wyoming. Hathaway was confirmed in June of 1975 by a 60-36 vote after five days of hearings by the Senate Interior Committee. But he resigned July 25 "for reasons of personal health."

Ford's selection for the Supreme Court, federal Appeals Judge John Paul Stevens, was speedily confirmed Dec. 17 after his nomination Nov. 28, 1975, to fill the seat left vacant by the retirement of William O. Douglas.

The Senate Commerce Committee Nov. 13, 1975, killed the renomination of Isabel A. Burgess to a second five-year term on the National Transportation Safety Board. Opposition to her developed when a committee staff report showed that she had purchased stock in an airline regulated by the board and accepted free transportation, meals and lodging from other regulated companies. She also had unusually high travel expenses and absenteeism.

One day earlier, the Senate Banking, Housing and Urban Affairs Committee rejected the nomination of former Rep. Ben B. Blackburn (R Ga. 1967-75) to be chairman of the Federal Home Loan Bank Board. Foes of the nomination objected to his negative attitude toward blacks and public housing tenants and his opposition to civil rights legislation during his years in the House. The Senate Commerce Committee Oct. 30 tabled, and thus killed, the nomination of Colorado beer executive Joseph Coors to the board of the Corporation for Public Broadcasting (CPB). The question of a possible conflict of interest based upon

Coors' membership on the board of Television News, Inc. (TVN) and his conservative political philosophy led to the committee's action.

In 1974, President Ford withdrew four controversial nominations. Two were holdovers from the Nixon administration. Ford withdrew his nomination of Andrew E. Gibson to be federal energy administrator following the publication of reports that he had been promised $880,000 in severance pay from his former employer, an oil shipping company with interests related to matters he would have to monitor. He also did not resubmit three other controversial nominations after the October-November congressional election recess. Under Senate Rule 38, any nomination must be resubmitted when the Senate adjourns or is in recess for more than 30 days. The nominations not resubmitted were those of Peter M. Flanigan to be ambassador to Spain, Stanton B. Anderson to be ambassador to Costa Rica, and Daniel T. Kingsley to be a member of the Federal Power Commission. Anderson and Kingsley had been nominated by Nixon.

Chapter 20

Power of Removal

Controversy over the role of the Senate in the removal of public officers began in the early days of the Republic and continued intermittently into the 20th century.

The Constitution contained no language governing removals except for the impeachment provisions of Article II, Section 4. Hamilton, writing in *The Federalist* (No. 77), contended that the consent of the Senate "would be necessary to displace as well as to appoint," but this view was soon challenged and rejected by Congress.[20]

Debate over the power of removal began in the First Congress, during consideration of a bill to establish the Department of Foreign Affairs. Two principal theories were advanced. One group insisted that since the Constitution gave the Senate a share in the appointment power, the Senate must also give its advice and consent to removals. The other group, led by Madison, maintained that the power of removal was an executive function, necessarily implied in the power to nominate, and that Senate participation would violate the principle of separation of powers.

Madison's view prevailed in the House, which passed the bill by a 29-22 vote after striking out language specifically vesting removal power in the President and substituting a provision that deliberately implied recognition of the President's exclusive power of removal under the Constitution.

After a lengthy and spirited debate in closed session, the Senate narrowly acceded to the House interpretation. A motion to strike out the House language recognizing the President's sole power of removal was rejected on a tie vote, with Vice President Adams—voting for the first time—recorded in opposition. The fact that the Senate agreed to limit its own powers was widely attributed to senatorial respect for President Washington.

Early Presidents exercised great restraint in use of the removal power, even after the enactment in 1820 of the "Four Years" law. This law, ostensibly designed to ensure accountability of federal officers, established a fixed four-year term for district attorneys, customs collectors and many other officers who previously had served at the pleasure of the President.

Presidents James Monroe and John Quincy Adams followed a policy of renominating all such persons when their terms expired unless they had been guilty of misconduct. However, senatorial pressure for patronage was on the rise, and Adams' self-restraint was met by Senate demands for a broader role in appointments and removals.

Jackson's Clashes With Senate

Andrew Jackson's sweeping and partisan use of the removal power soon brought renewed Senate demands for an increased share in the patronage pie. Controversy over the issue led to a series of Senate resolutions requesting the President to inform the Senate of his reasons for removing various officials. Jackson complied with several of these requests, but by 1835 he had had enough. A Senate resolution, adopted by a 23-22 vote, requesting information on the "charges, if any," against the recently removed surveyor general of South Tennessee brought the following response:

"It is now, however, my solemn conviction that I ought no longer, from any motive, nor in any degree, to yield to these unconstitutional demands. Their continued repetition imposes on me, as the representative and trustee of the American people, the painful but imperious duty of resisting to the utmost any further encroachment on the rights of the Executive.... The President in cases of this nature possesses the exclusive power of removal from office; and under the sanctions of his official oath, and of his liability to impeachment, he is bound to exercise it whenever the public welfare shall require. On no principle known to our institutions can he be required to account for the manner in which he discharges this portion of his public duties, save only in the mode and under the forms prescribed by the Constitution."[21]

Meanwhile, the Senate had appointed a committee "to inquire into the extent of Executive patronage; the circumstances which contributed to its increase of late; the expediency and practicability of reducing the same, and the means of such reduction."[22] The committee reported a bill to repeal the first two sections of the Four Years Law and to require the President to submit to the Senate the reasons for each removal. John Quincy Adams called this an effort "to cut down the executive power of the president and to grasp it for the Senate."[23] Supported by Calhoun, Webster and Clay, the measure won Senate approval, 31-16, but was never taken up in the House. Webster and Clay disputed the interpretation of the removal power established by the First Congress. Attributing that interpretation largely to congressional confidence in President Washington, Clay said it had not been reconsidered only because prior to Jackson's administration it had not been abused.

Presidential Opposition to Tenure Acts

The next great clash between Senate and President over the removal power occurred in the administration of Andrew Johnson. Among its consequences were the Tenure of Office Act of 1867 and Johnson's impeachment trial.

The conflict grew out of Johnson's fight with the radical Republican leaders of Congress over reconstruction policy and his use of the removal power to make places for his own followers.

As passed by the Senate, the Tenure of Office bill enabled civil officers, excluding members of the Cabinet, appointed by and with the advice and consent of the Senate, to remain in office until their successors were appointed by the President and confirmed by the Senate. It permitted the President to suspend an officer during a recess of the Senate and appoint a temporary successor but provided that the suspended officer should resume his post if the Senate failed to approve the suspension. The Senate rejected an amendment to delete the clause excluding Cabinet members, as well as one to require Senate confirmation of the appointment of all officers with salaries exceeding $1,000. However, the House deleted the exclusion for Cabinet members, and in conference it was agreed that Cabinet members should hold office for the term of the President who appointed them and for one month thereafter, subject to removal by and with the advice and consent of the Senate.

President Johnson vetoed the bill on the ground that it would unconstitutionally restrict the President's power of removal, but Congress enacted the measure over the veto—by a 35-11 vote in the Senate and a 133-37 vote in the House.

Johnson promptly put the Tenure of Office Act to the test. First, he suspended Secretary of War Stanton, but the Senate refused to concur in the suspension. Johnson then attempted to dismiss Stanton and make another appointment to the post. The House immediately initiated impeachment proceedings, the principal charge being that Johnson had violated the new law by dismissing Stanton. On this charge, the Senate failed to convict by only one vote; seven Republicans and 12 Democrats voted for acquittal, while 35 Republicans voted for conviction. A two-thirds majority was required to convict.

Early in Grant's administration in 1869, Congress amended the Tenure of Office Act by repealing its provisions regulating suspensions. The new law provided that the President might suspend officers "in his discretion"—without, as before, reporting to the Senate the reasons for his action—but required prompt nomination of successors.[24] A further dispute between President Cleveland and the Republican controlled Senate finally led to repeal of what was left of the Tenure of Office Act of 1867 and of the amended 1869 version.

While Congress was in recess in the summer of 1885, Cleveland suspended 643 officers subject to senatorial confirmation. When Congress reconvened, he submitted to the Senate the names of their replacements to whom he had given recess appointments. The committees handling these nominations then called upon the executive departments for information concerning the reasons for the suspensions, information which the departments refused to give. Action on the nominations was stalled by the dispute.

The climax to the controversy came over the nomination of a U.S. attorney in Alabama. The Justice Department refused demands by the Senate Judiciary Committee for information concerning the reasons for removal of his predecessor. The Senate responded with a resolution, adopted on a party-line vote, censuring the Attorney General for his refusal to transmit the desired papers. A second resolution, adopted by a one-vote margin, said it was "the duty of the Senate to refuse its advice and consent to proposed removals of officers" in cases where information requested by the Senate was withheld.[25]

The Senate debated the resolutions heatedly over a two-week period. While they were pending, Cleveland sent a special message to the Senate reasserting the President's authority:

"The requests and demands which by the score have for nearly three months been presented to the different departments of the government, whatever their form, have but one complexion. They assume the right of the Senate to sit in judgment upon the exercise of my exclusive function, for which I am solely responsible to the people from whom I have so lately received the sacred trust of office....

"The pledges I have made were made to the people, and to them I am responsible. I am not responsible to the Senate, and I am unwilling to submit my actions and official conduct to them for judgment...."[26]

Public opinion responded to the President's message, and the nomination logjam was broken. The following year Sen. E. R. Hoar (R Mass.) introduced legislation to repeal the Tenure of Office Acts, and the bill was speedily enacted into law.

Wilson and Coolidge on Removals

Another big controversy over the removal power occurred in 1920, when President Wilson vetoed the forerunner of the Budget and Accounting Act of 1921. That measure, as transmitted to Wilson, provided that the comptroller general and assistant comptroller general were to be appointed by the President subject to Senate confirmation, but were to be subject to removal by concurrent resolution of Congress. A concurrent resolution does not require the President's approval; thus the President would have had no control over the removal of these officers. Wilson's veto message was emphatic:

"I am convinced that the Congress is without constitutional power to limit the appointing power and its incident power of removal derived from the Constitution."[27]

The following year, the Budget and Accounting Act of 1921 became law with the signature of President Harding. The final legislation, however, differed from the 1920 version in providing for removal of the comptroller general and assistant comptroller general by joint resolution, which requires the signature of the President, or passage over his veto, to go into effect.

Senate pressure for a role in removals does not always take the form of resistance to removals desired by the President. The Senate also has attempted to force removals, although without notable success. President Lincoln was able to head off efforts by a caucus of Republican senators to force the resignation of Secretary of State Seward in 1862. More recently, in 1924, the Senate adopted a resolution "that it is the sense of the United States Senate that the President of the United States immediately request the resignation of Edwin Denby as secretary of the Navy."[28] Denby had been implicated in the naval oil lease scandals, and Senate Democrats hoped to press similar resolutions against other members of President Coolidge's Cabinet. The Denby resolution was adopted on a 47-34 roll call and a copy was sent to the President. Coolidge promptly issued a statement:

"No official recognition can be given to the passage of the Senate resolution relative to their opinion concerning members of the cabinet or other officers under executive control....

"The dismissal of an officer of the government, such as is involved in this case, other than by impeachment, is exclusively an executive function."[29]

A few days later Denby resigned.

Another Senate removal effort, with a different twist, involved appointees to the newly created Federal Power Commission during the 71st Congress. Dissatisfied with the actions of FPC members it had confirmed shortly before the Christmas recess, the Senate in January 1931 tried to recall the nominations for reconsideration. President Hoover refused, saying:

"I am advised that these appointments were constitutionally made, with the consent of the Senate, formally communicated to me, and that the return of the documents by me and reconsideration by the Senate would be ineffective to disturb the appointees in their offices."[30]

Court Decisions on Removal Power

The courts upheld the President. After nearly 140 years of controversy over the President's power of removal, the Supreme Court had finally met the issue head on in 1926. In the words of Chief Justice Taft, the court had "studiously avoided deciding the issue until it was presented in such a way that it could not be avoided."[31]

The case involved a postmaster who had been removed from office by President Wilson in 1920, without consultation with the Senate, although the 1876 law under which the man had been appointed stipulated: "Postmasters of the first, second and third classes shall be appointed and may be removed by the President, by and with the advice and consent of the Senate, and shall hold their offices for four years, unless sooner removed or suspended according to law."[32]

In a 6-3 decision, the court upheld in 1926 the President's unrestricted power of removal as inherent in the executive power invested in him by the Constitution. The court concluded: "It therefore follows that the Tenure of Office Act of 1867, in so far as it attempted to prevent the President from removing executive officers who had been appointed by him by and with the consent of the Senate was invalid, and that subsequent legislation of the same effect was equally so.... The provision of the law of 1876, by which the unrestricted power of removal of first-class postmasters is denied to the President, is in violation of the Constitution and invalid."[33] *(Myers v. U.S.,* 272 U.S. 52)

In a unanimous 1935 decision, the court modified this position. The 1935 case involved a Federal Trade Commissioner whom President Roosevelt had tried to remove because "I do not feel that your mind and my mind go along together on either the policies or the administration"[34] of the FTC. The court held that the FTC was "an administrative body created by Congress to carry into effect legislative policies" and thus could not "in any proper sense be characterized as an arm or an eye of the Executive." It continued:

"Whether the power of the President to remove an officer shall prevail over the authority of Congress to condition the power by fixing a definite term and precluding a removal except for cause will depend upon the character of the office; the Myers decision, affirming the power of the President alone to make the removal, is confined to purely executive officers, and as to officers of the kind here under consideration, we hold that no removal can be made during the prescribed term for which the officer is appointed, except for one or more of the causes named in the applicable statute.[35] *(Humphrey's Executor v. U.S.,* 295 U.S. 602)

In ruling that Roosevelt had exceeded his authority in removing Humphrey, the court indicated that except for certain types of officials (such as those immediately responsible to the President and those exercising non-discretionary or ministerial functions), Congress could apply such limitations on removal as it chose.

In a later decision *(Wiener v. U.S.,* 357 U.S. 349), the court built on the *Humphrey* decision. That case involved the refusal of a member of the War Claims Commission, named by President Truman, to resign when the Eisenhower administration came to power so that a Republican could be named to the position.

Congress created the commission with "jurisdiction to receive and adjudicate according to law" certain damage claims resulting from World War II. The law made no provision for removal of commissioners.

Wiener was removed by the new President and sought his pay in court. The Supreme Court agreed with him. It noted the similarity between the *Wiener* and *Humphrey* cases: in both situations, Presidents had removed persons from quasi-judicial agencies without showing cause for the sole purpose of naming persons of their own choosing. The court said it understood the *Humphrey* decision to "draw a sharp line of cleavage between officials who were part of the executive establishment and were thus removable by virtue of the President's constitutional powers, and those who are members of a body 'to exercise its judgment without the leave or hindrance of any other official or any department of the government,'...as to whom a power of removal exists only if Congress may fairly be said to have conferred it. This sharp differentiation derives from the difference in functions between those who are part of the executive establishment and those whose tasks require absolute freedom from executive interference." The court also noted the "intrinsic judicial character" of the commission.

As a result of this case and the *Myers* and *Humphrey* cases, the rule has developed that a President can remove a member of a quasi-judicial agency only for cause, even if Congress has not so provided. This is a major limitation on a President's normal power of removal that may be exercised at his discretion.

Nomination Procedures

It has been customary since the time of Washington for the President to submit nominations to the Senate in written form. By exception, Harding in 1921 proceeded directly from the inaugural ceremonies to the Senate chamber to present his Cabinet nominations in person.

Before submitting a nomination the President normally consults with key members of Congress, political organizations and special interest groups in an effort to obtain informal clearance for his candidate. Because the President usually wants to avoid a confirmation fight, serious opposition at this stage may lead him to choose another person for the post.

In recent years the Federal Bureau of Investigation has conducted investigations of potential candidates, and there have been frequent controversies between the President and the Senate over access to FBI reports. Potential Supreme Court nominees have been evaluated by the American Bar Association's standing committee on the federal judiciary. President Nixon abandoned this procedure in 1969 but decided to return to it in 1970, after the Haynsworth and Carswell defeats.

Committee Hearings

Since 1868, most nominations have been referred to committee. The committee, or a subcommittee, may hold hearings at which the nominee and others may testify. Most such hearings are purely routine, although some turn into grueling inquisitions. Nominees have been known to ask the

President to withdraw their names rather than face such an ordeal.

Until 30 years or so ago, it was unusual for Supreme Court nominees to be invited to appear before the Judiciary Committee. Felix Frankfurter, who received such an invitation in 1939, noted that on only one previous occasion had a Supreme Court nominee testified before the committee. Frankfurter originally declined the committee's invitation but later appeared at the committee's request. Ten years later the committee by a 5-4 vote invited court nominee Sherman Minton to appear before it, but when Minton questioned the propriety of such an appearance, the committee reversed itself and reported the nomination favorably to the Senate. These precedents notwithstanding, in recent years Supreme Court nominees have been expected to testify at hearings on their nominations. Justice Abe Fortas in 1968 became the first nominee for chief justice ever to appear before the committee and the first sitting justice, except for recess appointees, ever to do so.

When hearings on a nomination have been completed, the subcommittee votes and sends the nomination to the full committee. The committee may report the nomination favorably, unfavorably or without recommendation, or it may simply take no action at all. Nominations that fail to gain approval usually meet defeat at this stage.

Floor Action. Nominations that reach the floor are called up on the executive calendar, frequently en bloc, and usually are approved without objection. The question takes the following form: "Will the Senate advise and consent to this nomination?"[36] Controversial nominations may be debated at length, but few nominations are brought to the floor unless sufficient votes for confirmation can be mustered.

Since 1929, Senate rules (Rule 38) have provided that nominations shall be considered in open session unless the Senate, in closed session and by majority vote, decides to consider a particular nomination in closed session. In such a case any senator is permitted to make public his own vote.

Prior to 1929, the customary practice was to consider nominations in closed executive session, and the votes taken were not supposed to be made public.

Nominations may not be put to a vote on the day they are received or on the day they are reported from committee, except by unanimous consent. They may be approved, rejected or returned to committee.

All nominations still pending at the end of the session in which they are made die with that session. If the Senate recesses or adjourns for more than 30 days, all pending nominations must be returned to the President; they cannot be considered again unless he resubmits them.

When a nomination has been confirmed or rejected, a motion to reconsider may be made on the day the vote is taken or on either of the next two days of actual executive session.

Recess Appointments

Recess appointments present special problems. The Constitution provides that "the President shall have power to fill up all vacancies that may happen during the recess of the Senate, by granting commissions which shall expire at the end of their next session." *(Article II, Section 2)*

The ambiguities of this section have produced repeated controversies between the President and the Senate. Chief point at issue is the constitutional meaning of the word "happen." If it means "happen to occur," then the President can only fill offices that become vacant after the Senate adjourns. If it means "happen to exist," he can fill any vacancy, whatever the cause.[37]

President Washington, taking a strict view of his powers, sought specific Senate authorization to make recess appointments of military officers created by a bill enacted near the end of a session. Madison opted for a broad construction. His recess appointment of envoys to negotiate a peace treaty with Great Britain brought outcries from the Senate that a recess appointment could not be made to an office never before filled. However, resolutions protesting Madison's action never came to a vote, and the appointments ultimately were confirmed.

Although the recess appointment debate continued for years, it gradually became accepted that the President could make recess appointments to fill any vacancies, no matter how they arose. However, federal law prohibits payment of salary to any person appointed during a recess of the Senate to fill an existing vacancy, if the vacancy existed while the Senate was in session, until the appointee has been confirmed by the Senate. This prohibition does not apply if the vacancy occurred during the last 30 days of the session, or if the Senate failed to act on a nomination submitted to it before adjournment.

PART VII
Amending Power

Chapter 21

The Constitutional Convention

It was the difficulty of adapting the Articles of Confederation to changing conditions—a process which required unanimous approval of amendments by the states, as well as the consent of the Continental Congress—which led to the framing of the Constitution. In drafting the amending provision, the delegates to the Philadelphia Convention of 1787 had little to serve as a guide. Six of the 13 early state constitutions had been drawn up as "perpetual charters" and made no provision for amendment. In only three states were the legislatures empowered to propose changes. In four, the amending power was vested solely in popular conventions.

The unwritten British constitution, by contrast, could be effectively amended by act of Parliament. Although the fundamentals of British government were understood as constitutional, and functioned in practice to contain and guide the operation of governing institutions, there was neither a document to define nor an agency to declare what was "unconstitutional." Whatever was enacted in Parliament was the supreme law of the land.

For a variety of reasons the Founding Fathers were unwilling to rely on so flexible a base for their new nation. The 13 independent states could not be expected to resign a part of their newly won sovereignty without a clear, written understanding of what kind of union they were joining.

Furthermore, they would need substantial guarantees that the new national government would not unilaterally alter the terms of the agreement, in particular by reducing the sovereignty retained by the states. The reliance on separation of powers, and on checks and balances, for protection against arbitrary government required that the arrangement not be subject to easy alteration, lest the separation and the balance be destroyed. Experience with arbitrary acts of Parliament convinced the former colonists that certain rights must be declared inviolable by any agency of government, and must be controlled by a law which no one of those agencies could itself change.

These and other reasons prompted the Constitutional Convention to write a document that was expected to endure as the fundamental law of the land. And yet those assembled in Philadelphia realized that they could not foresee all the future needs of the new nation, nor regard their labors as perfect. They devised, therefore, a Constitution which would be easier to amend than the Articles of Confederation, but more difficult to revise than the British constitution. They built into the amendment process the principle of checks and balances basic to the Constitution itself, and they reserved to the states the ultimate power to alter the agreement into which they had originally entered.

The plan for a national government presented by Edmund Randolph of Virginia on May 29, 1787, the fourth day of the Convention, set forth that "provision ought to be made for the amendment of the Articles of Union whensoever it shall seem necessary" and that "the assent of the National Legislature ought not to be required thereto." A plan proposed by Charles Pinckney of South Carolina on the same day provided that amendments "to invest future additional Powers in the United States" should be proposed by conventions and ratified by an unspecified percentage of the state legislatures.[1] *(Footnotes, p. 324)*

When Randolph's proposal was brought forward in the convention on June 5, Pinckney expressed doubt as to its "propriety or necessity," while Elbridge Gerry of Masschusetts favored it. "The novelty and difficulty of the experiment requires periodical revision," Gerry said. "The prospect of such a revision would also give intermediate stability to the Government." George Mason of Virginia supported the Randolph proposal, holding that:

"The plan now to be formed will certainly be defective, as the Confederation has been found, on trial, to be. Amendments, therefore, will be necessary and it will be better to provide for them in an easy, regular and constitutional way, than to trust to chance and violence. It would be improper to require the consent of the National Legislature, because they may abuse their power and refuse their consent on that very account."

On June 20, Mason said that "the Convention, though comprising so many distinguished characters, could not be expected to make a faultless government," and that he would prefer "trusting to posterity the amendment of its defects, rather than to push the experiment too far." The Convention agreed, on July 23, that "provisions ought to be made for future amendments...whensoever it shall seem necessary" and referred the matter to the Committee of Detail. In its report of Aug. 6, the committee recommended the provision that: "On the application of the legislatures of two-thirds of the states in the Union, for an amendment of this Constitution, the Legislature of the United States shall call a convention for that purpose." This recommendation was adopted by the Convention on Aug. 30, in spite of the contention of Gouverneur Morris of Pennsylvania that "the Legislature should be left at liberty to call a convention, whenever they please."

Reconsideration of the amendment provision was voted by the Convention on Sept. 10, on the motion of Gerry, who objected to it on the ground that, since the Constitution was to be paramount to the state constitutions "two-thirds of the states can bind the Union to innovations that may subvert the state constitutions altogether." Alexander Hamilton of New York likewise favored reconsideration, although he "did not object to the consequence stated by Mr. Gerry."

"There was no greater evil in subjecting the people of the United States to the major voice than the people of a particular state [Hamilton said]. It had been wished by many and was much to have been desired that an easier mode for introducing amendments had been provided by the Articles of Confederation. It was equally desirable now that an easy mode should be established for supplying defects which will probably appear in the new system. The mode proposed was not adequate. The state legislatures will not apply for alterations but with a view to increase their own powers. The national Legislature will be most sensible to the necessity of amendments, and ought also to be empowered, whenever two-thirds of each branch should concur, to call a convention." This was one of the few suggestions made by Hamilton which found a place in the finished Constitution.

Roger Sherman of Connecticut moved to add to the provision the following clause: "or the Legislature may propose amendments to the several states for their approbation, but no amendments shall be binding until consented to by the several states." James Wilson of Pennsylvania moved to reduce the requirement of unanimous consent of the states to a two-thirds majority. Six states—Connecticut, Georgia, Massachusetts, New Jersey, North Carolina and South Carolina—voted against this motion and five states—Delaware, Maryland, New Hampshire, Pennsylvania and Virginia—in favor of it, but a later motion by Wilson to permit three-fourths of the states to make an amendment effective was adopted without dissent.

Madison then proposed a substitute for the entire article, and this was adopted with only one state dissenting. Madison's plan provided that amendments should be proposed by Congress whenever two-thirds of both houses considered it necessary or when two-thirds of the state legislatures made application, such amendments to be valid when ratified by three-fourths of the state legislatures or three-fourths of the state conventions, as Congress might designate.

When this provision was reported by the Committee on Style, Sept. 15, Morris and Gerry objected that both methods of amendment depended upon Congress. They urged a provision requiring Congress, when requested by two-thirds of the states, to call a convention to propose amendments. This provision was accepted without dissent.

John Rutledge of South Carolina protested that he "could never agree to give a power by which the articles relating to slaves might be altered by the states not interested in that property and prejudiced against it." The Convention consequently agreed to a provision prohibiting amendment before 1808 of the clauses concerned with slavery (the counting of slaves as three-fifths of the population for assessment of direct taxes and authorization of the slave trade). At the last minute, Sherman voiced the fear that "three-fourths of the states might be brought to do things fatal to particular states, as abolishing them altogether or depriving them of their equality in the Senate." He sought another proviso prohibiting any amendment by which any state would "be affected in its internal policy, or deprived of its equal suffrage in the Senate." Madison warned against adding special provisos restricting the amending power, lest every state insist on protecting its boundaries or exports. However, "the circulating murmurs of the small states" prompted Morris to propose protecting equal representation in the Senate from amendment, a proviso adopted unanimously. These were the only two limitations on the substance of amendments which could be adopted.

Constitutional Provision

As finally agreed upon, Article V of the Constitution provided that: "The Congress, whenever two-thirds of both Houses shall deem it necessary, shall propose Amendments to this Constitution, or, on the Application of the Legislatures of two-thirds of the several States, shall call a Convention for proposing Amendments, which, in either Case, shall be valid to all Intents and Purposes, as Part of this Constitution, when ratified by the Legislatures of three-fourths of the several States, or by Conventions in three-fourths thereof, as the one or the other Mode of Ratification may be proposed by the Congress; Provided that no Amendment which may be made prior to the Year One thousand eight hundred and eight shall in any Manner affect the first and fourth Clauses in the Ninth Section of the first Article; and that no State, without its Consent, shall be deprived of its equal Suffrage in the Senate."

Thus, the Constitution allows either Congress or the state legislatures to initiate the amending process, either Congress or a general convention to propose amendments, and either state legislatures or state conventions to ratify amendments. Congress determines which method of ratification will be employed, and what form a general convention would take if requested by the state legislatures.

The President has no formal authority over constitutional amendments (his veto power does not extend to them); nor can governors veto approval of amendments by their respective legislatures.

Ratification. Notification of state ratification is transmitted by the states to the head of the General Services Administration. (Until 1950, the Secretary of State performed this function.) His action in proclaiming the adoption of an amendment on receipt is purely ministerial; the amendment is brought into effect by the ratifying action of the necessary number of states on the day when the required number of ratifications is reached. (However, the Eighteenth Amendment had an unusual provision postponing its effectiveness for one year after ratification.

Ratification of the Constitution

Omission of a Bill of Rights constituted the principal source of dissatisfaction with the new Constitution in the state ratifying conventions held in 1788. The demand for amendments to establish these rights, and to effect various other changes in the Constitution, made the provisions of Article V an issue in the struggle for ratification. In the Virginia convention, Patrick Henry and George Mason raised vehement objections to the amending process prescribed in Article V.

"When I come to contemplate this part [Henry said], I suppose that I am mad or that my countrymen are so. The way to amendment is, in my conception, shut.... Two-thirds of Congress or of the state legislatures are necessary even to propose amendments. If one-third of these be unworthy men, they may prevent the application for amendments; but what is destructive and mischievous is that three-fourths of the state legislatures, or of the state conventions, must concur in the amendments when proposed.... A bare majority in four small states may hinder the adoption of amendments.... Is this an easy mode of securing the public liberty? It is, sir, a most fearful situation, when the most contemptible minority could prevent the alteration of the most oppressive government, for it may in many respects prove to be such."[2]

Washington admitted that there were defects in the Constitution, but observed that "As a constitutional door is opened for future amendments and alterations, I think it would be wise in the people to accept what is offered to them...." Jefferson, at first hostile, came to support the Constitution, "contented to travel on towards perfection, step by step."[3]

The Federalist expressed the view that: "The mode (of amendment) preferred by the convention seems to be stamped with every mark of propriety. It guards equally against that extreme facility, which would render the Constitution too mutable; and that extreme difficulty which might perpetuate its discovered faults. It moreover equally enables the general and the state governments to originate the amendment of errors, as they may be pointed out by the experience on one side or the other."[4]

Change Without Amendment

Since the Constitution was drafted, the United States has been transformed beyond recognition. And yet this document remains the fundamental law of the land. The amending process has contributed to the remarkable durability of the Constitution.

But basic changes in the nature of the Constitution are by no means limited to those achieved through the amendment process. Each branch of the national government has contributed to transformation of the arrangement created at the Constitutional Convention.

The interpretation of the Constitution by the Supreme Court has been a major source of change. The principle of judicial review of legislation established the high court as the authoritative interpreter of the Constitution.

In 1803 Chief Justice Marshall, in *Marbury v. Madison* (5 U.S. 137), first asserted the Supreme Court's power to declare acts of Congress unconstitutional. In an *obiter dictum*, Marshall said: "The powers of the Legislature are defined and limited; and that those limits may not be mistaken, or forgotten, the Constitution is written. To what purpose are powers limited, and to what purpose is that limitation committed to writing, if these limits may at any time be passed by those intended to be restrained?"

"It is a proposition too plain to be contested," the Chief Justice continued, "that the Constitution controls any legislative act repugnant to it, or that the Legislature may alter the Constitution by an ordinary act. Between these alternatives there is no middle ground. The Constitution is either a superior paramount law, unchangeable by ordinary means, or it is on a level with ordinary legislative acts, and, like other acts, is alterable when the Legislature shall please to alter it.... If an act of the Legislature, repugnant to the

Constitution, is void, does it, notwithstanding its invalidity, bind the courts, and oblige them to give it effect? ...It is emphatically the province and duty of the judicial department to say what the law is.... So if a law be in opposition to the Constitution; if both the law and the Constitution apply to a particular case, so that the Court must either decide that case conformably to the law, disregarding the Constitution; or conformably to the Constitution, disregarding the law; the Court must determine which of these conflicting rules governs the case. This is of the very essence of judicial duty."[5]

The Constitution has also been affected by the growth in this century of the President's powers during national emergencies.

Chapter 22

Use of Amending Process

While profound changes in the foundations of American government have been wrought by Congress, the judiciary and the executive, formal amendments also have contributed to the process of constitutional transformation. Indeed, some of the amendments, such as the Eleventh and the Sixteenth, reversed judicial interpretations of the Constitution.

A number of the 26 amendments made only technical adjustments in the mechanisms of government. For example, the Twelfth Amendment provided for separate balloting for President and Vice President in the electoral college, and the Twentieth Amendment revised the dates for the beginning of presidential terms and the convening of Congress. Other amendments advanced the course of democracy by extending the vote to blacks (Fifteenth) and women (Nineteenth), lowering the voting age from 21 to 18 (Twenty-sixth) and providing for the direct election of senators (Seventeenth). The economy was profoundly affected by the Income Tax Amendment (Sixteenth) and social mores by the Prohibition Amendment (Eighteenth, repealed by the Twenty-first). The relationship between the national and state governments was altered by the Fourteenth Amendment, the most fundamental formal revision of the Constitution; its consequences are still unfolding in Supreme Court decisions.

The constitutional amendments have come in clusters. The first ten, the Bill of Rights, were practically a part of the original Constitution. Two amendments designed to correct the functioning of the Constitution were soon precipitated by a Supreme Court decision and by a crisis arising from a flaw in the procedure for electing the President and Vice President.

The Civil War prompted the Thirteenth, Fourteenth and Fifteenth Amendments. Apart from those three, which grew out of the nation's gravest crisis, more than a century elapsed between constitutional amendments. From 1913 to 1920, largely as the culmination of the progressive movement, four amendments of fundamental importance were ratified—giving the United States the income tax, direct election of senators, Prohibition, and women's suffrage.

The next two amendments, rescinding Prohibition and altering the dates for the beginning of a new Congress and of the presidential term, went into effect in 1933. There have been five amendments since World War II, none of them profoundly revising the system of government.

The best known amendment unsuccessfully pressed during the 1940s and 1950s was the so-called Bricker Amendment that would have limited the treaty-making power and the President's authority to enter into executive agreements. The amendment came within one vote of securing the necessary two-thirds Senate majority in 1950.

Another goal persistently sought by constitutional amendment has been reform of the system for electing the President by abolishing or revising the electoral college and providing for direct popular elections.

Anti-abortion and anti-busing amendments have been other controversial proposals put forward in the 1970s by segments of Congress and outside pressure groups.

Leadership of Congress

Although the Constitutional Convention envisioned a substantial role for the states in the amendment process, Congress has dominated the rewriting of the Constitution. Not once have the states been successful in calling for a convention to propose an amendment. as they are authorized to do by petitions to Congress from two-thirds of the legislatures. During the first 100 years of its existence,

Congress received only 10 such petitions from state legislatures, but between 1893 and 1974, more than 300 such petitions were received.[6] The states, while approving 26 amendments proposed by Congress, by early 1976 had failed to ratify only five.

Undoubtedly, the need to obtain the approval of as many as three-fourths of the states has served as a brake on congressional inclinations to alter the Constitution. On at least one occasion, the prospect that the states might take the initiative drove Congress to act. The Seventeenth Amendment, providing for direct election of senators, was continually blocked in the Senate until the state legislatures were on the verge of requiring a convention. Even in this case, however, Congress had for years provided the principal public arena for debate of the issue.

Congress has the power to determine by which of the two procedures the states shall ratify a proposed amendment. In every case except one, approval by the state legislatures has been prescribed. Only for the Twenty-first Amendment, the repeal of Prohibition, did Congress call for ratification by state conventions. The provision for ratification by conventions in that instance was primarily the result of three factors: (1) a desire for speedy ratification; (2) the contention of advocates of repeal that the state legislatures ratifying the Eighteenth Amendment had yielded to the pressure tactics of Prohibition forces, had overrepresented rural areas favoring Prohibition and had not represented the views of the majority of the people; and (3) the desire to remove permanently from the political arena a question which had divided states, regions and political parties. Submitted to the states in February 1933, the Twenty-first Amendment was ratified by conventions in 36 of the then total of 48 states by December of the same year.

The Supreme Court and Procedural Questions. As C. H. Pritchett has noted, the Supreme Court generally has regarded the amending process as "almost entirely a concern of Congress."[7] Until 1939, however, the court did rule on procedural questions relating to the adoption of amendments. In 1920 in the *National Prohibition Cases* (253 U.S. 350), it ruled that the two-thirds vote in each house required to propose an amendment meant two-thirds of the members present—assuming the presence of a quorum—and not a vote of two-thirds of the entire membership.[8] The Supreme Court has ruled that Congress has the power to set a "reasonable" time limit on the ratification period and has left it up to Congress to determine what that is.

Proposing and Ratifying: Undecided Questions

Convention Formula. Of the two methods of proposing amendments—via a convention called by Congress at the request of the legislatures of two-thirds of the states, or by a two-thirds majority of each house of Congress—only the latter has been employed. State legislatures have petitioned Congress to call a convention on numerous occasions, but all efforts have been unsuccessful.

In the 1960s, however, the Council of State Governments mounted a campaign to secure a constitutional amendment that would allow one house of a state legislature to be apportioned on some basis other than population. Although the effort died out, it pointed to the many uncertainties surrounding use of the convention formula for proposing amendments—questions that have not been resolved. Among the uncertainties are the following questions:

● What constitutes a valid call of two-thirds of the state legislatures?

● In what time span must the required two-thirds of the states submit their resolutions?

● Can a state rescind a previous call for a convention?

● If the required two-thirds of the states issue a convention call but Congress fails to call the convention, how is the issue resolved?

● How should the apportionment of delegates to the convention be decided? How should the delegates be selected?

Ratification Procedures. There are also undecided questions concerning ratification of amendments. Constitutional authorities have disagreed on whether Congress or the state legislatures should determine the procedures for ratification by state conventions.

Bills have been introduced in Congress to spell out procedures, but none of them have passed. The state legislatures were divided on this question. At least 21 of them provided by statute that state officials were to follow the procedures specified in a federal law if Congress should enact one. Sixteen legislatures, assuming that the procedural question was within their jurisdiction, passed laws applicable not merely to the convention summoned for the Twenty-first Amendment, but for all future conventions called to ratify amendments to the U.S. Constitution. One state, New Mexico, claimed exclusive authority on the matter and directed its officials to resist any attempt at congressional encroachment on that authority.

Time for Ratification. Another uncertainty concerning ratification concerns the definition of a "reasonable" time period for ratification, a question which the Supreme Court has left to Congress.

The Eighteenth Amendment (Prohibition) was the first to specify a period of years—in this case, seven—within which ratification had to be effected. In 1921 in *Dillon v. Gloss* (256 U.S. 368), the court held that Congress had the power to fix a definite ratification period "within reasonable limits." In 1939 in *Coleman v. Miller* (307 U.S. 433), the court held that the decision as to what was a "reasonable" period was an essentially political one which Congress—and not the court—had to determine.

The Child Labor Amendment proposed in 1924, with no time limit, might technically still be open for ratification. To date, 28 states have ratified the amendment. Even if 10 more states were to ratify (the three-fourths applies to the number of states presently in the Union, not the number at the time the amendment was proposed), it seems unlikely that Congress would consider this a "reasonable" time period.

In March of 1976, Kentucky ratified the Thirteenth, Fourteenth and Fifteenth Amendments—more than 100 years after they became part of the Constitution.

A state which has refused to ratify a proposed amendment may later change its mind and vote affirmatively. However, the weight of opinion is that once a state has approved a proposed amendment, it cannot reverse its decision and "unratify." This question could become an issue in the ratification campaign for the Equal Rights Amendment.

Appraisal of the Amending Process. As Burns, Peltason and Cronin have noted in their book, *Government by the People*, "The entire amending procedure has been criticized because neither a majority of the voters at large nor even a majority of the voters in a majority of the states

Time Taken to Ratify Amendments

The time elapsing between the submission by Congress of a constitutional amendment and its ratification by the requisite number of states has averaged about one and one-half years. The first ten amendments were proposed and ratified as a group, the process taking two years and 81 days. The longest time of all—three years and 340 days—was needed to complete ratification of the Twenty-second Amendment. In contrast, the Twenty-sixth Amendment was ratified in 100 days, and eight other amendments were ratified in less than one year. The detailed record follows:

Amendment	Passed Congress	Ratified	Time Elapsed Years	Days
1-10 (Bill of Rights)	Sept. 25, 1789	Dec. 15, 1791	2	81
11 (Suits Against States)	March 4, 1794	Feb. 7, 1795		340
12 (Presidential Electors)	Dec. 9, 1803	June 15, 1804		189
13 (Abolition of Slavery)	Jan. 31, 1865	Dec. 6, 1865		309
14 (Civil Rights: Due Process)	June 13, 1866	July 9, 1868	2*	26
15 (Black Suffrage)	Feb. 26, 1869	Feb. 3, 1870		342
16 (Income Tax)	July 12, 1909	Feb. 3, 1913	3*	206
17 (Direct Election of Senators)	May 13, 1912	April 8, 1913		330
18 (Prohibition)	Dec. 18, 1917	Jan. 16, 1919	1	29
19 (Women's Suffrage)	June 4, 1919	Aug. 18, 1920	1*	75
20 ("Lame Duck")	March 2, 1932	Jan. 23, 1933		327
21 (Prohibition Repeal)	Feb. 20, 1933	Dec. 5, 1933		288
22 (Presidential Tenure)	March 24, 1947	Feb. 27, 1951	3*	340
23 (D.C. Vote)	June 16, 1960	March 29, 1961		286
24 (Poll Tax)	Sept. 14, 1962	Jan. 23, 1964	1	131
25 (Presidential Disability)	July 6, 1965	Feb. 10, 1967	1	219
26 (18-Year-Old Vote)	March 23, 1971	July 1, 1971		100

* *Includes a leap year.*

Source: Congressional Research Service, Library of Congress, *The Constitution of the United States of America: Analysis and Interpretation* (Government Printing Office, 1973).

can formally alter the Constitution. But when a majority of
the people are serious in their desire to bring about changes
in our constitutional system, their wishes are usually implemented either by formal amendment or by the more sub-
tle methods of interpretation and adaptation."[9]

Pritchett has commented, "The adoption of three
amendments in six years—the Twenty-third, Twenty-fourth
and Twenty-fifth—is evidence that the amending
machinery is not hard to operate if there is a genuine consensus on the need, and may even lead to some concern that
amendments are too easy to achieve.... It is of prime importance that the Constitution retain its brevity and be limited
to basic structural arrangements and the protection of individual liberties. It would be disastrous if it became,
through the amending power, a vehicle by which pressure
groups and crackpots could impose their nostrums on the
nation."[10]

PART VIII

Electing the President

Chapter 23

Historical Background

Congress under the Constitution has two key responsibilities relating to the election of the President and Vice President of the United States. First, it is directed to receive and in joint session count the electoral votes certified by the states. Second, if no candidate has a majority of the electoral vote, the House of Representatives must elect the President and the Senate the Vice President.

Although many of the framers of the Constitution apparently thought that most elections would be decided by Congress, the House actually has chosen a President only twice, in 1801 and 1825. But in the course of the nation's history a number of campaigns have been deliberately designed to throw elections into the House, where each state has one vote and a majority of states is needed to elect; apprehension over such an outcome has nurtured electoral reform efforts over the years.

In modern times the formal counting of electoral votes has been largely a ceremonial function, but the congressional role can be decisive when votes are contested. The preeminent example is the Hayes-Tilden contest of 1876, when congressional decisions on disputed electoral votes from four states gave the election to Republican Rutherford B. Hayes despite the fact that Democrat Samuel J. Tilden had a majority of the popular vote. From the very beginning, the constitutional provisions governing the selection of the President have had few defenders, and many efforts at electoral-college reform have been undertaken.

In addition to its role in electing the President, Congress bears responsibility in the related areas of presidential succession and disability. The Twentieth Amendment empowers Congress to decide what to do if the President-elect and the Vice President-elect both fail to qualify by the date prescribed for commencement of their terms; it also gives Congress authority to settle problems arising from the death of candidates in cases where the election devolves upon Congress. Under the Twenty-fifth Amendment, Congress has ultimate responsibility for resolving disputes over presidential disability. It also must confirm presidential nominations to fill a vacancy in the vice presidency.

The power of the President to appoint a new Vice President under the terms of the Twenty-fifth Amendment has been used twice since the amendment was ratified on Feb. 10, 1967. It was used for the first time in 1973 when Vice President Spiro T. Agnew resigned and President Richard M. Nixon nominated Gerald R. Ford as the new Vice President. It was used again after the Nixon resignation in 1974 when Ford succeeded to the presidency and chose as his new Vice President, former Gov. Nelson A. Rockefeller of New York.

The method of selecting a President was the subject of long debate at the Constitutional Convention of 1787. Several plans were proposed and rejected before a compromise solution, which was modified only slightly in future years, was adopted (Article II, Section 1, Clause 2).[1]

Facing the Convention when it convened May 25 was the question of whether the chief executive should be chosen by direct popular election, by the Congress, by state legislatures or by intermediate electors. Direct election was opposed because it was generally felt that the people lacked sufficient knowledge of the character and qualifications of possible candidates to make an intelligent choice. Many delegates also feared that the people of the various states would be unlikely to agree on a single person, usually casting their votes for favorite-son candidates well-known to them. Southerners opposed direct election for the additional reason that suffrage was more widespread in the North than in the South, where black slaves did not vote.

The possibility of giving Congress the power to pick the President also received consideration. However, this plan also was rejected, largely because of fear that it would jeopardize the principle of executive independence. Similarly, a plan favored by many delegates, to let state legislatures choose the President, was turned down because it was feared that the President might feel so indebted to the states as to allow them to encroach on federal authority.

Unable to agree on a plan, the Convention on Aug. 31 appointed a "Committee of Eleven" to propose a solution to the problem. The committee on Sept. 4 suggested a compromise under which each state would appoint presidential electors (known as the electoral college), equal to the total number of its representatives and senators. The electors, chosen in a manner set forth by each state legislature, would meet in their own states and each cast votes for two persons. The votes would be counted in Congress, with the candidate receiving a majority elected President, and the second highest candidate becoming Vice President.

No distinction was made between ballots for President and Vice President. The development of national political parties and the nomination of tickets for President and Vice President caused confusion in the electoral system. All the electors of one party would tend to cast ballots for their two party nominees. But with no distinction between the presidential and vice presidential nominees, the danger arose of a tie vote between the two. This actually happened in 1800, leading to a change in the original electoral system with the Twelfth Amendment.

The committee plan constituted a great concession to the less populous states, since they were assured two extra votes (corresponding to their senators) regardless of how small their populations might be. The plan also left important powers with the states by giving complete discretion to state legislatures to determine the method of choosing electors.

Only one provision of the committee's plan aroused serious opposition—that giving the Senate the right to decide elections in which no candidate received a majority of electoral votes. Some delegates feared that the Senate, which already had been given treaty ratification powers and the responsibility to "advise and consent" to all important executive appointments, might become too powerful. Therefore, a counterproposal was made, and accepted, to let the House decide in instances when the electors failed to give a majority of their votes to a single candidate. The interests of the small states were preserved by giving each delegation only one vote in the House on roll calls to elect a President.

The system adopted by the Constitutional Convention was a compromise born out of problems involved in diverse state voting requirements, the slavery problem, big- versus small-state rivalries and the complexities of the balance of power among different branches of the government. It also was apparently as close to a direct popular election as the men who wrote the Constitution thought possible and appropriate at the time. Some scholars have suggested that the electoral college, as it came to be called, was a "jerry-rigged improvisation" which really left it to future generations to work out the best form of presidential election.[2] *(Footnotes, p. 324)*

The Twelfth Amendment

Only once since ratification of the Constitution has an amendment been adopted which substantially altered the method of electing the President. In the 1800 presidential election, the Republican (anti-Federalist) electors inadvertently caused a tie in the electoral college by casting equal numbers of votes for Thomas Jefferson, whom they wished to be elected President, and Aaron Burr, whom they wished to elect Vice President. The election was thrown into the House of Representatives and 36 ballots were required before Jefferson was finally elected President. The Twelfth Amendment, ratified in 1804, sought to prevent a recurrence of this incident by providing that the electors should vote separately for President and Vice President.[3]

Other changes in the system evolved over the years.[4] The authors of the Constitution, for example, had intended that each state should choose its most distinguished citizens as electors and that they would deliberate and vote as individuals in electing the President. But as strong political parties began to appear, the electors came to be chosen merely as representatives of the parties; independent voting by electors almost disappeared.

However, sometimes in American political history an elector has broken ranks to vote for a candidate other than his party's. In 1796, a Pennsylvania Federalist elector voted for Democratic-Republican Thomas Jefferson instead of Federalist John Adams. And in 1820, the New Hampshire Democratic-Republican elector voted for John Quincy Adams instead of the party nominee, James Monroe.

There was no further occurrence until 1948, when Preston Parks, a Truman elector in Tennessee, voted for Gov. Strom Thurmond of South Carolina, the States' Rights Democratic Party (Dixiecrat) presidential nominee. Since then, there have been the following additional instances:

● In 1956, when W. F. Turner, a Stevenson elector in Alabama, voted for a local judge, Walter E. Jones.

● In 1960, when Henry D. Irwin, a Nixon elector in Oklahoma, voted for Sen. Harry F. Byrd Jr. (D Va.).

● In 1968, when Dr. Lloyd W. Bailey, a Nixon elector in North Carolina, voted for George C. Wallace, the American Independent Party candidate.

● In 1972, when Roger L. McBride, a Nixon elector in Virginia, voted for John Hospers, the Libertarian candidate.

The original system underwent further change as democratic sentiment mounted early in the 19th century, bringing with it the demand that electors should be chosen by direct popular vote of the people, instead of by the state legislatures. By 1804, the majority of state legislatures had adopted popular-vote provisions.

Initially, most "popular-election" states provided that electors should be chosen from districts similar to congressional districts, with the electoral votes of a state split if the various districts differed in their political sentiment. This "district plan" of choosing electors was supported by the leading statesmen of both parties, including Thomas Jefferson, Alexander Hamilton, James Madison, John Quincy Adams, Andrew Jackson and Daniel Webster.[5]

The district plan, however, tended to dilute the power of political bosses and dominant majorities in state legislatures, who found themselves unable to "deliver" their states for one candidate or another. These groups brought pressure for a change and the states moved toward a winner-take-all popular ballot. Under this system, all of a state's electoral votes went to the party which won a plurality of popular votes statewide.

By 1804, six of the 11 "popular-election" states cast their electoral votes under the statewide popular ballot; by 1824, 12 out of 18. By 1836 all states except South Carolina had adopted the system of choosing electors statewide by popular vote. (After the Civil War, South Carolina switched from the practice of selecting its electors through the state legislature to a system of statewide, popular vote selection.)

However, since no mention of the statewide, popular election system was ever written into the Constitution, the state legislatures retained the power to specify any method of choosing presidential electors and to determine how their votes would be divided. In 1969, for example, Maine adopted a partial district system for use in the 1972 presidential election.

Election by Congress

The election of 1800 was the first in which the contingent election procedures of the Constitution were put to the test and the President was elected by the House of Representatives.[6]

The Federalists, a declining but still potent political force, nominated John Adams for a second term and chose Charles Cotesworth Pinckney as his running mate. A Republican congressional caucus chose Vice President Thomas Jefferson for President and Aaron Burr, who had been instrumental in winning the New York legislature for the Republicans earlier in 1800, for Vice President.

The bitterly fought campaign was marked by efforts in several states to change for partisan advantage the methods of selecting electors. In New York, where electors previously had been chosen by the legislature, Hamilton proposed that Governor John Jay call the lame-duck Federalist legislature into special session to adopt a proposal for popular election of electors under a district system, thus denying the incoming Republicans an opportunity to appoint electors. Jay declined, and in the end the new Republican legislature cast all 12 New York electoral votes for Jefferson and Burr.

The Federalists were more successful in Pennsylvania, another critical state. The state senate, where holdover members maintained Federalist control, refused to renew legislation providing for selection of electors by statewide popular vote. The Republican house of representatives was forced to accept a compromise that gave the Federalists seven electors and the Republicans eight.

Jefferson-Burr Deadlock

The electors met in each state on Dec. 4, and the results gradually became known throughout the country: Jefferson and Burr, 73 electoral votes each; Adams, 65; Pinckney, 64; John Jay, 1. The Federalists had lost, but because the Republicans had neglected to withhold one electoral vote from Burr, their presidential and vice presidential candidates were tied and the election was thrown into the House.

The lame-duck Congress, with a strong Federalist majority, would still be in office for the electoral count, and the possibilities for intrigue were only too apparent. After toying with and rejecting a proposal to block any election until March 4 when Adams' term expired, the Federalists decided to throw their support to Burr and thus elect a cynical and pliant politician over a man they considered a "dangerous radical." Alexander Hamilton opposed this move: "I trust the Federalists will not finally be so mad as to vote for Burr," he wrote. "I speak with intimate and accurate knowledge of his character. His elevation can only promote the purposes of the desperate and the profligate. If there be a man in the world I ought to hate, it is Jefferson. With Burr I have always been personally well. But the public good must be paramount to every private consideration."[7]

On Feb. 11, 1801, Congress met in joint session—with Jefferson in the chair—to count the electoral vote. This ritual ended, the House retired to its own chamber to elect a President. When the House met, it became apparent that the advice of Hamilton had been rejected. A majority of Federalists in the House insisted on backing Burr over Jefferson, the man they despised more. Indeed, if Burr had given clear assurances he would run the country as a Federalist, he might well have been elected. But Burr was unwilling to make those assurances; and, as one chronicler put it, "no one knows whether it was honor or a wretched indecision which gagged Burr's lips."[8]

In all, there were 106 members of the House at the time, consisting of 58 Federalists and 48 Republicans. If the ballots had been cast per capita, Burr would have been elected, but the Constitution provided that each state should cast a single vote and that a majority of states was necessary for election.

On the first ballot, Jefferson received the votes of eight states, one short of a majority of the 16 states then in the Union. Six states backed Burr, while the representatives of Vermont and of Maryland were equally divided, so they lost their votes. By midnight of the first day of voting, 19 ballots had been taken and the deadlock remained.

In all, 36 ballots were taken before the House came to a decision on Feb. 17. Predictably, there were men who sought to exploit the situation for personal gain. Jefferson wrote on Feb. 15: "Many attempts have been made to obtain terms and promises from me. I have declared to them une-quivocally that I would not receive the Government on capitulation; that I would not go in with my hands tied."[9]

The impasse was finally broken when Vermont and Maryland switched to support of Jefferson. Delaware and South Carolina also withdrew their support from Burr by casting blank ballots. The final vote: 10 states for Jefferson, four (all New England) for Burr. Thus Jefferson became President, and Burr, under the Constitution as it then stood, automatically became Vice President.

Federalist James A. Bayard of Delaware, who had played a key role in breaking the deadlock, wrote to Hamilton: "The means existed of electing Burr, but this required his cooperation. By deceiving one man (a great blockhead) and tempting two (not incorruptible), he might have secured a majority of the states. He will never have another chance of being President of the United States; and the little use he has made of the one which has occurred gives me but an humble opinion of the talents of an unprin-cipled man."[10]

The Jefferson-Burr contest clearly illustrated the dangers of the double-balloting system established by the original Constitution, and pressure began to build for an amendment requiring separate votes for President and Vice President. Congress approved the Twelfth Amendment in December 1803, and the states—acting with unexpected speed—ratified it in time for the 1804 election.

John Quincy Adams' Election

The only other time a President was elected by the House of Representatives was in 1825. There were many contenders for the presidency in the 1824 election, but four predominated: John Quincy Adams, Henry Clay, William H. Crawford and Andrew Jackson. Crawford, Secretary of the Treasury under Monroe, was the early front-runner, but his candidacy faltered after he suffered a paralytic stroke in 1823.[11]

When the electoral votes were counted, Jackson had 99, Adams 84, Crawford 41 and Clay 37. With 18 of the 24 states choosing their electors by popular vote, Jackson also led in the popular voting, although the significance of the popular vote was open to challenge. Under the Twelfth Amendment, the names of the three top contenders—Jackson, Adams and the ailing Crawford—were placed before the House of Representatives. Clay's support was vital to the two front-runners.

From the start, Clay apparently intended to support Adams as the lesser of two evils. But before the House voted, a great scandal erupted. A Philadelphia newspaper printed an anonymous letter alleging that Clay had agreed to support Adams in return for being made Secretary of State. The letter alleged also that Clay would have been willing to make the same deal with Jackson. Clay immediately denied the charge and pronounced the writer of the letter "a base and infamous calumniator, a dastard and a liar."[12] But Jackson believed the charges and found his suspicions vindicated when Adams, after the election, did appoint Clay as Secretary of State. "Was there ever witnessed such a bare-faced corruption in any country before?" Jackson wrote to a friend.[13]

When the House met to vote, Adams was supported by the six New England states and New York and, in large part through Clay's backing, by Maryland, Ohio, Kentucky, Illinois, Missouri and Louisiana. Thus a majority of 13 delegations voted for him—the bare minimum he needed for election, since there were 24 states in the Union at the time. The election was accomplished on the first ballot, but Adams took office under a cloud from which his administration never recovered.

Jackson's successful 1828 campaign made much of his contention that the House of Representatives had thwarted the will of the people by denying him the presidency in 1825 even though he had been the leader in popular and electoral votes.

271

Vice Presidential Election in Senate

On only one occasion has the Senate had to decide a vice presidential contest. That was in 1837, when Van Buren was elected President with 170 of the 294 electoral votes while his vice presidential running mate, Richard M. Johnson, received only 147 electoral votes—one less than a majority. This discrepancy occurred because Van Buren electors from Virginia boycotted Johnson. (Johnson's nomination had been opposed by southern Democrats because of his longstanding involvement with a mulatto woman.)[14] The Senate elected Johnson, 33-16, over Francis Granger of New York, the runner-up in the electoral vote for Vice President.

Threat of Election by House

Although only two presidential elections actually have been decided by the House, a number of others—including those of 1836, 1856, 1860, 1892, 1948, 1960 and 1968—could have been thrown into the House by only a small shift in the popular vote.

The threat of House election was clearly evident in 1968, when George C. Wallace of Alabama ran as a third-party candidate.[15] For the record, Wallace frequently asserted that he could win an outright majority in the electoral college by the addition of key midwestern and mountain states to his hoped-for base in the Deep South and border states. In reality, the Wallace campaign had a narrower goal: to win the balance of power in electoral college voting, thus depriving either major party of the clear electoral majority required for election. Wallace made it clear that he would then expect one of the major party candidates to make concessions in return for enough votes from Wallace electors to win the election. Wallace indicated that he expected the election to be settled in the electoral college and not in the House of Representatives. At the end of the campaign it was disclosed that Wallace had obtained written affidavits from all of his electors in which they promised to vote for Wallace "or whomsoever he may direct" in the electoral college.

In response to the Wallace challenge, both major party candidates, Republican Richard M. Nixon and Democrat Hubert H. Humphrey, maintained that they would refuse to bargain with Wallace for his electoral votes. Nixon asserted that the House, if the decision rested there, should elect the popular-vote winner. Humphrey said the representatives should select "the President they believe would be best for the country." Bipartisan efforts to obtain advance agreements from House candidates to vote for the national popular-vote winner if the election should go to the House ended in failure. Neither Nixon nor Humphrey replied to suggestions that they pledge before the election to swing enough electoral votes to the popular-vote winner to assure his election without help from Wallace.

In the end, Wallace received only 13.5 per cent of the popular vote and 46 electoral votes (including the vote of one Republican defector), all from southern states. He failed to win the balance of power in the electoral college which he had hoped to use to wring policy concessions from one of the major party candidates. If Wallace had won a few border states, or if a few thousand more Democratic votes had been cast in northern states barely carried by Nixon, thus reducing Nixon's electoral vote below 270, Wallace would have been in a position to bargain off his electoral votes or to throw the election into the House for final settlement.

The near-success of the Wallace strategy provided dramatic impetus for electoral college reform efforts. *(p. 279)*

Counting the Electoral Vote

Congress has mandated a variety of dates for the casting of popular votes, the meeting of the electors to cast ballots in the various states and the official counting of the electoral votes before both houses of Congress.[16]

The Continental Congress made the provisions for the first election. On Sept. 13, 1788, the Congress directed that each state choose its electors on the first Wednesday in January 1789. It further directed these electors to cast their ballots on the first Wednesday in February 1789.

In 1792, the Second Congress passed legislation setting up a permanent calendar for choosing electors. Allowing some flexibility in dates, the law directed that states choose their electors within the 34 days preceding the first Wednesday in December of each presidential election year. Then the electors would meet in their various states and cast their ballots on the first Wednesday in December. On the second Wednesday of the following February, the votes were to be opened and counted before a joint session of Congress. Provision also was made for a special presidential election in case of the removal, death, resignation or disability of both the President and Vice President.

Under this system, states chose presidential electors at various times. For instance, in 1840 the popular balloting for electors began in Pennsylvania and Ohio on Oct. 30 and ended in North Carolina on Nov. 12. South Carolina, the only state still choosing presidential electors through the state legislature, appointed its electors on Nov. 26.

Congress modified the system in 1845, providing that each state choose its electors on the same day—the Tuesday next after the first Monday in November—a provision that still remains in force. Otherwise, the days for casting and counting the electoral votes remained the same.

The next change occurred in 1887, when Congress provided that electors were to meet and cast their ballots on the second Monday in January instead of the first Wednesday in December. Congress also dropped the provision for a special presidential election.

In 1934, Congress again revised the law. The new arrangements, still in force, directed the electors to meet on the first Monday after the second Wednesday in December. The ballots are opened and counted before Congress on Jan. 6 (the next day if Jan. 6 falls on a Sunday).

The Constitution provides that "The President of the Senate shall, in the presence of the Senate and House of Representatives, open all the certificates, and the votes shall then be counted...." It offers no guidance on handling disputed ballots.

Before counting the electoral votes in 1865, Congress adopted the Twenty-second Joint Rule, which provided that no electoral votes objected to in joint session could be counted except by concurrent votes of both the Senate and House. The rule was pushed by congressional Republicans to ensure rejection of the electoral votes from the newly reconstructed states of Louisiana and Tennessee. Under this rule Congress in 1873 also threw out the electoral votes of Louisiana and Arkansas and three from Georgia.

However, the rule lapsed at the beginning of 1876 when the Senate refused to readopt it because the House was in

Democratic control. Thus, following the 1876 election, when it became apparent that for the first time the outcome of an election would be determined by decisions on disputed electoral votes, Congress had no rules to guide it.

Hayes-Tilden Contest

The 1876 campaign pitted Republican Rutherford B. Hayes against Democrat Samuel J. Tilden. Early election night returns indicated that Tilden had been elected. He had won normally Republican Indiana, New York, Connecticut and New Jersey; those states plus his expected southern support would give him the election. However, by the following morning it became apparent that if the Republicans could hold South Carolina, Florida and Louisiana, Hayes would be elected with 185 electoral votes to 184 for Tilden. But if a single elector in any of these states voted for Tilden, he would throw the election to the Democrats. Tilden led in the popular-vote count by more than a quarter of a million votes.[17]

The situation was much the same in each of the three contested states. Historian Eugene H. Roseboom described it as follows: "The Republicans controlled the state governments and the election machinery, had relied upon the Negro masses for votes, and had practiced frauds as in the past. The Democrats used threats, intimidation, and even violence when necessary, to keep Negroes from the polls; and where they were in a position to do so they resorted to fraud also. The firm determination of the whites to overthrow carpetbag rule contributed to make a full and fair vote impossible; carpetbag hold on the state governments made a fair count impossible. Radical reconstruction was reaping its final harvest."[18]

Both parties pursued the votes of the three states with a fine disregard for propriety or legality, and in the end double sets of elector returns were sent to Congress from all three. Oregon also sent two sets of returns. Although Hayes carried that state, the Democratic governor discovered that one of the Hayes electors was a postmaster and therefore ineligible to be an elector under the Constitution, so he certified the election of the top-polling Democratic elector. However, the Republican electors met, received the resignation of their ineligible colleague, then reappointed him to the vacancy since he had in the meantime resigned his postmastership.

Had the Twenty-second Joint Rule remained in effect, the Democratic House of Representatives could have ensured Tilden's election by objecting to any of Hayes' disputed votes. But, since the rule had lapsed, Congress had to find some new method of resolving electoral disputes. A joint committee was created to work out a plan, and the resulting Electoral Commission Law was approved by large majorities and signed into law Jan. 29, 1877—only two days before the date scheduled for counting the electoral votes.

The law, which applied only to the 1876 electoral vote count, established a 15-member Electoral Commission which was to have final authority over disputed electoral votes, unless both houses of Congress agreed to overrule it. The commision was to consist of five senators, five representatives and five Supreme Court justices. Each chamber was to select its own members of the commission, with the understanding that the majority party would have three members and the minority two. Four justices, two from each party, were named in the bill, and these four were to select the fifth. It was expected that they would pick Justice David Davis, who was considered a political independent, but he was disqualified when the Illinois legislature named him to a seat in the Senate. Justice Joseph P. Bradley, a Republican, then was named to the 15th seat on the commission. The Democrats supported his selection, because they considered him the most independent of the remaining justices, all of whom were Republicans. However, he was to vote with the Republicans on every dispute and thus assure the victory of Hayes.

The electoral vote count began in Congress Feb. 1, and the proceedings continued until March 2. States were called in alphabetical order, and as each disputed state was reached, objections were raised to both the Hayes and Tilden electors. The question was then referred to the Electoral Commission, which in every case voted 8-7 for Hayes. In each case, the Democratic House rejected the commission's decision, but the Republican Senate upheld it, so the decision stood.

As the count went on, Democrats in the House threatened to launch a filibuster to block resumption of joint sessions so that the count could not be completed before Inauguration Day. The threat was never carried out, because of an agreement reached between the Hayes forces and southern conservatives. The southerners agreed to let the electoral count continue without obstruction. In return Hayes agreed that, as President, he would withdraw federal troops from the South, end Reconstruction and make other concessions. The southerners, for their part, pledged to respect the rights of blacks, a pledge they proved unable to carry out.

Thus, at 4 a.m., March 2, 1877, the president of the Senate was able to announce that Hayes had been elected President with 185 electoral votes, as against 184 for Tilden. Later that day Hayes arrived in Washington. The following evening he took the oath of office privately at the White House because March 4 fell on a Sunday. His formal inauguration followed on Monday. The country acquiesced. Thus ended a crisis that easily could have resulted in civil war.

Not until 1887 did Congress enact permanent legislation on the handling of disputed electoral votes. The Electoral Count Act of that year gave each state final authority in determining the legality of its choice of electors and required a concurrent majority of both the Senate and House to reject any electoral votes. It also establishd procedures for counting electoral votes in Congress.

Application of 1887 Law in 1969

The procedures relating to disputed electoral votes were utilized for the first time following the election of 1968. When Congress met in joint session Jan. 6, 1969, to count the electoral votes, Sen. Edmund S. Muskie (D Maine) and Rep. James G. O'Hara (D Mich.), joined by six other senators and 37 other representatives, filed a written objection to the vote cast by a North Carolina elector, Dr. Lloyd W. Bailey of Rocky Mount, who had been elected as a Republican but chose to vote for Wallace and Curtis E. LeMay instead of Nixon and Agnew.

Acting under the 1887 law, Muskie and O'Hara objected to Bailey's vote on the grounds that it was "not properly given" because a plurality of the popular vote in North Carolina were cast for Nixon-Agnew, and the state's voters had chosen electors to vote for Nixon and Agnew only. Muskie and O'Hara asked that Bailey's vote not be counted at all by Congress.

The 1887 statute, currently incorporated in the U.S. Code, Title 3, Section 15, stipulated that "no electoral vote or votes from any state which shall have been regularly given by electors whose appointment has been lawfully certified,...but from which but one return has been received shall be rejected, but the two houses concurrently may reject the vote or votes when they agree that such vote or votes have not been so certified." The statute did not define the term "regularly given," though at the time of its adoption chief concern centered on problems of dual sets of electoral vote returns from a state, votes cast on an improper day or votes disputed because of uncertainty about whether a state lawfully was in the Union on the day that the electoral vote was cast.

The 1887 statute provided that if written objection to any state's vote was received from at least one member of both the Senate and House, the two legislative bodies were to retire immediately to separate sessions, debate for two hours with a five-minute limitation on speeches, and that each chamber was to decide the issue by vote before resuming the joint session. The statute made clear that both the Senate and House had to reject a challenged electoral vote (or votes) for such action to prevail.

At the Jan. 6 joint session, convened at 1 p.m. in the House chamber with Senate President pro tempore Richard B. Russell (D Ga.) presiding, the counting of the electoral vote proceeded smoothly through the alphabetical order of states until the North Carolina result was announced, at which time O'Hara rose to announce filing of the complaint. The two houses then proceeded to separate sessions, at the end of which the Senate, by 33-58 roll-call vote, and the House, by a 170-228 roll-call vote, refused to sustain the challenge to Bailey's vote. The two houses then reassembled in joint session at which the results of the separate deliberations were announced and the count of the electoral vote by state proceeded without event. At the conclusion, Russell announced the vote and declared Nixon and Agnew elected.

Although Congress did not sustain the challenge to Bailey's vote, the case of the "faithless" elector led to increased pressure for electoral reform.

Chapter 24

Electoral Reform

Since Jan. 6, 1797, when Rep. William L. Smith (S.C.) introduced in Congress the first proposed constitutional amendment for reform of the electoral college system, hardly a session of Congress has passed without the introduction of one or more resolutions of this nature. But only one—the Twelfth Amendment, ratified in 1804—ever has been approved.

In recent years, public interest in a change in the electoral college system was spurred by the close 1960 and 1968 elections, by a series of Supreme Court rulings relating to apportionment and districting and by introduction of unpledged elector systems in the southern states.

Early in 1969, President Nixon asked Congress to take prompt action on electoral college reform. He said he would support any plan that would eliminate individual electors and distribute among the presidential candidates the electoral vote of every state and the District of Columbia in a manner more closely approximating the popular vote.[19]

Later that year the House approved, 338-70, a resolution proposing a constitutional amendment to eliminate the electoral college and to provide instead for direct popular election of the President and Vice President. The measure set a minimum of 40 per cent of the popular vote as sufficient for election and provided for a runoff election between the two top candidates for the presidency if no candidate received 40 per cent of the vote. Under this plan the House of Representatives could no longer be called upon to select a President. The proposed amendment also authorized Congress to provide a method of filling vacancies caused by the death, resignation or inability of presidential nominees before the election and a method of filling post-election vacancies caused by the death of the President-elect or Vice President elect.

Blocking of Proposed Amendment

President Nixon, who previously had favored a proportional plan of allocating each state's electoral votes, endorsed the House resolution and urged the Senate to adopt it. To become effective, the proposed amendment had to be approved by a two-thirds majority in both the Senate and House and be ratified by the legislatures of three-fourths of the states.

When the proposal reached the Senate floor in September 1970, small-state and southern senators succeeded in blocking final action on it. The resolution was laid aside Oct. 5, following two unsuccessful efforts to cut off debate by invoking cloture.

Presidential Disability

A decade of congressional concern over the question of presidential disability was eased in 1967 by ratification of the Twenty-fifth Amendment to the Constitution. The amendment for the first time provided for continuity in carrying out the functions of the presidency in the event of presidential disability and for filling a vacancy in the vice presidency.[20]

Congressional consideration of the problem of presidential disability had been prompted by President Dwight D. Eisenhower's heart attack in 1955. The ambiguity of the language of the disability clause (Article II, Section 1, Clause 5) of the Constitution had provoked occasional debate ever since the Constitutional Convention of 1787. But it had never been decided how far the term "disability" extended or who would be the judge of it.

Clause 5 provided that Congress should decide who was to succeed to the presidency in the event that both the President and the Vice President died, resigned or became disabled. Congress enacted succession laws three times. By the Act of March 1, 1792, it provided for succession (after the Vice President) of the president pro tempore of the Senate, then of the House Speaker; if those offices were vacant, states were to send electors to choose a new President.

That law stood until passage of the Presidential Succession Act of Jan. 19, 1886, which changed the line of succession to run from the Vice President to the Secretary of State, Secretary of the Treasury and so on through the Cabinet in order of rank. Sixty-one years later, the Act of July 18, 1947 (still in force), placed the Speaker of the House and the president pro tempore of the Senate ahead of Cabinet officers in succession after the Vice President.

Prior to ratification of the Twenty-fifth Amendment in 1967, no procedures had been laid down to govern situations arising in the event of presidential incapacity or of a vacancy in the office of the Vice President. Two Presidents had sustained serious disabilities—President James A. Garfield, who was shot in 1881 and was confined to his bed until he died two and one-half months later, and President Woodrow Wilson, who suffered a stroke in 1919. In each case the Vice President did not assume any duties of the presidency for fear he would appear to be usurping the power of that office. As for a vice presidential vacancy, the United States has been without a Vice President 18 times, for a total of 40 years through 1974, after the elected Vice President either succeeded to the presidency, died or on two occasions resigned. (John C. Calhoun resigned as Vice President Dec. 28, 1832, to become a U.S. senator and Agnew resigned Oct. 10, 1973.)

Ratification of the Twenty-fifth Amendment established procedures that clarified these areas of uncertainty in the Constitution. The amendment provided that the Vice President should become Acting President under either one of two circumstances. If the President informed Congress that he was unable to perform his duties, the Vice President would become Acting President until the President could resume his responsibilities.

If the Vice President and a majority of the Cabinet, or other body designated by Congress, found the President to be incapacitated, the Vice President would become Acting President until the President informed Congress that his disability had ended. Congress was given 21 days to resolve any dispute over the President's disability; a two-thirds vote of both chambers was required to overrule the President's declaration that he was no longer incapacitated.

Whenever a vacancy occurred in the office of Vice President, either by death, succession to the presidency or resignation, the President was to nominate a Vice President and the nomination was to be confirmed by a majority vote of both houses of Congress.

The proposed Twenty-fifth Amendment was approved by the Senate and House in 1965. It took effect Feb. 10, 1967, following ratification by 38 states.

Amendment Used Twice

Since its ratification in 1967, the Twenty-fifth Amendment has been used twice to fill a vacancy in the office of the Vice President.[21] The first time was in 1973 after Vice President Agnew's resignation. Agnew—under investigation for multiple charges of alleged conspiracy, extortion and bribery—agreed to resign and avoided imprisonment by pleading *nolo contendere* (no contest) to a single charge of federal income tax evasion.

On Oct. 12, President Nixon nominated House Minority Leader Gerald R. Ford (R Mich.) for Vice President. Ford became the 40th Vice President of the United States Dec. 6, an hour after the House of Representatives voted 387-5 to confirm him. The Senate had approved the nomination Nov. 27 by a 92-3 vote. Ford's confirmation followed hearings and approval by the House Judiciary and Senate Rules Committees.

The Twenty-fifth Amendment was used a second time in 1974 when Nixon resigned as President Aug. 9, 1974, to avoid impeachment because of the Watergate scandal. Ford succeeded to the presidency, becoming the first unelected President in American history, and on Aug. 20 nominated former Gov. Nelson A. Rockefeller of New York as the new Vice President.

Rockefeller became the 41st Vice President of the United States Dec. 19, 1974, after the House confirmed his nomination, 287-128. The Senate had given its approval to the nomination Dec. 10, on a 90-7 vote. Rockefeller's nomination had been approved by the House Judiciary and Senate Rules Committees after several days of hearings.

With both the President and Vice President holding office through appointment rather than election, members of Congress and the public expressed concern about the power of a President to, in effect, appoint his own successor. Among those proposing change was Sen. John O. Pastore (D R.I.) who sponsored a resolution for a new constitutional amendment to provide for a special national election for President whenever an appointed Vice President became President with more than one year remaining in a presidential term. Hearings on proposed changes were held in February 1975 by the Senate Judiciary Subcommittee on Constitutional Amendments.

Constitution
of the United States

We the People of the United States, in Order to form a more perfect Union, establish Justice, insure domestic Tranquility, provide for the common defence, promote the general Welfare, and secure the Blessings of Liberty to ourselves and our Posterity, do ordain and establish this Constitution for the United States of America.

Article I

Section. 1. All legislative Powers herein granted shall be vested in a Congress of the United States, which shall consist of a Senate and House of Representatives.

Section. 2. The House of Representatives shall be composed of Members chosen every second Year by the People of the several States, and the Electors in each State shall have the Qualifications requisite for Electors of the most numerous Branch of the State Legislature.

No Person shall be a Representative who shall not have attained to the age of twenty five Years, and been seven Years a Citizen of the United States, and who shall not, when elected, be an Inhabitant of that State in which he shall be chosen.

Representatives and direct Taxes shall be apportioned among the several States which may be included within this Union, according to their respective Numbers, which shall be determined by adding to the whole Number of free Persons, including those bound to Service for a Term of Years, and excluding Indians not taxed, three fifths of all other Persons. The actual Enumeration shall be made within three Years after the first Meeting of the Congress of the United States, and within every subsequent Term of ten Years, in such Manner as they shall by Law direct. The Number of Representatives shall not exceed one for every thirty Thousand, but each State shall have at Least one Representative; and until such enumeration shall be made, the State of New Hampshire shall be entitled to chuse three, Massachusetts eight, Rhode-Island and Providence Plantations one, Connecticut five, New-York six, New Jersey four, Pennsylvania eight, Delaware one, Maryland six, Virginia ten, North Carolina five, South Carolina five, and Georgia three.

When vacancies happen in the Representation from any State, the Executive Authority thereof shall issue Writs of Election to fill such Vacancies.

The House of Representatives shall chuse their Speaker and other Officers; and shall have the sole Power of Impeachment.

Section. 3. The Senate of the United States shall be composed of two Senators from each State, chosen by the Legislature thereof, for six Years; and each Senator shall have one Vote.

Immediately after they shall be assembled in Consequence of the first Election, they shall be divided as equally as may be into three Classes. The Seats of the Senators of the first Class shall be vacated at the Expiration of the second Year, of the second Class at the Expiration of the fourth Year, and of the third Class at the Expiration of the sixth Year, so that one third may be chosen every second Year; and if Vacancies happen by Resignation, or otherwise, during the Recess of the Legislature of any State, the Executive thereof may make temporary Appointments until the next Meeting of the Legislature, which shall then fill such Vacancies.

No Person shall be a Senator who shall not have attained to the Age of thirty Years, and been nine Years a Citizen of the United States, and who shall not, when elected, be an Inhabitant of that State for which he shall be chosen.

The Vice President of the United States shall be President of the Senate, but shall have no Vote, unless they be equally divided.

The Senate shall chuse their other Officers, and also a President pro tempore, in the Absence of the Vice President, or when he shall exercise the Office of President of the United States.

The Senate shall have the sole Power to try all Impeachments. When sitting for that Purpose, they shall be on Oath or Affirmation. When the President of the United States is tried the Chief Justice shall preside: And no Person shall be convicted without the Concurrence of two thirds of the Members present.

Judgment in Cases of Impeachment shall not extend further than to removal from Office, and disqualification to hold and enjoy any Office of honor, Trust or Profit under the United States: but the Party convicted shall nevertheless be liable and subject to Indictment, Trial, Judgment and Punishment, according to Law.

Section. 4. The Times, Places and Manner of holding Elections for Senators and Representatives, shall be prescribed in each State by the Legislature thereof; but the Congress may at any time by Law make or alter such Regulations, except as to the Places of chusing Senators.

The Congress shall assemble at least once in every Year, and such Meeting shall be on the first Monday in December, unless they shall by Law appoint a different Day.

Section. 5. Each House shall be the Judge of the Elections, Returns and Qualifications of its own Members, and a Majority of each shall constitute a Quorum to do Business; but a smaller Number may adjourn from day to day, and may be authorized to compel the Attendance of absent Members, in such Manner, and under such Penalties as each House may provide.

Each House may determine the Rules of its Proceedings, punish its Members for disorderly Behaviour, and, with the Concurrence of two thirds, expel a Member.

Each House shall keep a Journal of its Proceedings, and from time to time publish the same, excepting such Parts as may in their Judgment require Secrecy; and the Yeas and

Nays of the Members of either House on any question shall, at the Desire of one fifth of those Present, be entered on the Journal.

Neither House, during the Session of Congress, shall, without the Consent of the other, adjourn for more than three days, nor to any other Place than that in which the two Houses shall be sitting.

Section. 6. The Senators and Representatives shall receive a Compensation for their Services, to be ascertained by Law, and paid out of the Treasury of the United States. They shall in all Cases, except Treason, Felony and Breach of the Peace, be privileged from Arrest during their Attendance at the Session of their respective Houses, and in going to and returning from the same; and for any Speech or Debate in either House, they shall not be questioned in any other Place.

No Senator or Representative shall, during the Time for which he was elected, be appointed to any civil Office under the Authority of the United States, which shall have been created, or the Emoluments whereof shall have been encreased during such time; and no Person holding any Office under the United States, shall be a Member of either House during his Continuance in Office.

Section. 7. All Bills for raising Revenue shall originate in the House of Representatives; but the Senate may propose or concur with amendments as on other Bills.

Every Bill which shall have passed the House of Representatives and the Senate, shall, before it become a Law, be presented to the President of the United States; If he approve he shall sign it, but if not he shall return it, with his Objections to that House in which it shall have originated, who shall enter the Objections at large on their Journal, and proceed to reconsider it. If after such Reconsideration two thirds of that House shall agree to pass the Bill, it shall be sent, together with the Objections, to the other House, by which it shall likewise be reconsidered, and if approved by two thirds of that House, it shall become a Law. But in all such Cases the Votes of both Houses shall be determined by yeas and Nays, and the Names of the Persons voting for and against the Bill shall be entered on the Journal of each House respectively. If any Bill shall not be returned by the President within ten Days (Sunday excepted) after it shall have been presented to him, the Same shall be a Law, in like Manner as if he had signed it, unless the Congress by their Adjournment prevent its Return, in which Case it shall not be a Law.

Every Order, Resolution, or Vote to which the Concurrence of the Senate and House of Representatives may be necessary (except on a question of Adjournment) shall be presented to the President of the United States; and before the Same shall take Effect, shall be approved by him, or being disapproved by him, shall be repassed by two thirds of the Senate and House of Representatives, according to the Rules and Limitations prescribed in the Case of a Bill.

Section. 8. The Congress shall have Power To lay and collect Taxes, Duties, Imposts and Excises, to pay the Debts and provide for the common Defence and general Welfare of the United States; but all Duties, Imposts and Excises shall be uniform throughout the United States;

To borrow Money on the credit of the United States;

To regulate Commerce with foreign Nations, and among the several States, and with the Indian Tribes;

To establish an uniform Rule of Naturalization, and uniform Laws on the subject of Bankruptcies throughout the United States;

To coin Money, regulate the Value thereof, and of foreign Coin, and fix the Standard of Weights and Measures;

To provide for the Punishment of counterfeiting the Securities and current Coin of the United States;

To establish Post Offices and post Roads;

To promote the Progress of Science and useful Arts, by securing for limited Times to Authors and Inventors the exclusive Right to their respective Writings and Discoveries;

To constitute Tribunals inferior to the supreme Court;

To define and punish Piracies and Felonies commited on the high Seas, and Offences against the Law of Nations;

To declare War, grant Letters of Marque and Reprisal, and make Rules concerning Captures on Land and Water;

To raise and support Armies, but no Appropriation of Money to that Use shall be for a longer Term than two Years;

To provide and maintain a Navy;

To make Rules for the Government and Regulation of the land and naval Forces;

To provide for calling forth the Militia to execute the Laws of the Union, suppress Insurrections and repel Invasions;

To provide for organizing, arming, and disciplining, the Militia, and for governing such Part of them as may be employed in the Service of the United States, reserving to the States respectively, the Appointment of the Officers, and the Authority of training the Militia according to the discipline prescribed by Congress;

To exercise exclusive Legislation in all Cases whatsoever, over such District (not exceeding ten Miles square) as may, by Cession of Particular States, and the Acceptance of Congress, become the Seat of the Government of the United States, and to exercise like Authority over all Places purchased by the Consent of the Legislature of the State in which the Same shall be, for the Erection of Forts, Magazines, Arsenals, dock-Yards, and other needful Buildings;—And

To make all Laws which shall be necessary and proper for carrying into Execution the foregoing Powers, and all other Powers vested by this Constitution in the Government of the United States, or in any Department or Officer thereof.

Section. 9. The Migration or Importation of such Persons as any of the States now existing shall think proper to admit, shall not be prohibited by the Congress prior to the Year one thousand eight hundred and eight, but a Tax or duty may be imposed on such Importation, not exceeding ten dollars for each Person.

The Privilege of the Writ of Habeas Corpus shall not be suspended, unless when in Cases of Rebellion or Invasion the public Safety may require it.

No Bill of Attainder or ex post facto Law shall be passed.

No Capitation, or other direct, Tax shall be laid, unless in Proportion to the Census of Enumeration herein before directed to be taken.

No Tax or Duty shall be laid on Articles exported from any State.

No Preference shall be given by any Regulation of Commerce or Revenue to the Ports of one State over those of another; nor shall Vessels bound to, or from, one State, be obliged to enter, clear or pay Duties in another.

No Money shall be drawn from the Treasury, but in Consequence of Appropriations made by Law; and a regular Statement and Account of the Receipts and Expenditures of all public Money shall be published from time to time.

No Title of Nobility shall be granted by the United States: And no Person holding any Office of Profit or Trust under them, shall, without the Consent of the Congress, accept of any present, Emolument, Office, or Title, of any kind whatever, from any King, Prince or foreign State.

Section. 10. No State shall enter into any Treaty, Alliance, or Confederation; grant Letters of Marque and Reprisal; coin Money; emit Bills of Credit; make any Thing but gold and silver Coin a Tender in Payment of Debts; pass any Bill of Attainder, ex post facto Law, or Law impairing the Obligation of Contracts, or grant any Title of Nobility.

No State shall, without the Consent of the Congress, lay any Imposts or Duties on Imports or Exports, except what may be absolutely necessary for executing it's inspection Laws: and the net Produce of all Duties and Imposts, laid by any State on Imports or Exports, shall be for the Use of the Treasury of the United States; and all such Laws shall be subject to the Revision and Controul of the Congress.

No State shall, without the Consent of Congress, lay any Duty of Tonnage, keep Troops, or Ships of War in time of Peace, enter into any Agreement or Compact with another State, or with a foreign Power, or engage in War, unless actually invaded, or in such imminent Danger as will not admit of delay.

Article II

Section. 1. The executive Power shall be vested in a President of the United States of America. He shall hold his Office during the Term of four Years, and, together with the Vice President, chosen for the same Term, be elected, as follows

Each State shall appoint, in such Manner as the Legislature thereof may direct, a Number of Electors, equal to the whole Number of Senators and Representatives to which the State may be entitled in the Congress: but no Senator or Representative, or Person holding an Office of Trust or Profit under the United States, shall be appointed an Elector.

The Electors shall meet in their respective States, and vote by Ballot for two Persons, of whom one at least shall not be an Inhabitant of the same State with themselves. And they shall make a List of all the Persons voted for, and of the Number of Votes for each; which List they shall sign and certify, and transmit sealed to the Seat of the Government of the United States, directed to the President of the Senate. The President of the Senate shall, in the Presence of the Senate and House of Representatives, open all the Certificates, and the Votes shall then be counted. The Person having the greatest Number of Votes shall be the President, if such Number be a Majority of the whole Number of Electors appointed; and if there be more than one who have such Majority, and have an equal Number of Votes, then the House of Representatives shall immediately chuse by Ballot one of them for President; and if no Person have a Majority, then from the five highest on the list the said House shall in like Manner chuse the President. But in chusing the President, the Votes shall be taken by States, the Representation from each State having one Vote; a quorum for this Purpose shall consist of a Member or Members from two thirds of the States, and a Majority of all the States shall be necessary to a Choice. In every Case, after the Choice of the President, the Person having the greatest Number of Votes of the Electors shall be the Vice President. But if there should remain two or more who have equal Votes, the Senate shall chuse from them by Ballot the Vice President.

The Congress may determine the Time of chusing the Electors, and the Day on which they shall give their Votes; which Day shall be the same throughout the United States.

No Person except a natural born Citizen, or a Citizen of the United States, at the time of the Adoption of this Constitution, shall be eligible to the Office of President; neither shall any Person be eligible to that Office who shall not have attained to the Age of thirty five Years, and been fourteen Years a Resident within the United States.

In Case of the Removal of the President from Office, or of his Death, Resignation, or Inability to discharge the Powers and Duties of the said Office, the Same shall devolve on the Vice President, and the Congress may by Law provide for the Case of Removal, Death, Resignation or Inability, both of the President and Vice President, declaring what Officer shall then act as President, and such Officer shall act accordingly, until the Disability be removed, or a President shall be elected.

The President shall, at stated Times, receive for his Services, a Compensation, which shall neither be encreased nor dimished during the Period for which he shall have been elected, and he shall not receive within that Period any other Emolument from the United States, or any of them.

Before he enter on the Execution of his Office, he shall take the following Oath or Affirmation: —"I do solemnly swear (or affirm) that I will faithfully execute the Office of President of the United States, and will to the best of my Ability, preserve, protect and defend the Constitution of the United States."

Section. 2. The President shall be Commander in Chief of the Army and Navy of the United States, and of the Militia of the several States, when called into the actual Service of the United States; he may require the Opinion, in writing, of the principal Officer in each of the executive Departments, upon any Subject relating to the Duties of their respective Offices, and he shall have Power to grant Reprieves and Pardons for Offenses against the United States, except in Cases of Impeachment.

He shall have Power, by and with the Advice and Consent of the Senate, to make Treaties, provided two thirds of the Senators present concur; and he shall nominate, and by and with the Advice and Consent of the Senate, shall appoint Ambassadors, other public Ministers and Consuls, Judges of the supreme Court, and all other Officers of the United States, whose Appointments are not herein otherwise provided for, and which shall be established by Law: but the Congress may by Law vest the Appointment of such inferior Officers, as they think proper, in the President alone, in the Courts of Law, or in the Heads of Departments.

The President shall have Power to fill up all Vacancies that may happen during the Recess of the Senate, by granting Commissions which shall expire at the End of their next Session.

Section. 3. He shall from time to time give to the Congress Information of the State of the Union, and recommend to their Consideration such Measures as he shall judge necessary and expedient; he may, on extraordinary Occasions, convene both Houses, or either of them, and in Case of Disagreement between them, with Respect to the Time of Adjournment, he may adjourn them to such Time as he shall think proper; he shall receive Ambassadors and other public Ministers; he shall take Care that the Laws be faithfully executed, and shall Commission all the Officers of the United States.

Section. 4. The President, Vice President and all Civil Officers of the United States, shall be removed from office on Impeachment for, and Conviction of, Treason, Bribery, or other high Crimes and Misdemeanors.

Article III

Section. 1. The judicial Power of the United States, shall be vested in one supreme Court, and in such inferior Courts as the Congress may from time to time ordain and establish. The Judges, both of the supreme and inferior Courts, shall hold their Offices during good Behaviour, and shall, at stated Times, receive for their Services, a Compensation, which shall not be diminished during their Continuance in Office.

Section. 2. The judicial Power shall extend to all Cases, in Law and Equity, arising under this Constitution, the Laws of the United States, and Treaties made, or which shall be made, under their Authority;—to all Cases affecting Ambassadors, other public Ministers and Consuls;—to all Cases of admiralty and maritime Jurisdiction;—to Controversies to which the United States shall be a Party;—to Controversies between two or more States;—between a State and Citizens of another State;—between Citizens of different States;—between Citizens of the same State claiming Lands under Grants of different States, and between a State, or the Citizens thereof, and foreign States, Citizens or Subjects.

In all Cases affecting Ambassadors, other public Ministers and Consuls, and those in which a State shall be Party, the supreme Court shall have original Jurisdiction. In all the other Cases before mentioned, the supreme Court shall have appellate Jurisdiction, both as to Law and Fact, with such Exceptions, and under such Regulations as the Congress shall make.

The Trial of all Crimes, except in cases of Impeachment, shall be by Jury; and such Trial shall be held in the State where the said Crimes shall have been committed; but when not committed within any State, the Trial shall be at such Place or Places as the Congress may by Law have directed.

Section. 3. Treason against the United States, shall consist only in levying War against them, or in adhering to their Enemies, giving them Aid and Comfort. No Person shall be convicted of Treason unless on the Testimony of two Witnesses to the same overt Act, or on Confession in open Court.

The Congress shall have Power to declare the Punishment of Treason, but no Attainder of Treason shall work Corruption of Blood, or Forfeiture except during the Life of the Person attainted.

Article IV

Section. 1. Full Faith and Credit shall be given in each State to the public Acts, Records, and judicial Proceedings of every other State. And the Congress may by general Laws prescribe the Manner in which such Acts, Records and Proceedings shall be proved, and the Effect thereof.

Section. 2. The Citizens of each State shall be entitled to all Privileges and Immunities of Citizens in the several States.

A Person charged in any State with Treason, Felony, or other Crime, who shall flee from Justice, and be found in another State, shall on Demand of the executive Authority of the State from which he fled, be delivered up, to be removed to the State having Jurisdiction of the Crime.

No Person held to Service or Labour in one State, under the Laws thereof, escaping into another, shall, in Consequence of any Law or Regulation therein, be discharged from such Service or Labour, but shall be delivered up on Claim of the Party to whom such Service or Labour may be due.

Section. 3. New States may be admitted by the Congress into this Union; but no new State shall be formed or erected within the Jurisdiction of any other State; nor any State be formed by the Junction of two or more States, or Parts of States, without the Consent of the Legislatures of the States concerned as well as of the Congress.

The Congress shall have Power to dispose of and make all needful Rules and Regulations respecting the Territory or other Property belonging to the United States; and nothing in this Constitution shall be so construed as to Prejudice any Claims of the United States, or of any particular State.

Section. 4. The United States shall guarantee to every State in this Union a Republican Form of Government, and shall protect each of them against Invasion; and on Application of the Legislature, or of the Executive (when the Legislature cannot be convened) against domestic Violence.

Article V

The Congress, whenever two thirds of both Houses shall deem it necessary, shall propose Amendments to this Constitution, or, on the Application of the Legislatures of two thirds of the several States, shall call a Convention for proposing Amendments, which, in either Case, shall be valid to all Intents and Purposes, as Part of this Constitution, when ratified by the Legislatures of three fourths of the several States, or by Conventions in three fourths thereof, as the one or the other Mode of Ratification may be proposed by the Congress; Provided that no Amendment which may be made prior to the Year One thousand eight hundred and eight shall in any Manner affect the first and fourth Clauses in the Ninth Section of the first Article; and that no State, without its Consent, shall be deprived of its equal Suffrage in the Senate.

Article VI

All Debts contracted and Engagements entered into, before the Adoption of this Constitution, shall be as valid against the United States under this Constitution, as under the Confederation.

This Constitution, and the Laws of the United States which shall be made in Pursuance thereof; and all Treaties made, or which shall be made, under the Authority of the United States, shall be the supreme Law of the Land; and the Judges in every State shall be bound thereby, any Thing in the Constitution or Laws of any State to the Contrary notwithstanding.

The Senators and Representatives before mentioned, and the Members of the several State Legislatures, and all executive and judicial Officers, both of the United States and of the several States, shall be bound by Oath or Affirmation, to support this Constitution; but no religious Test shall ever be required as a Qualification to any Office or public Trust under the United States.

Article VII

The Ratification of the Conventions of nine States, shall be sufficient for the Establishment of this Constitution between the States so ratifying the Same. Done in Convention by the Unanimous Consent of the States present the Seventeenth Day of September in the Year of our Lord one thousand seven hundred and Eighty seven and of the Independence of the United States of America the Twelfth In witness whereof We have hereunto subscribed our Names, George Washington, President and deputy from Virginia.

New Hampshire:　　　John Langdon,
　　　　　　　　　　　　　Nicholas Gilman.

Massachusetts: Nathaniel Gorham,
                          Rufus King.

Connecticut: William Samuel Johnson,
                          Roger Sherman.

New York: Alexander Hamilton.

New Jersey: William Livingston,
                          David Brearley,
                          William Paterson,
                          Jonathan Dayton.

Pennsylvania: Benjamin Franklin,
                          Thomas Mifflin,
                          Robert Morris,
                          George Clymer,
                          Thomas FitzSimons,
                          Jared Ingersoll,
                          James Wilson,
                          Gouverneur Morris.

Delaware: George Read,
                          Gunning Bedford Jr.,
                          John Dickinson,
                          Richard Bassett,
                          Jacob Broom.

Maryland: James McHenry,
                          Daniel of St. Thomas Jenifer,
                          Daniel Carroll.

Virginia: John Blair,
                          James Madison Jr.

North Carolina: William Blount,
                          Richard Dobbs Spaight,
                          Hugh Williamson.

South Carolina: John Rutledge,
                          Charles Cotesworth Pinckney,
                          Charles Pinckney,
                          Pierce Butler.

Georgia: William Few,
                          Abraham Baldwin.

Amendments

Amendment I

(First ten amendments ratified Dec. 15, 1791.)

Congress shall make no law respecting an establishment of religion, or prohibiting the free exercise thereof; or abridging the freedom of speech, or of the press; or the right of the people peaceably to assemble, and to petition the Government for a redress of grievances.

Amendment II

A well regulated Militia, being necessary to the security of a free State, the right of the people to keep and bear Arms, shall not be infringed.

Amendment III

No Soldier shall, in time of peace be quartered in any house, without the consent of the Owner, nor in time of war, but in a manner to be prescribed by law.

Amendment IV

The right of the people to be secure in their persons, houses, papers, and effects, against unreasonable searches and seizures, shall not be violated, and no Warrants shall issue, but upon probable cause, supported by Oath or affirmation, and particularly describing the place to be searched, and the persons or things to be seized.

Amendment V

No person shall be held to answer for a capital, or otherwise infamous crime, unless on a presentment or indictment of a Grand Jury, except in cases arising in the land or naval forces, or in the Militia, when in actual service in time of War or public danger; nor shall any person be subject for the same offence to be twice put in jeopardy of life or limb; nor shall be compelled in any criminal case to be a witness against himself, nor be deprived of life, liberty, or property, without due process of law; nor shall private property be taken for public use, without just compensation.

Amendment VI

In all criminal prosecutions, the accused shall enjoy the right to a speedy and public trial, by an impartial jury of the State and district wherein the crime shall have been committed, which district shall have been previously ascertained by law, and to be informed of the nature and cause of the accusation; to be confronted with the witnesses against him; to have compulsory process for obtaining witnesses in his favor, and to have the Assistance of Counsel for his defence.

Amendment VII

In Suits at common law, where the value in controversy shall exceed twenty dollars, the right of trial by jury shall be preserved, and no fact tried by a jury, shall be otherwise re-examined in any Court of the United States, than according to the rules of the common law.

Amendment VIII

Excessive bail shall not be required, nor excessive fines imposed, nor cruel and unusual punishments inflicted.

Amendment IX

The enumeration in the Constitution, of certain rights, shall not be construed to deny or disparage others retained by the people.

Amendment X

The powers not delegated to the United States by the Constitution, nor prohibited by it to the States, are reserved to the States respectively, or to the people.

Amendment XI *(Ratified Feb. 7, 1795)*

The Judicial power of the United States shall not be construed to extend to any suit in law or equity, commenced or prosecuted against one of the United States by Citizens of another State, or by Citizens or Subjects of any Foreign State.

Amendment XII *(Ratified June 15, 1804)*

The Electors shall meet in their respective states and vote by ballot for President and Vice-President, one of whom, at least, shall not be an inhabitant of the same state with themselves; they shall name in their ballots the person voted for as President, and in distinct ballots the person voted for as Vice-President, and they shall make distinct lists of all persons voted for as President, and of all persons voted for as Vice-President, and of the number of votes for each, which lists they shall sign and certify, and transmit sealed to the seat of the government of the United States, directed to the President of the Senate;—The President of the Senate shall, in the presence of the Senate and House of Representatives, open all the certificates and the votes shall then be counted;—The person having the greatest number of votes for President, shall be the President, if such number be a majority of the whole number of Electors appointed; and if no person have such majority, then from the persons having the highest numbers not exceeding three on the list of those voted for as President, the House of Representatives shall choose immediately, by ballot, the President. But in choosing the President, the votes shall be taken by states, the representation from each state having one vote; a quorum for this purpose shall consist of a member or members from two-thirds of the states, and a majority of all the states shall be necessary to a choice. And if the House of Representatives shall not choose a President whenever the right of choice shall devolve upon them, before the fourth day of March next following, then the Vice-President shall act as President, as in the case of the death or other constitutional disability of the President—The person having the greatest number of votes as Vice-President, shall be the Vice-President, if such number be a majority of the whole number of Electors appointed, and if no person have a majority, then from the two highest numbers on the list, the Senate shall choose the Vice-President; a quorum for the purpose shall consist of two-thirds of the whole number of Senators, and a majority of the whole number shall be necessary to a choice. But no person constitutionally ineligible to the office of President shall be eligible to that of Vice-President of the United States.

Amendment XIII *(Ratified Dec. 6, 1865)*

Section 1. Neither slavery nor involuntary servitude, except as a punishment for crime whereof the party shall have been duly convicted, shall exist within the United States, or any place subject to their jurisdiction.

Section 2. Congress shall have power to enforce this article by appropriate legislation.

Amendment XIV *(Ratified July 9, 1868)*

Section 1. All persons born or naturalized in the United States and subject to the jurisdiction thereof, are citizens of the United States and of the State wherein they reside. No State shall make or enforce any law which shall abridge the privileges or immunities of citizens of the United States; nor shall any State deprive any person of life, liberty, or property, without due process of law; nor deny to any person within its jurisdiction the equal protection of the laws.

Section 2. Representatives shall be apportioned among the several States according to their respective numbers, counting the whole number of persons in each State, excluding Indians not taxed. But when the right to vote at any election for the choice of electors for President and Vice President of the United States, Representatives in Congress, the Executive and Judicial officers of a State, or the members of the Legislature thereof, is denied to any of the male inhabitants of such State, being twenty-one years of age, and citizens of the United States, or in any way abridged, except for participation in rebellion, or other crime, the basis of representation therein shall be reduced in the proportion which the number of such male citizens shall bear to the whole number of male citizens twenty-one years of age in such State.

Section 3. No person shall be a Senator or Representative in Congress, or elector of President and Vice President, or hold any office, civil or military, under the United States, or under any State, who, having previously taken an oath, as a member of Congress, or as an officer of the United States, or as a member of any State legislature, or as an executive or judicial officer of any State, to support the Constitution of the United States, shall have engaged in insurrection or rebellion against the same, or given aid or comfort to the enemies thereof. But Congress may by a vote of two-thirds of each House, remove such disability.

Section 4. The validity of the public debt of the United States, authorized by law, including debts incurred for payment of pensions and bounties for services in suppressing insurrection or rebellion, shall not be questioned. But neither the United States nor any State shall assume or pay any debt or obligation incurred in aid of insurrection or rebellion against the United States, or any claim for the loss or emancipation of any slave; but all such debts, obligations and claims shall be held illegal and void.

Section 5. The Congress shall have power to enforce, by appropriate legislation, the provisions of this article.

Amendment XV *(Ratified Feb. 3, 1870)*

Section 1. The right of citizens of the United States to vote shall not be denied or abridged by the United States or by any State on account of race, color, or previous condition of servitude.

Section 2. The Congress shall have power to enforce this article by appropriate legislation.

Amendment XVI *(Ratified Feb. 3, 1913)*

The Congress shall have power to lay and collect taxes on incomes, from whatever source derived, without apportionment among the several States, and without regard to any census or enumeration.

Amendment XVII *(Ratified Apr. 8, 1913)*

The Senate of the United States shall be composed of two Senators from each State, elected by the people thereof, for six years; and each Senator shall have one vote. The electors in each State shall have the qualifications requisite for electors of the most numerous branch of the State legislatures.

When vacancies happen in the representation of any State in the Senate, the executive authority of such State shall issue writs of election to fill such vacancies: *Provided,* That the legislature of any State may empower the executive thereof to make temporary appointments until the people fill the vacancies by election as the legislature may direct.

This amendment shall not be so construed as to affect the election or term of any Senator chosen before it becomes valid as part of the Constitution.

Amendment XVIII *(Ratified Jan. 16, 1919)*

Section 1. After one year from the ratification of this article the manufacture, sale, or transportation of intoxicating liquors within, the importation thereof into, or the exportation thereof from the United States and all territory subject to the jurisdiction thereof for beverage purposes is hereby prohibited.

Section 2. The Congress and the several States shall have concurrent power to enforce this article by appropriate legislation.

Section 3. This article shall be inoperative unless it shall have been ratified as an amendment to the Constitution by the legislatures of the several States, as provided in the Constitution, within seven years from the date of the submission hereof to the States by the Congress.

Amendment XIX *(Ratified Aug. 18, 1920)*

The right of citizens of the United States to vote shall not be denied or abridged by the United States or by any State on account of sex.

Congress shall have power to enforce this article by appropriate legislation.

Amendment XX *(Ratified Jan. 23, 1933)*

Section 1. The terms of the President and Vice President shall end at noon on the 20th day of January, and the terms of Senators and Representatives at noon on the 3d day of January, of the years in which such terms would have ended if this article had not been ratified; and the terms of their successors shall then begin.

Section 2. The Congress shall assemble at least once in every year, and such meeting shall begin at noon on the 3d day of January, unless they shall by law appoint a different day.

Section 3. If, at the time fixed for the beginning of the term of the President, the President elect shall have died, the Vice President elect shall become President. If a President shall not have been chosen before the time fixed for the beginning of his term, or if the President elect shall have failed to qualify, then the Vice President elect shall act as President until a President shall have qualified; and the Congress may by law provide for the case wherein neither a President elect nor a Vice President elect shall have qualified, declaring who shall then act as President, or the manner in which one who is to act shall be selected, and such person shall act accordingly until a President or Vice President shall have qualified.

Section 4. The Congress may by law provide for the case of the death of any of the persons from whom the House of Representatives may choose a President whenever the right of choice shall have devolved upon them, and for the case of the death of any of the persons from whom the Senate may choose a Vice President whenever the right of choice shall have devolved upon them.

Section 5. Sections 1 and 2 shall take effect on the 15th day of October following the ratification of this article.

Section 6. This article shall be inoperative unless it shall have been ratified as an amendment to the Constitution by the legislatures of three-fourths of the several States within seven years from the date of its submission.

Amendment XXI *(Ratified Dec. 5, 1933)*

Section 1. The eighteenth article of amendment to the Constitution of the United States is hereby repealed.

Section 2. The transportation or importation into any State, Territory or possession of the United States for delivery or use therein of intoxicating liquors, in violation of the laws thereof, is hereby prohibited.

Section 3. This article shall be inoperative unless it shall have been ratified as an amendment to the Constitution by conventions in the several States, as provided in the Constitution, within seven years from the date of the submission hereof to the States by the Congress.

Amendment XXII *(Ratified Feb. 27, 1951)*

Section 1. No person shall be elected to the office of the President more than twice, and no person who has held the office of President, or acted as President, for more than two years of a term to which some other person was elected President shall be elected to the office of the President more than once. But this Article shall not apply to any person holding the office of President when this Article was proposed by the Congress, and shall not prevent any person who may be holding the office of President, or acting as President, during the term within which this Article becomes operative from holding the office of President or acting as President during the remainder of such term.

Section 2. This Article shall be inoperative unless it shall have been ratified as an amendment to the Constitution by the legislatures of three-fourths of the several States within seven years from the date of its submission to the States by the Congress.

Amendment XXIII *(Ratified March 29, 1961)*

Section 1. The District constituting the seat of Government of the United States shall appoint in such manner as the Congress may direct:

A number of electors of President and Vice President equal to the whole number of Senators and Representatives in Congress to which the District would be entitled if it were a State, but in no event more than the least populous State; they shall be in addition to those appointed by the States, but they shall be considered, for the purposes of the election of President and Vice President, to be electors appointed by a State; and they shall meet in the District and perform such duties as provided by the twelfth article of amendment.

Section 2. The Congress shall have power to enforce this article by appropriate legislation.

Amendment XXIV *(Ratified Jan. 23, 1964)*

Section 1. The right of citizens of the United States to vote in any primary or other election for President or Vice President, for electors for President or Vice President, or for Senator or Representative in Congress, shall not be denied or abridged by the United States or any State by reason of failure to pay any poll tax or other tax.

Section 2. The Congress shall have power to enforce this article by appropriate legislation.

Amendment XXV *(Ratified Feb. 10, 1967)*

Section 1. In case of the removal of the President from

office or of his death or resignation, the Vice President shall become President.

Section 2. Whenever there is a vacancy in the office of the Vice President, the President shall nominate a Vice President who shall take office upon confirmation by a majority vote of both Houses of Congress.

Section 3. Whenever the President transmits to the President pro tempore of the Senate and the Speaker of the House of Representatives his written declaration that he is unable to discharge the powers and duties of his office, and until he transmits to them a written declaration to the contrary, such powers and duties shall be discharged by the Vice President as Acting President.

Section 4. Whenever the Vice President and a majority of either the principal officers of the executive departments or of such other body as Congress may by law provide, transmit to the President pro tempore of the Senate and the Speaker of the House of Representatives their written declaration that the President is unable to discharge the powers and duties of his office, the Vice President shall immediately assume the powers and duties of the office as Acting President.

Thereafter, when the President transmits to the President pro tempore of the Senate and the Speaker of the House of Representatives his written declaration that no inability exists, he shall resume the powers and duties of his office unless the Vice President and a majority of either the principal officers of the executive department or of such other body as Congress may by law provide, transmit within four days to the President pro tempore of the Senate and the Speaker of the House of Representatives their written declaration that the President is unable to discharge the powers and duties of his office. Thereupon Congress shall decide the issue, assembling within forty-eight hours for that purpose if not in session. If the Congress, within twenty-one days after receipt of the latter written declaration, or, if Congress is not in session, within twenty-one days after Congress is required to assemble, determines by two-thirds vote of both houses that the President is unable to discharge the powers and duties of his office, the Vice President shall continue to discharge the same as Acting President; otherwise, the President shall resume the powers and duties of his office.

Amendment XXVI *(Ratified July 1, 1971)*

Section 1. The right of citizens of the United States, who are eighteen years of age or older, to vote shall not be denied or abridged by the United States or by any State on account of age.

Section 2. The Congress shall have power to enforce this article by appropriate legislation.

Reference Notes

Part I—Fiscal Powers

Chapter One—Taxation and Spending

1. George B. Galloway, *The Legislative Process in Congress* (Thomas Y. Crowell Co., 1955), p. 91.
2. C. Herman Pritchett, *The American Constitution* (McGraw-Hill Book Co. Inc., 1959), p. 233.
3. For a discussion, see Daniel T. Selko, *The Federal Financial System* (The Brookings Institution, 1940), pp. 30-37.
4. See Pritchett, *The American Constitution,* pp. 420-442.
5. *Ibid.,* p. 237.
6. Lewis H. Kimmel, *Federal Budget and Fiscal Policy 1789-1958* (Brookings Institution, 1959), p. 63.
7. Frederick A. Ogg and P. Orman Ray, *Introduction to American Government* (Appleton-Century-Crofts Inc., 1951), p. 518.
8. For a history of tariff legislation, see Selko, *The Federal Financial System,* pp. 60, 557-572.
9. For a concise summary of tax policy, see Ogg and Ray, *Introduction to American Government,* pp. 514-526.
10. For background, see Joseph A. Pechman, *Federal Tax Policy* (The Brookings Institution, 1966), pp. 247-252.
11. Pechman, *Federal Tax Policy,* p. 248.
12. *Ibid.*
13. For background, see Pechman, pp. 249-250.
14. *Ibid.,* pp. 250-252.
15. Congressional Quarterly, *Congress and the Nation,* Vol. *III,* p. 79.
16. Pechman, *Federal Tax Policy,* pp. 252-254.
17. *Ibid.,* p. 254.

Chapter Two—Tax Bills in Congress

18. Background on tax bills in Congress, see Ray Blough, *The Federal Taxing Process* (Prentice-Hall Inc., 1952), pp. 61-91, and Pechman, *Federal Tax Policy*, pp. 32-50.

19. Congressional Quarterly, 1975 *Weekly Report*, p. 2410.

20. *Ibid.*, p. 419.

21. *Ibid.*, p. 2440.

22. For background, see Congressional Quarterly, *Congress and the Nation, Vol. II* (1969), pp. 149-153.

23. Congressional Quarterly, *1969 Almanac*, pp. 589-649.

24. Congressional Quarterly, *Congress and the Nation, Vol. III*, pp. 78-85.

Chapter Three—Power Over Spending

25. Pritchett, *The American Constitution*, p. 246.

26. On spending power limits, general welfare, see Selko, *The Federal Financial System*, pp. 36-37; Ogg and Ray, *Introduction to American Government*, pp. 518-519; Pritchett, *The American Constitution*, pp. 245-248.

27. See Stephen Horn, *Unused Power: The Work of the Senate Committee on Appropriations* (Brookings Institution, 1970); and Jeffrey L. Pressman, *House vs. Senate* (Yale University Press, 1966).

28. Fisher, *President and Congress*, pp. 92-93.

29. Kimmel, *Federal Budget and Fiscal Policy*, p. 2.

30. *Ibid.*, p. 3.

31. *Ibid.*, p. 4.

32. *Ibid.* For additional background on spending powers, see Fisher, *President and Congress*, pp. 85-100; and *Presidential Spending Power*, pp. 9-35; Selko, *The Federal Financial System*, pp. 77-102.

33. On growth of expenditures, see Kimmel, *Federal Budget and Fiscal Policy*, pp. 4-5; and Ogg and Ray, *Introduction to American Government*, pp. 512-514.

34. Fisher, *Presidential Spending Power*, p. 39.

35. For background on 1921 act and development, see Kimmel, *Federal Budget and Fiscal Policy;* Ogg and Ray, *Introduction to American Government*, pp. 505-12; Fisher, *Presidential Spending Power*, pp. 36-58; and Selko, *The Federal Financial System*, pp. 101-31. For modern procedures, see David J. Ott and Attiat F. Ott, *Federal Budget Policy*, revised edition (Brookings Institution, 1969).

36. On Nixon changes, see Fisher, *Presidential Spending Power*, pp. 46-59.

37. Ott and Ott, *Federal Budget Policy*, p. 41. See also Richard E. Brown, *The GAO* (University of Tennessee Press, 1970).

38. For a thorough discussion of the process, see Richard F. Fenno Jr., *The Power of the Purse* (Little, Brown and Co. Inc., 1966), Pressman, *House vs. Senate*, Robert Ash Wallace, *Congressional Control of Federal Spending* (Wayne State University Press, 1960); and Horn, *Unused Power*.

39. Congressional Quarterly, *1974 Almanac*, pp. 961-963.

40. Congressional Quarterly, 1975 *Weekly Report*, p. 2410.

Chapter Four—1974 Budget Act

41. For a discussion of current powers, see Louis Fisher, *Presidential Spending Power* (Princeton University Press, 1975).

42. For background, see Congressional Quarterly, *Congress and the Nation, Vol. I*, pp. 349, 352, 354.

43. For background, see Galloway, *The Legislative Process*, pp. 123-24; Wallace, *Congressional Control of Federal Spending*, pp. 131-36.

44. Congressional Quarterly, *1974 Almanac*, pp. 145-53.

Chapter Five—The National Debt

45. For a discussion of constitutional debt powers, see Pritchett, *The American Constitution*, pp. 248-51.

46. Ogg and Ray, *Introduction to American Government*, p. 527.

47. Ott and Ott, *Federal Budget Policy*, p. 110.

48. Kimmel, *Federal Budget and Fiscal Policy*, p. 305.

49. *Ibid.*, p. 55.

50. *Ibid.*, p. 306.

51. For background, see Congressional Quarterly, *Congress and the Nation, Vol. I*, pp. 393-395.

52. Congressional Quarterly, *1963 Almanac*, p. 570.

Part II—Foreign Affairs

Chapter Six—Legislative-Executive Antagonism

1. For a general discussion of legislative-executive antagonism, see Edward S. Corwin, *The President: Office and Powers, 1787-1957* (New York, 1957), Chapter V.

2. On the views of Madison and Hamilton, see Arthur M. Schlesinger Jr., *The Imperial Presidency* (Houghton-Mifflin Co., 1973), pp. 18-20; Louis Fisher, *President and Congress* (The Free Press, 1972), pp. 32-33; Raoul Berger, *Executive Privilege* (Harvard University Press, 1974), pp. 135-38; Bryant Putney, "Participation by Congress in Control of Foreign Policy," *Editorial Research*

Reports, Nov. 9, 1939, pp. 342-43; and Corwin, *The President: Office and Powers,* pp. 178-84.

3. Louis Henkin, *Foreign Affairs and the Constitution* (W.W. Norton & Co. Inc., 1972), pp. 76-80.

4. See Joseph P. Harris, *The Advice and Consent of the Senate* (Greenwood Press, 1968), Chapter XVI.

5. For a general discussion, see C. Herman Pritchett, *The American Constitution* (McGraw-Hill Book Co. Inc., 1959), pp. 360-62.

6. For an account of the historical development, see Schlesinger, *The Imperial Presidency;* Rexford G. Tugwell, *The Enlargement of the Presidency* (Doubleday and Co. Inc., 1960); and Corwin, *The President: Office and Powers.*

7. Francis O. Wilcox, *Congress, the Executive and Foreign Policy* (Harper and Row, 1971), p. 8.

8. Congressional Quarterly, *Congress and the Nation, 1969-1972,* Vol. III, pp. 857-59, 866-68; and Fisher, *President and Congress,* pp. 199-200.

9. For details on military sales controls, see Congressional Quarterly, 1975 *Weekly Report,* pp. 2817-19.

10. Wilcox, *Congress, the Executive and Foreign Policy,* p. 5. Writing in 1973, however, Schlesinger questions this assertion; following the Vietnam War, he said, "The assertions of sweeping and unilateral presidential authority remained official doctrine in foreign affairs." (*The Imperial Presidency,* p. ix).

Chapter Seven—The Treaty Power

11. For a general discussion of the treaty power, see Schlesinger, *The Imperial Presidency,* pp. 79-85; Henkin, *Foreign Affairs and the Constitution,* pp. 130-73; George H. Haynes, *The Senate of the United States* (Houghton-Mifflin Co., 1938), Chapter XII.

12. Haynes. *The Senate,* pp. 629-33; Daniel S. Cheever and H. Field Haviland Jr., *American Foreign Policy and the Separation of Powers* (Harvard University Press, 1952).

13. On the range of commitments, see Roland A. Paul, *American Military Commitments Abroad* (Rutgers University Press, 1973); and Congressional Quarterly, *Global Defense.*

14. Haynes, *The Senate,* p. 574.

15. *Ibid.* pp. 573-75; and Charles Warren, *The Making of the Constitution* (Little-Brown, 1928), pp. 651-58.

16. Haynes, *The Senate,* p. 575.

17. *Ibid.,* pp. 62-66.

18. *Ibid.,* pp. 583-84.

19. *Ibid.,* p. 692.

20. Harris, *The Advice and Consent of the Senate,* p. 282.

21. Background, see Haynes, *The Senate, p. 583.*

22. *Ibid.,* p. 584.

23. *Ibid.,* p. 591; and F.M. Brewer, "Advice and Consent of the Senate," *Editorial Research Reports,* June 1, 1943, p. 348.

24. Haynes *The Senate,* pp. 586-87, 600.

25. Quoted in Haynes, *The Senate,* p. 581.

26. For a discussion of the decision, see Schlesinger, *The Imperial Presidency,* pp. 100-4; Pritchett, *The American Constitution,* pp. 356-57; and Louis W. Koenig, *The Chief Executive* (Harcourt, Brace and World Inc., 1964), Chapter 9, for a discussion of the President as "chief diplomat."

27. Haynes, *The Senate,* p. 529.

28. *Ibid.,* p. 593.

29. *Ibid.,* p. 595; Harris, *The Advice and Consent of the Senate,* p. 285; and Brewer, "Advice and Consent of the Senate," p. 350.

30. Jefferson to Madison, March 15, 1798; quoted in Brewer, "Advice and Consent of the Senate," p. 350.

31. Jefferson to Genet, Nov. 22, 1793; quoted in Brewer, "Advice and Consent of the Senate," p. 350.

32. *Ibid.*

33. *Ibid.,* p. 352.

34. *Ibid.*

35. Haynes, *The Senate,* p. 596.

36. Brewer, "Advice and Consent of the Senate," p. 353.

37. Haynes, *The Senate,* p. 597.

38. Brewer, "Advice and Consent of the Senate," p. 354.

39. Wilcox, *Congress, The Executive and Foreign Policy,* p. 55.

40. See Haynes, *The Senate,* pp. 602 ff. for a discussion.

41. *Ibid.,* p. 666.

42. *Ibid.,* pp. 636-39.

43. Senate Foreign Relations Committee, *Background Information on the Committee on Foreign Relations,* U.S. Senate (U.S. Government Printing Office, 1975), p. 24.

44. Haynes, *The Senate,* pp. 665-70.

45. *Ibid.,* pp. 663-64.

46. Senate Foreign Relations Committee, *Background Information,* pp. 24-25.

47. Haynes, *The Senate,* pp. 604-6.

48. *Ibid.,* p. 608.

49. *Ibid.,* p. 657.

50. *Ibid.,* p. 609.

51. *Ibid.*

52. For a discussion of the Connally reservation, see Congressional Quarterly, *Congress and the Nation, 1945-1964,* Vol. I, pp. 98, 126.

53. Senate Foreign Relations Committee, *Background Information,* p. 24.

54. On proposed changes, see Brewer, "Advice and Consent of the Senate," and "The Treaty Power," *Editorial Research Reports,* Jan. 18, 1943; and Cheever and Haviland, *American Foreign Policy,* pp. 178-85.

55. Brewer, "The Treaty Power," p. 44.

56. *Ibid.*

57. *Ibid.*, pp. 40-41.

58. *Congress and the Nation,* Vol. I, p. 98.

59. On the Bricker amendment, see *ibid.*, pp. 110-12, 119.

60. For a general discussion of executive agreements, see Corwin, *The President: Office and Powers,* pp. 204-17; Schlesinger, *The Imperial Presidency,* pp. 86-88; Berger, *Executive Privilege,* pp. 140-62; Henkin, *Foreign Affairs and the Constitution,* pp. 176-86. For legislative proposals, see Congressional Quarterly, 1975 *Weekly Report,* pp. 1712 ff.

61. Haynes, *The Senate,* pp. 639-51; Henkin, p. 428; Schlesinger, p. 103.

62. The Rush-Bagot Agreement, which limited arms on the Great Lakes, the Boxer rebellion settlements, and the open door policy were executive agreements. See Haynes, *The Senate,* p. 644 and Henkin, *Foreign Affairs and the Constitution,* pp. 179, 428.

63. Senate Judiciary Subcommittee on the Separation of Powers, *Congressional Oversight of Executive Agreements* (U.S. Government Printing Office, 1973), p. 3.

64. Congressional Quarterly, *1970 Almanac,* p. 1008; Paul, *American Military Commitments Abroad.*

Chapter Eight—The War Power

65. For a discussion of convention proceedings, see Corwin, *The President: Office and Powers,* pp. 194 ff; and Berger, *Executive Privilege,* pp. 65 ff.

66. *Ibid.*

67. *Ibid.*, p. 64.

68. *Ibid.*, p. 63.

69. *Ibid.*, p. 64.

70. *Ibid.*, p. 60.

71. Fisher, *President and Congress,* p. 175.

72. Pritchett, *The American Constitution,* pp. 357-58.

73. Fisher, *President and Congress,* p. 179.

74. Cited in Berger, *Executive Privilege,* p. 75.

75. Cited in Fisher, *President and Congress,* p. 177.

76. Berger, *Executive Privilege,* pp. 76-77; Schlesinger, *The Imperial Presidency,* p. 51.

77. Berger, *Executive Privilege,* p. 75; Schlesinger, *The Imperial Presidency,* p. 21.

78. Berger, *Executive Privilege,* p. 82.

79. Senate Foreign Relations Committee, *Hearings on War*

Powers Legislation, 91st Congress, 1st session, 1971 (U.S. Government Printing Office, 1972), p. 254.

80. Fisher, *President and Congress*, p. 187.

81. Corwin, *The President: Office and Powers*, p. 237.

82. Fisher, *President and Congress*, p. 189.

83. Corwin, *The President: Office and Powers*, p. 242.

84. Fisher, *President and Congress*, p. 190.

85. *Ibid.*, p. 193.

86. Congressional Quarterly, *1973 Almanac*, p. 779.

87. *Ibid.*, p. 778. The Senate in 1974 passed a bill terminating four emergencies. The House passed a similar bill in 1975.

88. Fisher, *President and Congress*, p. 193.

89. Schlesinger, *The Imperial Presidency*, p. 135.

90. *Ibid.*, p. 181.

91. *Ibid.*, p. 193.

92. For a discussion of the Korean War, see Schlesinger, Chapter 6; and James A. Robinson, *Congress and Foreign Policy Making* (Dorsey Press, 1962), pp. 48-50.

93. Berger, *Executive Privilege*, p. 76.

94. Fisher, *President and Congress*, p. 194.

95. *Ibid.;* and Eagleton, *War and Presidential Power*, pp. 70-72.

96. Congressional Quarterly, *Global Defense*, pp. 72-73.

97. Berger, *Executive Privilege*, p. 111.

98. For discussion of Vietnam and additional references, see Congressional Quarterly, 1975 *Weekly Report*, pp. 842-46.

99. For a discussion of anti-war proposals, see Eagleton, *War and Presidential Power*, pp. 107 ff.

100. Quoted in Berger, *Executive Privilege*, p. 87.

101. On the war powers bill, see Congressional Quarterly, *1973 Almanac*, pp. 905-17; Schlesinger, *The Imperial Presidency*, pp. 301-07; Eagleton, *War and Presidential Power*.

102. Quoted in Schlesinger, *The Imperial Presidency*, p. 332.

103. *Ibid.*, p. 335.

104. *Ibid.*, p. 339.

105. *Ibid.*, p. 338.

106. Quoted in Schlesinger, p. 354.

107. *Ibid.*, p. 359.

108. For details, see Congressional Quarterly, *1972 Almanac*, pp. 858-62.

109. Congressional Quarterly, *1973 Almanac*, p. 787.

110. Berger, *Executive Privilege*, pp. 279-80.

111. *Ibid.*, p. 284.

112. Senate Foreign Relations Committee, *Hearings on War Powers Legislation*, 1971, p. 43.

113. Wilcox, *Congress, the Executive and Foreign Policy*, pp. 48-49.

114. *Ibid.*, p. 136.

115. See Paul, *American Military Commitments Abroad.*
116. Berger, *Executive Privilege*, p. 158.
117. Schlesinger, *The Imperial Presidency*, p. 372.

Part III—Commerce Power

Chapter Nine—History of Commerce Clause

1. C. Herman Pritchett, *The American Constitution* (McGraw-Hill Book Co., 1968), p. 253.
2. *Ibid.*, p. 254.
3. *Ibid.*, p. 277. For a concise description of the commerce power, see Frederic A. Ogg and P. Orman Ray, *Introduction to American Government* (Appleton-Century-Crofts Inc., 1951), pp. 549-572.
4. Charles Warren, *The Making of the Constitution* (Little, Brown and Co., 1928), p. 16.
5. Bryant Putney, "Federal Powers under the Commerce Clause," *Editorial Research Reports*, Oct. 4, 1935, p. 292.
6. J. B. McMaster, *History of the People of the United States* (1893), p. 206; quoted in Putney, "Federal Powers," p. 293.
7. *Ibid.*
8. *Ibid.*
9. Warren, *The Making of the Constitution*, pp. 585-586.
10. *Ibid.*, p. 570.
11. *Ibid.*, pp. 699-702.
12. Background on the case, see Putney, "Federal Powers," pp. 295-97; Pritchett, *The American Constitution*, pp. 253-55; and Charles Warren, *The Supreme Court in United States History* (Little, Brown and Co., 1926), pp. 587-632.
13. Albert J. Beveridge, *The Life of John Marshall* (Houghton-Mifflin Co., 1919), Vol. 4, pp. 429-430.
14. Ogg and Ray, *Introduction to American Government*, p. 550.

Chapter Ten—Interstate and Foreign Commerce

15. *Ibid.*, p. 563.
16. Pritchett, *The American Constitution*, p. 260.
17. Ogg and Ray, *Introduction to American Government*, p. 565.
18. Pritchett, *The American Constitution*, p. 276.
19. *Ibid.*, p. 256.
20. Warren, *The Supreme Court*, pp. 735-736; see also Pritchett, p. 260.
21. Ogg and Ray, *Introduction to American Government*, p. 560.
22. Pritchett, *The American Constitution*, p. 261.

23. Quoted in Putney, "Federal Powers," p. 302.

24. Pritchett, *The American Constitution*, p. 262.

25. *Ibid.*, pp. 262-263.

26. The cases were *Heart of Atlanta Motel Inc. v. United States* (379 U.S. 241) and *Katzenbach v. McClung* (379 U.S. 294).

27. Congressional Quarterly, *1968 Almanac* (Washington, 1969), p. 152.

28. The following discussion of federal regulatory agencies relies on Richard L. Worsnop, "Federal Regulatory Agencies: Fourth Branch of Government," *Editorial Research Reports*, Feb. 5, 1969, pp. 83-102; and Congressional Quarterly, "Regulatory Agencies: Congress Taking a Fresh Look," 1973 *Weekly Report*, pp. 3447-52.

29. M.H. Bernstein, *Regulating Business by Independent Commission* (Princeton University Press, 1955), p. 67.

30. C. Herman Pritchett, "The Regulatory Commissions Revisited," *American Political Science Review* 43 (October 1949): 988-989.

31. Robert E. Cushman, *The Independent Regulatory Commissions* (Oxford University Press, 1941), pp. 681-682.

32. In 1949, the Senate, by a 15-53 vote, rejected President Truman's nomination of Leland Olds for a third term as a member of the FPC. Olds, who had played a key role in the development of federal regulation of the natural gas industry, was opposed by oil and natural gas interests who blamed him for the commission's "discriminatory and socialistic" attitude toward private power and fuel companies. The following year, the Senate, by a 59-14 vote, rejected Martin A. Hutchinson, a lawyer and political opponent of Sen. Harry Flood Byrd (D Va.) for a seat on the FTC. Hutchinson, who had run unsuccessfully in 1946 against Byrd, was opposed by the Virginia senator.

33. Congressional Quarterly, 1974 *Weekly Report*, pp. 3161, 3255.

34. Background on foreign commerce, see Ogg and Ray, *Introduction to American Government*, pp. 553-558.

Part IV—Impeachment

Chapter Eleven—Constitutional Background

1. Paul S. Fenton, "The Scope of the Impeachment Power," *Northwestern University Law Review*, Vol. 65, No. 5 (1970): pp. 719-58, reprinted in U.S. Congress, House, Committee on the Judiciary, *Impeachment: Selected Materials*, 93d Cong., 1st sess., October 1973, pp. 663-88.

2. Asher C. Hinds, *Hinds' Precedents of the House of Representatives of the United States*, Vol. 4 (Washington: U.S. Government Printing Office, 1907), pp. 1008-11.

3. For further detail, see Congressional Quarterly, *1974 Almanac,* pp. 867-902; Congressional Quarterly, *Watergate: Chronology of a Crisis,* in particular Part III.

4. *The Federalist Papers,* with an Introduction by Clinton Rossiter (New York: Mentor, 1961), No. 65, p. 397.

5. U.S. Congress, House, Committee on the Judiciary, *Impeachment: Selected Materials on Procedure,* 93d Cong., 2d sess., January 1974, pp. 687-740, 851-900.

6. *Impeachment: Selected Materials on Procedure,* pp. 697, 892

7. Joseph Story, *Commentaries on the Constitution of the United States* (Boston: Hilliard Gray and Co., 1833), Vol. 2, section 798.

8. Raoul Berger, *Impeachment: The Constitutional Problems* (Cambridge: Harvard University Press, 1973), p. 31, quoting G. M. Trevelyan's *Illustrated History of England* (London: Longmans Green, 1956), p. 391.

9. *The Federalist Papers,* No. 65, p. 398.

10. Max Farrand (ed.), *The Records of the Federal Convention of 1787* (New Haven: 1911), Vol. 1, p. 78; Vol. 2, pp. 116, 185-86, 292, 495, 545, 550-52.

11. *Impeachment: Selected Materials on Procedure,* pp. 687-89, citing *Hinds' Precedents,* Vol. 3, p. 981.

12. *Jefferson's Manual of Parliamentary Practice and Rules of the House of Representatives,* Section LIII, 603, reprinted in *Impeachment: Selected Materials,* pp. 21-22; also Clarence Cannon, *Cannon's Precedents of the House of Representatives of the United States,* Vol. 6 (Washington: U.S. Government Printing Office, 1935), p. 657.

13. *Impeachment: Selected Materials on Procedure,* pp. 343ff, 381ff, 411ff, 475ff, citing *Hinds' Precedents,* Vol. 3, pp. 644, 681, 711, 772.

14. *Impeachment: Selected Materials on Procedure,* pp. 477-78, 509-10, 609, 655, 795, 821.

15. *Ibid.,* pp. 345-47, 382-83, 416-17, 483-84, 511, 555, 607-09, 658-59, 797.

16. *Ibid.,* pp. 821-22, citing *Cannon's Precedents,* Vol. 6, p. 709.

17. *Ibid.,* pp. 563-65.

18. *Ibid.,* pp. 765-67, citing *Cannon's Precedents,* Vol. 6, p. 657.

19. *Ibid.,* pp. 716, 890.

20. *Ibid.,* pp. 4-15, 607-52.

21. *Ibid.,* pp. 733-37.

22. *Ibid.,* p. 383.

23. *Ibid.,* pp. 2-3.

24. *Congressional Record,* 91st Cong., 2d sess., April 15, 1970, p. 11913.

25. *Impeachment: Selected Materials on Procedure*, pp. 456-71, 597.

26. *Ibid.*, pp. 795-818.

27. *Impeachment: Selected Materials*, p. 688, citing *Proceedings of the United States Senate in the Trial of Impeachment of Halsted L. Ritter*, S. Doc. No. 200, 74th Cong., 2d sess., 1936.

Chapter Twelve—History of Impeachments

28. Background, *Impeachment: Selected Materials on Procedure*, pp. 525, 722-24, 876-82; Congressional Quarterly, *1953 Almanac*, p. 311; *1970 Almanac*, p. 1025.

29. Background, *Impeachment: Selected Materials*, pp. 682-88, citing *Senate Journal*, No. 2, pp. 435-37 (1798), *Hinds' Precedents*, Vol. 3, pp. 644-980, *Cannon's Precedents*, Vol. 6, pp. 684-742, 778-86, and *Proceedings in Ritter Trial. Impeachment: Selected Materials on Procedure*, pp. 343-524, 549-685, 795-850, 884-92.

Part V—Investigations

Chapter Thirteen—Origins of Investigations

1. Woodrow Wilson, *Congressional Government* (World Publishing Co., 1967), p. 303.

2. Quoted in Donald H. Riddle, *The Truman Committee* (Rutgers University Press, 1964), p. 12. Also in the *Congressional Record*, 78th Congress, 2nd session, Aug. 7, 1944, p. 6747.

3. C. Herman Pritchett, *The American Constitution* (McGraw-Hill Inc., 1968), p. 214, quoting Lippmann's *Public Opinion* (Harcourt, Brace and World Inc., 1922), p. 289.

4. Joseph P. Harris, *Congressional Control of Administration* (Doubleday and Co., 1964), p. 253; and Marshall E. Dimock, *Congressional Investigating Committees* (Johns Hopkins Press, 1929), p. 87.

5. Dimock, p. 104; and Telford Taylor, *Grand Inquest* (Simon and Schuster Inc., 1955), p. 33.

6. Taylor, p. 51. For a summary, see Congressional Quarterly, *Congress and the Nation, 1945-1964*, Vol. I, p. 1679.

7. For a discussion of development of the power and controversy surrounding it, see Dimock, *Investigating Committees*, pp. 46, 117-21, and Taylor, *Grand Inquest*, pp. 5-16.

8. For background, see Carl Beck, *Contempt of Congress* (Hauser Press, 1959); and Ronald L. Goldfarb, *The Contempt Power* (Columbia University Press, 1963).

9. Goldfarb, p. 25.

10. *Ibid.*, p. 30; Beck, *Contempt,* p. 3; Ernest J. Eberling, *Congressional Investigations* (Columbia University Press, 1928),pp. 37-42, 66-85.

11. Eberling, pp. 161-167; Beck, p. 191.

12. Dimock, *Investigating Committees*, pp. 121-123; Pritchett, *The American Constitution*, p. 217.

13. Taylor, *Grand Inquest*, p. 35; *Congress and the Nation*, Vol. I, p. 1783.

14. Goldfarb, *The Contempt Power*, p. 196; Beck, *Contempt*, appendix.

15. Beck, p. 185.

16. *Ibid.*, pp. 185-86, 189.

17. Congressional Quarterly, *Watergate: Chronology of a Crisis*, pp. 311, 637.

Chapter Fourteen—Investigative Procedures

18. Dimock, *Investigating Committees*, pp. 73-74.

19. *Ibid.*, p. 58.

20. *Ibid.*, p. 102.

21. M. Nelson McGeary, *The Development of Congressional Investigative Power* (Octagon Books Inc., 1966), p. 8.

22. Harris, *Congressional Control*, p. 264.

23. Congressional Quarterly, *Watergate*, p. 467.

24. *Ibid.*, p. 514.

25. *Ibid.*, p. 518, for text of resolution.

26. *Ibid.*, p. 356.

27. *Ibid.*, p. 103; Raoul Berger, *Executive Privilege* (Harvard University Press, 1974), pp. 187-94.

28. Harris, *Congressional Control*, pp. 264-265.

29. Congressional Quarterly, 1975 *Weekly Report*, pp. 496, 627.

30. Congressional Quarterly, *Watergate*, p. 652.

31. For a good discussion of procedure, see McGeary, *Investigative Power*, Chapter III; and Riddle, *The Truman Committee*.

32. McGeary, pp. 51-52.

33. Background on staff, *ibid.*, pp. 59-66.

34. See John E. Wiltz, *In Search of Peace* (Louisiana State University Press, 1963), a book about the Nye committee.

35. Riddle, *The Truman Committee*.

36. According to the Charles B. Brownson *1975 Congressional Staff Directory.*

37. Congressional Quarterly, *Watergate,* p. 543.

38. For a discussion of hearings, see McGeary, *Investigative Power*, pp. 73-81.

Chapter Fifteen—Witnesses' Rights

39. For background on rights of witnesses, see Taylor, *Grand Inquest*, Chapter VI; and Library of Congress, Legislative Reference Service, *Congressional Power of Investigation* (Washington: U.S. Government Printing Office, 1954), pp. 15-20.

40. *Ibid.*, p. 15.

41. Quoted in Taylor, *Grand Inquest*, p. 240.

42. *Congress and the Nation*, Vol. I, pp. 1683-85.

43. J.W. Fulbright, "Congressional Investigations: Significance for the Legislative Processes," *University of Chicago Law Review*, 1951, p. 442.

44. Taylor, *Grand Inquest*, pp. 215-16.

45. *Ibid.*

46. Pritchett, *The American Constitution*, p. 618.

47. *Congress and the Nation*, Vol. I, pp. 1658, 1685. For a critique see Taylor, *Grand Inquest*, pp. 218-21.

48. Congressional Quarterly, *Watergate*, p. 111.

49. *Ibid.*, p. 138.

50. For a summary, see Taylor, *Grand Inquest;* and *Congress and the Nation, 1945-1964*, Vol. I, pp. 1680-81, 1684.

51. Riddle, *The Truman Committee*, pp. 4-5.

52. Dimock, pp. 126-28.

53. *Ibid.*, pp. 137-45; Pritchett, p. 215.

54. McGeary, *Investigative Power*, pp. 97-100; Taylor, *Grand Inquest*, pp. 56-57.

55. Legislative Reference Service, *Congressional Power of Investigation*, p. 48.

56. Quoted in August Raymond Ogden, *The Dies Committee* (The Catholic University of America Press, 1945), p. 44.

57. Pritchett, p. 227.

Chapter Sixteen—Investigations and the Executive

58. Berger, *Executive Privilege*, p. 1.

59. Taylor, *Grand Inquest*, p. 101.

60. Berger, *Executive Privilege*, p. 1.

61. *Congress and the Nation*, Vol. I, p. 1681; Taylor, *Grand Inquest*, pp. 99-100.

62. *Ibid.*, p. 99; Berger, *Executive Privilege*, pp. 166-179.

63. Dimock, pp. 105-107; Legislative Reference Service, *Congressional Power of Investigation*, p. 51.

64. Berger, *Executive Privilege*, pp. 183-85; Asher C. Hinds, *Hinds' Precedents of the House of Representatives of the United States*, Vol. 3 (Washington: U.S. Government Printing Office, 1907), pp. 181-86.

65. Taylor, *Grand Inquest*, p. 101; Eberling, *Congressional Investigations*, pp. 256-58; *Hinds' Precedents* Vol. 3, pp. 190-93.

66. Clarence Cannon, *Cannon's Precedents of the House of Representatives of the United States,* Vol. 6, (Washington: U.S. Government Printing Office, 1935), pp. 597-99.

67. Taylor, *Grand Inquest,* p. 102; Goodman, *The Committee,* pp. 226-37.

68. *Congress and the Nation,* Vol. I, p. 1693.

69. Taylor, *Grand Inquest,* p. 133.

70. Reprinted in Berger, *Executive Privilege,* p. 373-86.

71. *Ibid.,* p. 377.

72. *Ibid.,* p. 381.

73. *Ibid.,* p. 382.

74. *Ibid.,* p. 384.

Chapter Seventeen—Watergate and Executive Privilege

75. Congressional Quarterly, *Watergate,* p. 47.

76. *Ibid.,* p. 103.

77. *Ibid.,* p. 189.

78. *Ibid.,* pp. 341-44.

79. *Ibid.,* p. 513.

80. *Ibid.*

81. *Ibid.*

82. *Ibid.,* p. 523.

83. *Ibid.*

84. *Ibid.,* p. 640.

Chapter Eighteen—Politics of Investigations

85. Harris, *Congressional Control,* p. 271.

86. May 25, 1933; quoted in McGeary, *Investigative Power,* p. 45.

87. James A. Perkins, "Congressional Investigation of Matters of International Import," *American Political Science Review,* Vol. 39, 1940, pp. 285-87; quoted in Harris, p. 272.

88. *Ibid.*

89. *Congress and the Nation,* Vol. I, pp. 1687-88.

90. *Ibid.,* p. 1745.

91. Congressional Quarterly, 1975 *Weekly Report,* pp. 180, 240, 367.

92. *Ibid.,* pp. 1285, 1480, 1551.

Part VI—Confirmations

Chapter Nineteen—Confirmation of Nominations

1. Joseph P. Harris, *The Advice and Consent of the Senate: A Study of the Confirmation of Appointments By The United States Senate* (Greenwood Press, 1968), p. 17.

2. *The Federalist Papers*, With an Introduction by Clinton Rossiter (Mentor, 1961), No. 66, p. 405.

3. Harris, *The Advice and Consent of the Senate*, p. 29.

4. George H. Haynes, *The Senate of the United States: Its History and Practice* (Houghton Mifflin, 1938), p. 724.

5. Harris, *The Advice and Consent of the Senate*, p. 39.

6. Haynes, *The Senate*, p. 727.

7. Harris, *The Advice and Consent of the Senate*, p. 45.

8. *Ibid.*, p. 50.

9. *Ibid.*, p. 51.

10. *Ibid.*, p. 75.

11. *Ibid.*, p. 91.

12. *Ibid.*, p. 146.

13. *Ibid.*, p. 148.

14. *Ibid.*

15. *Ibid.*, p. 176.

16. Congressional Quarterly, *1968 Almanac*, p. 536.

17. Congressional Quarterly, *Congress and the Nation, 1969-1972*, Vol. III, p. 294.

18. Congressional Quarterly, *1970 Almanac*, p. 160.

19. *Ibid.*, p. 154.

Chapter Twenty—Power of Removal

20. *The Federalist Papers*, No. 77, p. 459.

21. Haynes, *The Senate*, p. 796.

22. *Ibid.*, p. 797.

23. *Ibid.*

24. *Ibid.*, p. 805.

25. *Ibid.*, pp. 807-808.

26. *Ibid.*, p. 808.

27. *Ibid.*, p. 810.

28. *Ibid.*, p. 817.

29. *Ibid.*, p. 819.

30. *Ibid.*, p. 826.

31. *Ibid.*, p. 828.

32. *Ibid.*

33. *Ibid.*, p. 829.

34. *Ibid.*, p. 831.

35. *Ibid.*, p. 832.

36. Floyd M. Riddick, *The United States Congress: Organization and Procedure*, (National Capitol Publishers, 1949), p. 335.

37. Haynes, *The Senate*, p. 774.

Part VII—Amending Power

Chapter Twenty-one—Constitutional Convention

1. Background on the Constitutional Convention, see Bryant Putney, "Revision of the Constitution," *Editorial Research Reports,* April 21, 1937, pp. 285-303; Charles Warren, *The Making of the Constitution* (Little, Brown and Co., 1928), pp. 672-84.

2. Putney, "Revision of the Constitution," p. 293.

3. Warren, *The Making of the Constitution,* p. 735.

4. *The Federalist Papers,* (Mentor Books, New American Library, 1961), p. 278.

5. Wallace Mendelson, *The Constitution and the Supreme Court* (Dodd, Mead and Company, 1965), pp. 6-9.

Chapter Twenty-two—Use of Amending Process

6. James MacGregor Burns and J. W. Peltason, with Thomas E. Cronin, *Government by the People,* 9th edition (Prentice-Hall Inc., 1975), p. 64.

7. C. Herman Pritchett, *The American Constitution* (McGraw-Hill Company, 1968), p. 35.

8. *Ibid.,* p. 36.

9. Burns, et al., *Government by the People,* p. 67.

10. Pritchett, *The American Constitution,* p. 42.

Part VIII—Electing the President

Chapter Twenty-three—Historical Background

1. Background, Edward Stanwood, *A History of the Presidency from 1788 to 1897,* (Houghton Mifflin Co., 1898), pp. 1-9.

2. Neal R. Peirce, *The People's President: The Electoral College and the Emerging Consensus for a Direct Vote,* (Simon & Schuster, 1968), p. 52.

3. Background, Stanwood, *History of Presidency,* pp. 11-13, 77-82.

4. Background, Congressional Quarterly, *Guide to U.S. Elections,* pp. 202-205, 948-949.

5. Peirce, *People's President,* p. 76, citing Lucius Wilmerding, *The Electoral College,* (Rutgers University Press, 1958), p. 58.

6. Stanwood, *History of Presidency,* pp. 54-73.

7. *Ibid.,* p. 70.

8. Peirce, *People's President,* p. 69, citing Sidney Hyman, *The American President,* (New York, 1954), p. 128.

9. Arthur M. Schlesinger Jr., ed. *History of American Presidential Elections 1789-1968,* 4 Vols., (New York: Chelsea House Publishers and McGraw-Hill Book Co., 1971), Vol. 1, p. 133.

10. Eugene H. Roseboom, *A History of Presidential Election,* (New York: Macmillan Co., 1959), p. 47.

11. Background, Stanwood, *History of Presidency,* pp. 123-141.

12. *Ibid.,* p. 138.

13. Roseboom, *History of Presidential Elections,* p. 88.

14. Schlesinger, *History of American Presidential Elections,* Vol. 1, pp. 584, 596.

15. Background, Congressional Quarterly, 1968 *Weekly Report,* pp. 1811-23, 2955-56, 3171.

16. Background, Stanwood, *History of Presidency,* pp. 20, 38, 203-04, 242, 452; Roseboom, *History of Presidential Elections,* pp.246-47.

17. Background, Stanwood, *History of Presidency,* pp. 356-93.

18. Roseboom, *History of Presidential Elections,* pp. 243-44.

Chapter Twenty-four—Electoral Reform

19. Congressional Quarterly, *Congress and the Nation, 1969-1972,* Vol. III, pp. 1012-19.

20. Congressional Quarterly, *Congress and the Nation, 1965-1968,* Vol. II, pp. 645-48.

21. Background, Congressional Quarterly, *1973 Almanac,* pp. 1061-68; *1974 Almanac,* pp. 917-35.

Selected Bibliography

Part I—Fiscal Powers

Books

Blough, Ray. *The Federal Taxing Process.* Englewood Cliffs, N.J.: Prentice-Hall Inc., 1952.

Can Congress Control Spending? Proceedings of the Town Meeting on Domestic Affairs. Washington: American Enterprise Institute for Public Policy Research, 1973.

Fenno, Richard F. Jr. *The Power of the Purse: Appropriation Politics in Congress.* Boston: Little, Brown and Co. Inc., 1973.

Findley, William. *Review of the Revenue System Adopted by the First Congress.* Philadelphia: T. Dobson, 1794; reprint ed., New York: A. M. Kelley, 1971.

Fisher, Louis. *President and Congress.* New York: Free Press, 1972.

————. *Presidential Spending Power.* Princeton: Princeton University Press, 1975.

Galloway, George B. *The Legislative Process in Congress.* New York: Thomas Y. Crowell Co., 1955.

Harris, Joseph P. *Congressional Control of Administration.* Washington: Brookings Institution, 1964.

Horn, Stephen. *Unused Power: The Work of the Senate Committee on Appropriations.* Washington: Brookings Institution, 1970.

Kimmel, Lewis H. *Federal Budget and Fiscal Policy 1789-1958*. Washington: Brookings Institution, 1959.

Kirst, Michael W. *Government Without Passing Laws*. Chapel Hill: University of North Carolina Press, 1969.

MacLean, Joan C. *President and Congress: The Conflict of Powers*. Bronx: H. W. Wilson, 1955.

Manley, John F. *The Politics of Finance: The House Committee on Ways and Means*. Boston: Little, Brown & Co., 1970.

Myers, William Starr. *The Republican Party: A History*. New York: Century Co., 1928.

Ogg, Frederic A., and Ray, P. Orman. *Introduction to American Government*. New York: Appleton-Century-Crofts Inc., 1951.

Ott, David J. and Ott, Attiat F. *Federal Budget Policy*. rev. ed. Washington: Brookings Institution, 1969.

Pechman, Joseph A. *Federal Tax Policy*. rev. ed. Washington: Brookings Institution, 1971.

Pressman, Jeffrey L. *House vs. Senate: Conflict in the Appropriation Process*. New Haven: Yale University Press, 1966.

Pritchett, C. Herman. *The American Constitution*. New York: McGraw-Hill Book Co. Inc., 1959.

Saloma, John S. III. *The Responsible Use of Power*. Washington: American Enterprise Institute, 1964.

Schick, Allen. "The Battle of the Budget." In *Congress Against the President*, pp. 51-70. Edited by Harvey C. Mansfield Sr. New York: Praeger, 1975.

Selko, Daniel T. *The Federal Financial System*. Washington: Brookings Institution, 1940.

Sharkansky, Ira. *The Politics of Taxing and Spending*. New York: Bobbs-Merrill Co. Inc., 1969.

Smithies, Arthur. *The Budgeting Process in the United States*. New York: McGraw-Hill Book Co. Inc., 1955

Wallace, Robert Ash. *Congressional Control of Federal Spending*. Detroit: Wayne State University Press 1960.

Weidenbaum, Murray L. *Federal Budgeting, The Choice of Government Programs*. Washington: American Enterprise Institute, 1964.

Wilmerding, Lucius Jr. *The Spending Power: A History of the Efforts of Congress to Control Expenditures*. New Haven: Yale University Press, 1943.

Articles

Boeckel, Richard M. "The Deficit and the Public Debt."
Editorial Research Reports, May 2, 1936, pp. 317-35.
Finley, James J. "Congressional Budget Making." *Federal Accountant,* June 1974, pp. 22-34.
Fisher, Louis. "Congress, the Executive and the Budget."
Annals of the American Academy of Political and Social Science, January 1974, pp. 102-13.
Schick, Allen. "Budget Reform Legislation: Reorganizing Congressional Centers of Fiscal Power." *Harvard Journal on Legislation,* February 1974, pp. 303-50.
Webbink, Paul. "Deadlocks in Tariff Legislation." *Editorial Research Reports,* Nov. 1, 1929, pp. 865-79.

Government Publications

President's Commission on Budget Concepts. *Report of the President's Commission on Budget Concepts.* Washington: Government Printing Office, 1967.
U.S. Congress. House. Committee on the Budget. *Congressional Budget Reform, Committee Print, July 12, 1974.* Washington: Government Printing Office, 1975.
U.S. Congress. Joint Study Committee on Budget Control. *Improving Congressional Control Over Budgetary Outlay and Receipt Totals, Report, February 7, 1973.* Washington: Government Printing Office, 1973.
U.S. Congress, Library of Congress. Congressional Research Service. *An Analysis of Proposals to Improve Congressional Control of Spending,* by Allen Schick. Jan. 10, 1972.
U.S. Congress. Senate. *The Authority of the Senate to Originate Appropriations Bills.* S. Doc. 17, 88th Cong., 1st sess., 1963.
U.S. Congress. Senate. Committee on Government Operations. *Financial Management in the Federal Government.* S. Doc. 11, 87th Cong., 1st sess., 1961.
U.S. General Accounting Office. *Improving Congressional Control Over Federal Budget, GAO Report, Summer 1973,* by Elmer B. Staats. Washington: General Accounting Office, 1973.

Part II—Foreign Affairs

Books

Berger, Raoul. *Executive Privilege.* Cambridge: Harvard University Press, 1974. (Extensive bibliography.)

Butler, Charles H. *The Treaty Making Power of the United States.* New York: Banks Law Publishing Co., 1902.

Carroll, Holbert N. *The House of Representatives and Foreign Affairs.* Boston: Little, Brown & Co., 1966.

Cheever, Daniel S. and Haviland, H. Field Jr. *American Foreign Policy and the Separation of Powers.* Cambridge: Harvard University Press, 1952.

Congressional Quarterly. *Global Defense.* Washington, D.C.: September 1969.

Corwin, Edward S. *The President: Office and Powers, 1787-1957.* New York: New York University Press, 1957.

Crandall, Samuel B. *Treaties, Their Making and Enforcement.* New York: Columbia University Press, 1904.

Dahl, Robert A. *Congress and Foreign Policy.* New York: Harcourt, Brace & Co., 1950.

Dangerfield, Royden J. *In Defense of the Senate.* Norman, Okla.: University of Oklahoma Press, 1933.

Dennison, Eleanor E. *The Senate Foreign Relations Committee.* Stanford: Stanford University Press, 1942.

Eagleton, Thomas J. *War and Presidential Power.* New York: Liveright, 1974. (Extensive bibliography.)

Farnsworth, David N. *The Senate Committee on Foreign Relations.* Urbana: University of Illinois Press, 1961.

The Federalist Papers. Introduction by Clinton Rossiter. New York: Mentor, 1961.

Fisher, Louis. *President and Congress.* New York: The Free Press, 1972.

Fleming, Denna F. *The Treaty Veto of the American Senate.* New York: G. P. Putnam's Sons, 1930.

Harden, Ralston. *The Senate and Treaties 1789-1817.* New York: Macmillan Co., 1920.

Harris, Joseph P. *The Advice and Consent of the Senate.* Westport, Conn.: Greenwood Press, 1968.

Haynes, George H. *The Senate of the United States: Its History and Practice.* 2 vols. Boston: Houghton, Mifflin Co., 1938.

Henkin, Louis. *Foreign Affairs and the Constitution.* New York: W. W. Norton & Co., 1972.

Kolodziej, Edward A. "Congress and Foreign Policy: The Nixon Years." In *Congress Against the President.* Edited by Harvey C. Mansfield Sr. New York: Praeger Publishers, 1975.

Lehman, John. *The Executive, Congress, and Foreign Policy.* New York: Praeger Publishers, 1976.

Paul, Roland A. *American Military Commitments Abroad.* New Brunswick, N.J.: Rutgers University Press, 1973. (Extensive bibliography.)

Pritchett, C. Herman. *The American Constitution.* New York: McGraw-Hill Book Co. Inc., 1959.

Robinson, James A. *Congress and Foreign Policy Making.* Homewood, Ill.: Dorsey Press, 1962.

Schlesinger, Arthur M. Jr. *The Imperial Presidency.* Boston: Houghton, Mifflin Co., 1973.

Stennis, John C. *The Role of Congress in Foreign Policy.* Washington, D.C.: American Enterprise Institute for Public Policy Research, 1971.

Tugwell, Rexford G. *The Enlargement of the Presidency.* New York: Doubleday and Co. Inc., 1960.

Warren, Charles. *The Making of the Constitution.* Boston: Little, Brown & Co., 1928.

Westphal, C. F. *The House Committee on Foreign Affairs.* New York: Columbia University Press, 1942.

Wilcox, Francis O. *Congress, The Executive and Foreign Policy.* New York: Harper and Row, 1971.

Articles

Berry, John M. "Foreign Policy Making and the Congress." *Editorial Research Reports,* April 19, 1967, pp. 281-300.

Brewer, F. M. "Advice and Consent of the Senate." *Editorial Research Reports,* June 1, 1943, pp. 341-56; "The Treaty Power." *Editorial Research Reports,* Jan. 18, 1943, pp. 37-54.

"Congress and Foreign Relations." *Annals of the American Academy of Political and Social Science,* September 1953.

"Congress, the President and the Power to Commit Forces to Combat." *Harvard Law Review,* June 1968, pp. 1771-805.

Eagleton, Thomas F. "Congress and the War Power." *Missouri Law Review,* Winter 1972, pp. 1-32.

Gould, James W. "The Origins of the Senate Committee on Foreign Relations, 1789-1816." *Western Political Quarterly,* September 1959, pp. 670-82.

Humphrey, Hubert H. "The Senate in Foreign Policy." *Foreign Affairs,* July 1959.

Lee, Kendrick. "Congress and the Conduct of War." *Editorial Research Reports,* Aug. 24, 1942, pp. 125-40.

Manley, John F. "The Rise of Congress in Foreign Policy-Making." *Annals of the American Academy of Political and Social Science,* September 1971, pp. 60-70.

Patch, Buel W. "American Policy on the League of Nations and the World Court." *Editorial Research Reports,* Jan. 2, 1935, pp. 1-24; "The Power to Declare War." *Editorial Research Reports,* Jan. 6, 1938, pp. 1-18; "Treaties and Domestic Law." *Editorial Research Reports,* March 28, 1952, pp. 239-56.

"Presidential vs. Congressional War-Making Powers." *Boston University Law Review,* Special Issue, 1970, pp. 5-116.

Putney, Bryant. "Participation by Congress in Control of Foreign Policy." *Editorial Research Reports,* Nov. 9, 1939, pp. 337-55.

Reed, R. P. "Foreign Policy and the Initiation of War: The Congress and the Presidency in the Dispute Over War Powers." *Potomac Review,* Winter 1973, pp. 1-29.

Schlesinger, Arthur M. Jr. "Congress and the Making of American Foreign Policy." *Foreign Affairs,* October 1972, pp. 78-113.

Worsnop, Richard L. "War Powers of the President." *Editorial Research Reports,* March 14, 1966, pp. 181-200.

Government Publications

U.S. Congress. House. Committee on Foreign Affairs. *Background Information on the Use of United States Armed Forces in Foreign Countries.* (1970 revision by the Foreign Affairs Division, Legislative Reference Service, Library of Congress), 91st Cong., 2nd sess., 1970.

——. *Concerning the War Powers of Congress and the President.* H. Rept. 91-1547 to Accompany H. J. Res. 1355, 91st Cong., 2nd sess., 1970.

———. *Concerning the War Powers of Congress and the President.* H. Rept. 92-1302 to Accompany S. 2956, 92nd Cong., 2nd sess., 1972.

———. *Congress, the President and the War Powers: Hearings.* 91st Cong., 2nd sess., 1970.

———. *War Powers Legislation. Hearings before the Subcommittee on National Security Policy and Scientific Developments.* 93rd Cong., 1st sess., 1973.

U.S. Congress. Senate. Committee on Foreign Relations. *Background Information on the Committee on Foreign Relations, United States Senate.* 3rd rev. ed., 94th Cong., 1st sess., 1975.

———. *Documents Relating to the War Power of Congress, the President's Authority as Commander-in-Chief and the War in Indochina.* 91st Cong., 2nd sess., 1970.

———. *Hearings before the Subcommittee on U.S. Security Agreements and Commitments Abroad.* 91st Cong., 1969-1970.

———. *National Commitments.* S. Rept. 90-797 to Accompany S. Res. 187, 90th Cong., 1st sess., 1967.

———. *National Commitments.* S. Rept., 91-129 to Accompany S. Res. 85, 91st Cong., 1st sess., April 16, 1969.

———. *Termination of Southeast Asia Resolution.* S. Rept. 91-872 to Accompany S. Con. Res. 64, 91st Cong., 2nd sess., May 15, 1970.

———. *War Powers.* S. Rept. 92-606 to Accompany S. 2956, 92nd Cong., 2nd sess., 1972.

———. *War Powers Legislation: Hearings.* 92nd Cong., 1st sess., 1971.

———. *War Powers Legislation: Hearings.* 93rd Cong., 1st sess., April 11-12, 1973.

U.S. Congress. Senate. Committee on the Judiciary. Subcommittee on Separation of Powers. *Congressional Oversight of Executive Agreements.* S. Rept. to Accompany S. 1472, committee print, 93rd Cong., 1st sess., 1973.

Part III—Commerce Power

Books

Beard, Charles A. *Economic Interpretation of the Constitution of the United States.* New York: Macmillan, 1935.

Benson, Paul R. *Supreme Court and the Commerce Clause, 1937-1970.* Port Washington, N.Y.: Dunellen Publishing Co., 1971.

Bernstein, M. H. *Regulating Business by Independent Commission.* Princeton: Princeton University Press, 1955.

Beveridge, Albert J. *The Life of John Marshall.* 4 vols. Boston: Houghton Mifflin Co., 1919.

Bogart, Ernest L. *Economic History of the American People.* New York: Longmans, Green, 1942.

Corwin, Edward S. *The Commerce Power versus States Rights.* Princeton: Princeton University Press, 1936.

Crosskey, William W. *Politics and the Constitution in the History of the United States.* Chicago: University of Chicago Press, 1953.

Cushman, Robert E. *The Independent Regulatory Commissions.* New York: Oxford University Press, 1941.

Frankfurter, Felix. *The Commerce Clause under Marshall, Taney and Waite.* Chapel Hill: University of North Carolina Press, 1937.

Gavit, Bernard C. *Commerce Clause of the United States Constitution.* New York: AMS Press, 1970.

Haines, Charles Grove, and Sherwood, Foster H. *The Role of the Supreme Court in American Government and Politics, 1835-1864.* Berkeley: University of California Press, 1957.

Hamilton, Walton H. and Adair, Douglas. *The Power to Govern: The Constitution—Then and Now.* New York: W. W. Norton & Co. Inc., 1937.

Kallenbach, Joseph E. *Federal Cooperation with the States under the Commerce Clause.* Ann Arbor: University of Michigan Press, 1942.

Kelly, Alfred H. and Harbison, Winfred A. *The American Constitution: Its Origins and Development.* 3rd ed. New York: W. W. Norton & Co. Inc., 1963.

Liebhafsky, H. H. *American Government and Business.* New York: John Wiley & Sons, 1971.

Ogg, Frederick A. and Ray, P. Orman. *Introduction to American Government.* New York: Appleton-Century-Crofts Inc., 1951.

Pritchett, C. Herman. *The American Constitution.* 2nd ed. New York: McGraw-Hill Book Co., 1968.

_____ . *The Roosevelt Court: A Study in Judicial Politics and Values, 1937-1947.* New York: Macmillan Co., 1948.

Reynolds, George G. *Distribution of Power to Regulate Interstate Carriers Between the Nation and the States.* New York: AMS Press, 1928.

Warren, Charles. *The Making of the Constitution.* Boston: Little, Brown and Co., 1928.

_____ . *The Supreme Court in United States History.* rev. ed. 2 vols. Boston: Little, Brown and Co., 1926.

Articles

Apraia, Anthony F. "The Brass Tacks of the ICC Administration Problems." *Public Utilities Fortnightly,* March 31, 1960, pp. 433-42.

"Congressional Supervision of Interstate Commerce." *Yale Law Journal,* July 1966, pp. 1416-33.

Ely, Robert B. "Free Trade, American Style." *American Bar Association Journal,* May 1970, pp. 470-74.

Pritchett, C. Herman. "The Hoover Commission: A Symposium, Part VI. The Regulatory Commissions Revisited." *American Political Science Review,* vol. 43, 1949, pp. 978-1000.

Putney, Bryant. "Federal Powers Under the Commerce Clause." *Editorial Research Reports,* Oct. 4, 1935, pp. 289-304.

Worsnop, Richard L. "Federal Regulatory Agencies: Fourth Branch of Government." *Editorial Research Reports,* Feb. 5, 1969, pp. 83-102.

Government Publications

Udell, Gilman, comp. *Laws Relating to Interstate Commerce and Transportation.* Washington: Government Printing Office, 1966.

Part IV—Impeachment

Books

The Association of the Bar of the City of New York. *The Law of Presidential Impeachment and Removal.* 1974.

Bibliography

Benedict, Michael L. *The Impeachment and Trial of Andrew Johnson.* New York: W. W. Norton & Co., 1973.

Berger, Raoul. *Impeachment: The Constitutional Problem.* Cambridge: Harvard University Press, 1973.

Black, Charles L. *Impeachment: A Handbook.* New Haven: Yale University Press, 1974.

Brant, Irving. *Impeachment: Trials and Errors.* New York: Alfred A. Knopf, 1972.

Dewitt, David M. *Impeachment and Trial of Andrew Johnson.* New York: Russell & Russell, 1967.

Farrand, Max, ed. *The Records of the Federal Convention of 1787.* 4 vols. New Haven: Yale University Press, 1966.

The Federalist Papers. Introduction by Clinton Rossiter. New York: Mentor, 1961.

Haynes, George H. *The Senate of the United States: Its History and Practice.* 2 vols. Boston: Houghton Mifflin, 1938.

Riddick, Floyd M. *The United States Congress: Organization and Procedure.* Manassas, Va.: National Capitol Publishers Inc., 1949.

Simpson, Alexander Jr. *A Treatise of Federal Impeachments.* Philadelphia: 1916; reprint ed., Wilmington, Del.: Scholarly Resources Inc., 1974.

Articles

Bates, William. "Vagueness in the Constitution: The Impeachment Power." *Stanford Law Journal,* June 1973, pp. 908-26.

Berger, Raoul. "Executive Privilege vs. Congressional Inquiry." *UCLA Law Review,* vol. 12, 1965, p. 104.

Berger, Raoul. "Impeachment for 'High Crimes and Misdemeanors.' " *Southern California Law Review,* vol. 44, 1971, pp. 395-460.

Bishop, J. W. "The Executive's Right to Privacy: An Unresolved Constitutional Question." *Yale Law Journal,* vol. 66, 1957, p. 477.

Collins, P. R. "Power of Congressional Committees of Investigations to Obtain Information from the Executive Branch." *Georgia Law Journal,* vol. 39, 1951, p. 563.

Dougherty, J. H. "Inherent Limitations Upon Impeachment." *Yale Law Journal,* vol. 23, 1913, pp. 60-69.

Fenton, Paul S. "The Scope of the Impeachment Power." *Northwestern University Law Review,* November/ December 1970, pp. 719-58.

"The Impeachment of Andrew Johnson." *Annals of the American Academy of Political and Social Science,* vol. 10, 1968, pp. 126-33.

"President and Congress: Power of the President to Refuse Congressional Demand for Information." *Stanford Law Review,* vol. 1, 1949, p. 256.

Government Publications

Cannon, Clarence. *Cannon's Precedents of the House of Representatives.* Washington: Government Printing Office, 1935.

Hinds, Asher C. *Hinds' Precedents of the House of Representatives.* Washington, D.C.: Government Printing Office, 1907.

U.S. Congress. House. Committee on the Judiciary. *Constitutional Grounds for Presidential Impeachment.* 93rd Cong., 2nd sess., 1974.

U.S. Congress. House. Committee on the Judiciary. *Impeachment: Selected Materials.* 93rd Cong., 1st sess., 1973.

U.S. Congress. House. Committee on the Judiciary. *Impeachment: Selected Materials on Procedure.* 93rd Cong., 2nd sess., 1974.

U.S. Congress. Senate. Committee on the Judiciary. *Removal Power of Congress With Respect to the Supreme Court.* 80th Cong., 1st sess., 1947.

U.S. Department of Justice. Office of Legal Counsel. "Legal Aspects of Impeachment: An Overview." February 1974.

U.S. President. "An Analysis of the Constitutional Standard for Presidential Impeachment." Prepared by the attorneys for the President, The White House, February 1974.

Part V—Investigations

Books

Barth, Alan. *Government by Investigation.* New York: Viking Press, 1955.

Bibliography

Beck, Carl. *Contempt of Congress: A Study of the Prosecutions Initiated by the Committee on Un-American Activities, 1945-1957.* New Orleans: Hauser Press, 1959.

Bentley, Eric, ed. *Thirty Years of Treason: Excerpts from Hearings before the House Un-American Activities Committee, 1938-1968.* New York: Viking Press, 1971.

Berger, Raoul. *Executive Privilege.* Cambridge: Harvard University Press, 1974.

Carr, Robert K. *The House Committee on Un-American Activities, 1945-1950.* Ithaca: Cornell University Press, 1952.

Chambers, Whittaker. *Witness.* New York: Random House, 1952.

Congressional Quarterly. *Watergate: Chronology of a Crisis.* Washington: Congressional Quarterly Inc., 1975.

Dimock, Marshall E. *Congressional Investigating Committees.* Baltimore: Johns Hopkins Press, 1929.

Eberling, Ernest J. *Congressional Investigations: A Study of the Origin and Development of the Power of Congress to Investigate and Punish for Contempt.* New York: Columbia University Press, 1928.

Galloway, George B. *History of the House of Representatives.* New York: Thomas Y. Crowell Co., 1969.

Goldfarb, Ronald L. *The Contempt Power.* New York: Columbia University Press, 1963.

Goodman, Walter. *The Committee: The Extraordinary Career of the House Committee on Un-American Activities.* New York: Farrar, Straus and Giroux, 1968.

Hamilton, James. *The Power to Probe: A Study of Congressional Investigations.* New York: Random House, 1976.

Harris, Joseph P. *Congressional Control of Administration.* Washington: Brookings Institution, 1964.

McGeary, M. Nelson. *The Development of Congressional Investigative Power.* New York: Octagon Books Inc., 1966.

Ogden, August Raymond. *The Dies Committee: A Study of the Special House Committees for Investigation of Un-American Activities, 1938-1944.* Washington: Catholic University of America Press, 1945.

Pritchett, C. Herman. *The American Constitution.* New York: McGraw-Hill, 1968.

Riddle, Donald H. *The Truman Committee: A Study in Congressional Responsibility.* New Brunswick: Rutgers University Press, 1964.

Rovere, Richard H. *Senator Joe McCarthy.* Cleveland: World Publishing Co., 1968.

Schlesinger, Arthur M. Jr., and Burns, Roger, eds. *Congress Investigates: A Documentary History 1792-1974.* 5 vols. New York: Bowker, 1975.

Taylor, Telford. *Grand Inquest.* New York: Simon & Schuster Inc., 1955.

Wilson, Woodrow. *Congressional Government.* Cleveland: World Publishing Co., 1967 ed.

Wiltz, John E. *In Search of Peace: The Senate Munitions Inquiry, 1934-1936.* Baton Rouge: Louisiana State University Press, 1963.

Articles

"The Application of the Fourth Amendment to Congressional Investigations." *Minnesota Law Review,* January 1968, pp. 665-97.

"Congressional Investigations." *University of Chicago Law Review,* vol. 18, no. 3, 1951.

Cousens, Theodore W. "The Purpose and Scope of Investigation Under Legislative Authority." *Georgetown Law Journal,* vol. 26, 1938, p. 905.

Dilliard, Irving. "Congressional Investigations: The Role of the Press." *University of Chicago Law Review,* vol. 18, 1951, pp. 585-90.

Galloway, George. "Congressional Investigation: Proposed Reforms." *University of Chicago Law Review,* vol. 18, 1951, pp. 478-502.

Galloway, George B. "The Investigative Function of Congress." *American Political Science Review,* February 1927, pp. 47-70.

Kaplan, Lewis A. "The House Un-American Activities Committee and Its Opponents: A Study in Congressional Dissonance." *Journal of Politics,* August 1968, pp. 647-71.

McGeary, M. Nelson "Congressional Investigations: Historical Development." *University of Chicago Law Review,* vol. 18, 1951, pp. 425-39.

McGeary, M. Nelson "Congressional Power of Investigation." *Nebraska Law Review,* vol. 28, 1949, pp. 516-29.

Government Publications

U.S. Congress. Library of Congress. Legislative Research Service. *Congressional Power of Investigation.* Washington: Government Printing Office, 1954.

Part VI—Confirmations

Books

The Federalist Papers. Introduction by Clinton Rossiter. New York: Mentor, 1961.

Freidin, Seymour K. *A Sense of the Senate.* New York: Dodd, Mead and Co., 1972.

Harris, Joseph P. *The Advice and Consent of the Senate: A Study of the Confirmation of Appointments by the United States Senate.* New York: Greenwood Press, 1968.

Harris, Richard. *Decision.* New York: E. P. Dutton, 1971.

Haynes, George H. *The Senate of the United States: Its History and Practice.* 2 vols. Boston: Houghton Mifflin, 1938.

Mann, Dean E. *The Assistant Secretaries: Problems and Processes of Appointment.* Washington: Brookings Institution, 1965.

Riddick, Floyd M. *The United States Congress: Organization and Procedure.* Manassas, Va.: National Capitol Publishers, 1949.

Rogers, Lindsay. *The American Senate.* New York: Alfred A. Knopf, 1926.

Rothman, David J. *Politics and Power: The United States Senate, 1869-1901.* New York: Atheneum, 1969.

Warren, Charles. *The Supreme Court in United States History.* Boston: Little, Brown and Co., 1926.

Articles

Bickel, Alexander M. "The Making of Supreme Court Justices." *New Leader,* May 25, 1970, pp. 14-18.

Black, Charles L. Jr. "A Note on Senatorial Consideration of Supreme Court Nominees." *Yale Law Journal,* March 1970, pp. 657-64.

Carmen, Ira H. "The President, Politics and the Power of Appointment: Hoover's Nomination of Mr. Justice Cardozo." *Virginia Law Review,* May 1969, pp. 616-59.

Gimlin, Hoyt. "Challenging of Supreme Court." *Editorial Research Reports,* Oct. 9, 1968, pp. 741-60.

Griffin, Robert P. and Hart, Philip A. "The Fortas Controversy: The Senate's Role of Advice and Consent to Judicial Nominations ['The Broad Role' by Griffin and 'The Discriminating Role' by Hart]." *Prospectus,* April 1969, pp. 238-310.

McConnell, A. Mitchell Jr. "Haynsworth and Carswell: A New Senate Standard of Excellence." *Kentucky Law Journal,* Fall 1970, pp. 7-34.

Mendelsohn, Rona Hirsch. "Senate Confirmation of Supreme Court Appointments: the Nomination and Rejection of John J. Parker." *Howard Law Journal,* Winter 1967, pp. 105-48.

Rodell, Fred. "The Complexities of Mr. Justice Fortas." *New York Times Magazine,* July 28, 1968, pp. 67-68.

Steele, John L. "Haynsworth v. the U.S. Senate (1969)." *Fortune,* March 1970, pp. 90-93.

Swindler, William F. "The Politics of 'Advice and Consent:' The Senate's Role in Selection of Supreme Court Justices." *American Bar Association Journal,* June 1970, pp. 533-42.

Wukasch, Barry C. "The Abe Fortas Controversy: A Research Note on the Senate's Role in Judicial Selection." *Western Political Quarterly,* March 1971, pp. 24-27.

Government Publications

U.S. Congress. House. Committee on Government Operations. *Confirmation of the Director and Deputy Director of the Office of Management and Budget, Hearings, March 5, 9, 1973.* 93rd Cong., 1st sess., 1973.

U.S. Congress. Senate. Committee on Foreign Relations. *The Senate Role in Foreign Affairs Appointments, Committee Print.* 92nd Cong., 1st sess., 1971.

U.S. Congress. Senate. Committee on the Judiciary. *Nomination of Clement F. Haynsworth, Jr., of South Carolina, to be Associate Justice of the Supreme Court, Hearings, September 16-26, 1969.* 91st Cong., 1st sess., 1969.

U.S. Congress. Senate. Committee on the Judiciary. *Nomination of George Harrold Carswell, of Florida, to be Associate Justice of the Supreme Court, Hearings, January 27-February 3, 1970.* 91st Cong., 2nd sess, 1970.

U.S. Congress. Senate. Committee on the Judiciary. *Nomination of Harry A. Blackmun, of Minnesota, to be Associate Justice of the Supreme Court, Hearings, April 29, 1970.* 91st Cong., 2nd sess., 1970.

Part VII—Amending Power

Books

Boorstin, Daniel J. *An American Primer.* Chicago: University of Chicago Press, 1966.

Burns, James MacGregor, and Peltason, Jack Walter, with Cronin, Thomas E. *Government by the People. 9th* ed. Englewood Cliffs, N.J.: Prentice-Hall, 1975.

Crosskey, William W. *Politics and the Constitution in the History of the United States.* 2 vols. Chicago: University of Chicago Press, 1953.

Gillette, William. *Right to Vote: Politics and the Passage of the Fifteenth Amendment.* Baltimore: Johns Hopkins University Press, 1970.

Haynes, George H. *The Senate of the United States: Its History and Practice.* 2 vols. Boston: Houghton Mifflin Co., 1938.

Katz, William L. *Constitutional Amendments.* New York: Franklin Watts, 1974.

Kelly, Alfred H., and Harbison, Winfred A. *The American Constitution.* New York: W. W. Norton and Co., 1955.

Lasson, Nelson B. *History and Development of the Fourth Amendment to the United States Constitution.* New York: Plenum, 1970.

Mathews, John M. *Legislative and Judicial History of the Fifteenth Amendment.* New York: Da Capo Press, 1971.

Mendelson, Wallace. *The Constitution and the Supreme Court.* New York: Dodd, Mead and Co., 1965.

Morgan, Donald G. *Congress and the Constitution: A Study of Responsibility.* Cambridge: Harvard University Press, 1966.

Munro, William B., ed. *Initiative, Referendum and Recall.* New York: D. Appleton, 1912.

Oberholtzer, Ellis P. *Referendum in America.* New York: Da Capo Press, 1971.

Ogg, Frederic A., and Ray, P. Orman. *Introduction to American Government.* New York: Appleton-Century-Crofts Inc., 1951.

Orfield, Lester B. *Amending of the Federal Constitution.* New York: Da Capo Press, 1971.

Pritchett, C. Herman. *The American Constitution.* 2nd ed. New York: McGraw-Hill, 1968.

Vose, Clement E. *Constitutional Change: Amendment Politics and Supreme Court Litigation Since 1900.* Lexington, Mass.: Lexington Books, 1972.

Warren, Charles. *The Making of the Constitution.* Boston: Little, Brown and Co., 1928.

Articles

Feerick, John D. "Amending the Constitution Through a Convention." *American Bar Association Journal,* March 1974, pp. 258-88.

Forbush, Emory. "The Poll Tax." *Editorial Research Reports,* July 3, 1941, pp. 1-18.

Lacy, Donald P., and Martin, Philip L. "Amending the Constitution: The Bottleneck in the Judiciary Committees." *Harvard Journal on Legislation,* May 1972, pp. 666-93.

Martin, Philip L. "The Application Clause of Article Five." *Political Science Quarterly,* December 1970, pp. 616-28.

Patch, Buel W. "Tax and Debt Limitation." *Editorial Research Reports,* Feb. 13, 1952, pp. 121-40.

"Proposed Legislation on the Convention Method of Amending the United States Constitution." *Harvard Law Review,* June 1972, pp. 1612-48.

Putney, Bryant. "Revision of the Constitution." *Editorial Research Reports,* April 21, 1937, pp. 285-303.

Government Publications

U.S. Congress. Library of Congress. Congressional Research Service. *The Constitution of the United States: Analysis and Interpretation.* Washington, D.C.: Government Printing Office, 1973.

U.S. Congress. *The Proposed Amendments to the Constitution of the United States During the First Century of Its History,* by Herman V. Ames. H. Doc. 353, pt. 2, 54th Cong., 2nd sess., 1896.

U.S. Congress. *Proposed Amendments to the Constitution of the United States, 1889-1928,* by Michael A. Musmanno. H. Doc. 551, 70th Cong., 2nd sess., 1929.

U.S. Congress. Senate Library. *Proposed Amendments to the Constitution of the United States, 1926-1963.* S. Doc. 163, 87th Cong., 2nd sess., 1963.

U.S. Congress. Senate Library. *Proposed Amendments to the Constitution of the United States of America, 1963-1969.* S. Doc. 91-38, 91st Cong., 1st sess., 1969.

Part VIII—Electing the President

Books

American Bar Association. *Electing the President: A Report of the Commission on Electoral Reform.* Chicago: 1967.

Association of the Bar of the City of New York. *Report of the Committee on Federal Legislation: Proposed Constitutional Amendment Abolishing the Electoral College and Making Other Changes in the Election of the President and Vice-President.* New York: 1969.

Beman, L. T. *Abolishment of the Electoral College.* New York: H. W. Wilson, 1926.

Best, Judith. *The Case Against Direct Election of the President: A Defense of the Electoral College.* Ithaca, N.Y.: Cornell University Press, 1975.

Bickel, Alexander M. *The New Age of Political Reform: The Electoral College, the Convention and the Party System.* New York: Harper & Row, 1968.

Bickel, Alexander M. *Reform and Continuity: The Electoral College, the Convention and the Party System.* New York: Harper & Row, 1971.

Burnham, Walter D. *Presidential Ballots, 1836-1892.* Baltimore: Johns Hopkins Press, 1955.

Congressional Quarterly. *Guide to U.S. Elections.* Washington, D.C.: 1975.

Daniels, Walter M., ed. *Presidential Election Reforms.* New York: H. W. Wilson, 1953.

David, Paul T., ed. *The Presidential Election and Transition, 1960-1961.* Washington, D.C.: Brookings Institution, 1961.

Feerick, John D. *From Failing Hands: The Story of Presidential Succession.* Bronx, N.Y.: Fordham University Press, 1965.

Feerick, John D. *The Twenty-Fifth Amendment: Its Complete History and Earliest Applications.* Bronx, N.Y.: Fordham University Press, 1976.

Haworth, Paul L. *The Hayes-Tilden Disputed Presidential Election of 1876.* Cleveland: Burrows Bros., 1906.

Knoles, George H. *The Presidential Campaign and Election of 1892.* Stanford: Stanford University Press, 1942.

League of Women Voters. "Who Should Elect the President?" Washington, D.C.: 1969.

Longely, Lawrence D. *The Politics of Electoral College Reform.* New Haven: Yale University Press, 1972.

MacBride, Roger L. *The American Electoral College.* Caldwell, Idaho: Caxton Printers, 1953.

O'Neil, Charles A. *The American Electoral System.* New York: Putnam, 1887.

Peirce, Neal. *The People's President: The Electoral College and the Emerging Consensus for a Direct Vote.* New York: Simon & Schuster, 1968.

Polsby, Nelson. *Presidential Elections: Strategies of American Electoral Politics.* New York: Scribner, 1964.

Roseboom, Eugene H. *A History of Presidential Elections.* New York: Macmillan, 1957.

Sayre, Wallace S. *Voting for President: The Electoral College and the American Political System.* Washington, D.C.: Brookings Institution, 1970.

Schlesinger, Arthur M. Jr., ed. *The Coming to Power: Critical Presidential Elections in American History.* New York: McGraw-Hill, 1972.

Schlesinger, Arthur M. Jr., ed. *History of American Presidential Elections.* New York: McGraw-Hill, 1971.

Stanwood, Edward. *A History of the Presidency, 1788-1916*. 2 vols. Boston: Houghton Mifflin, 1889, 1916.

White, Theodore H. *The Making of the President, 1960*. New York: Atheneum Publishers, 1961.

White, Theodore H. *The Making of the President, 1968*. New York: Atheneum Publishers, 1969.

Wilmerding, Lucius Jr. *The Electoral College*. New Brunswick, N.J.: Rutgers University Press, 1958.

Zeidenstein, Harvey. *Direct Election of the President*. Lexington, Mass.: D. C. Heath, 1973.

Articles

Bayh, Birch. "Electing a President: The Case for Direct Popular Election." *Harvard Journal on Legislation*, January 1969, pp. 1-12.

Eshelman, Edwin D. "Congress and Electoral Reform: An Analysis of Proposals for Changing Our Method of Selecting a President." *Christian Century*, Feb. 5, 1969, pp. 178-81.

Feerick, John D. "The Electoral College: Why It Ought to Be Abolished." *Fordham Law Review*, October 1968, p. 43.

Freund, Paul A. "Direct Election of the President: Issues and Answers." *American Bar Association Journal*, August 1970, p. 733.

Gossett, William T. "Direct Popular Election of the President." *American Bar Association Journal*, March 1970, p. 230.

Huddle, F. P. "Electoral College: Historical Review and Proposals for Reforms." *Editorial Research Reports*, Aug. 18, 1944, vol. 2, pp. 99-114.

Lechner, Alfred J. "Direct Election of the President: The Final Step in the Constitutional Evolution of the Right to Vote." *Notre Dame Lawyer*, October 1971, pp. 122-52.

"Proposals to Change the Method of Electing the President: A Pro and Con Discussion on the Various Proposals for Change." *Congressional Digest*, November 1967, pp. 257-88.

Wildavsky, Aaron. "Choosing the Lesser Evils: The Policy-Maker and the Problem of Presidential Disability." *Parliamentary Affairs*, Winter 1959-1960, pp. 25-37.

Index

A

B

Index

Index

Index

Q, R

S